TYPESET IN THE
FUTURE

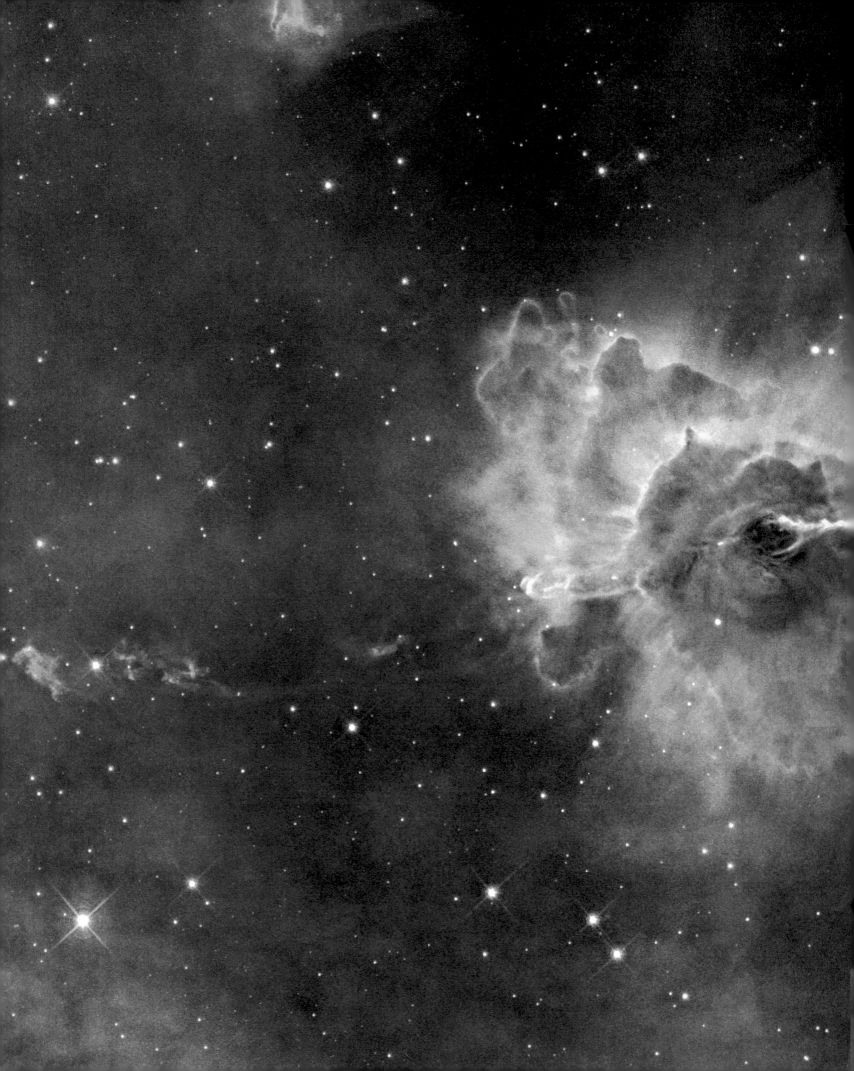

TYPESET IN THE FUTURE

TYPOGRAPHY AND DESIGN IN SCIENCE FICTION MOVIES

DAVE ADDEY

FOREWORD BY
MATT ZOLLER SEITZ

ABRAMS, NEW YORK

Alien's opening sequence introduces us to the *Nostromo*'s hypersleep pods, which can be found in the ship's cryogenic vault. We know that they are in the ship's cryogenic vault because of the inverted-blue-triangle-and-flat-red-person icon in the bottom center of this shot, which is clearly labeled "CRYOGENIC VAULT" in concept designer Ron Cobb's production sketches. This icon combines blue ("lowered thermal condition") with red ("viable, sound, alive, alertness") as part of Cobb's "Semiotic Standard" of iconography and color identification seen throughout the *Nostromo*'s interior. (We'll study Cobb's semiotic standard in more detail on page 60.)

CONTENTS

FOREWORD

Dave Addey made me miss a deadline.

It was a few years ago. I was trying to finish a rewrite of a long piece for *New York* magazine that had to go to press the next day. I don't remember how it happened—probably as the result of a movie discussion on social media—but I found myself googling the words *Futura* and *science fiction films* and somehow ended up on Typeset in the Future, the website that would ultimately become this book.

And it was there that I encountered the best of all possible discoveries: a thing so special and enthralling that I briefly wondered if it really existed or if I was dreaming it.

Typeset in the Future was an entire website about the use of fonts to put across the idea of "the future" in science fiction movies. That was its primary focus, and it was immediately clear that Addey was approaching his core mission with monk-like devotion. Starting with Stanley Kubrick's *2001: A Space Odyssey*, he pored over several classic science fiction films, freeze-framing compositions and zooming in on details, sometimes tilting or flipping the image to give us a better look at it. He looked at titles and subtitles, signage and manuals, computer screens and television chyrons, and scrutinized words and sentences, paragraphs and punctuation. He analyzed the spacing, the kerning, the serifs or lack thereof. He noticed where the filmmakers seemingly inserted one letter from a different typeface into a word that was otherwise uniform. It was the damnedest display of hyper-specific expertise that I'd seen in a long time.

I looked at the clock four hours later and realized I'd missed my deadline. I had to make up an excuse, because "I was up all night reading about fonts" doesn't usually cut it with editors.

I regret nothing. The word *fanatic* doesn't do justice to the experience of reading Addey on fonts. It's like reading Molly Haskell on screwball comedies or Roger Angell on baseball.

It's also like being in a class taught by the sort of professor that you instantly know you're going to think back on fondly for the rest of your days. It's clear that Addey knows as much about the particulars as any working designer, and that he also has that great teacher's ability to explain all he knows to somebody who knows very little, with concision, nuance, and lots of little jokes, many of them endearingly corny. ("Good news!" announces the opening of the second chapter. "While you were reading about *2001: A Space Odyssey*, a typographic study of *Alien* was gestating for your enjoyment.")

Another thing that distinguishes a great teacher is the ability to jump from the subject you're ostensibly studying to an adjacent subject and back again, without damaging the flow of the discussion. Addey is a master at that. You can see his skill put to fine use as you turn the pages of this book. Every page of *Typeset in the Future* is meant to be looked at as well as read, and the images and text are always working in tandem to express an idea. Much of the book is specifically focused on typefaces used within a given science fiction property (*2001*, the *Alien* franchise, *Blade Runner*, *Moon*, the various iterations of *Star Trek*), but on every other page you'll find Addey expanding his vision to accommodate the historical time period, social customs, and design clichés that a given film either echoed or pushed against. And, woven throughout the layout, you'll find examples of whatever he's discussing, reproduced in enough detail to be savored as objects and described in pithy two-line summaries or in clever captions.

This cryptic keypad from *Alien*'s self-destruct sequence looks meaningful and technical at a casual glance. In reality, its keys are labeled with arbitrary Sanskrit words and random Letraset iconography, proving that on-screen interfaces do not have to be functionally realistic in order to win over an audience.

This is a book so tightly focused that it can spend several pages discussing variants of Horizon, a font specifically created for use on the original *Star Trek*, or Pump Demi, a font often used in subtitles of "alien" languages; yet playful and loose enough to conduct lengthy interviews with important production designers like Mike Okuda and detour into discussions of the narrative function of dry on-screen factoids (such as the opening description of the *Alien* ore vessel *Nostromo*, which Addey describes as "foreshadowing inventory"), or the way science fiction filmmakers continue to put jagged-edge, pulsing scan lines on TV screens to signal that we're looking at a TV, even though televisions haven't done that since the turn of the millennium.

Treating *2001* as a cinematic big bang that advanced the arts of both motion-picture storytelling and visual design, Addey moves chronologically through later landmarks, showing how other filmmakers learned from, refined, and in some cases answered Kubrick's masterpiece. As Addey points out, *2001*'s main contribution to typography was its use of typeface, which had such a profound influence on science fiction that the presence of Eurostile now subconsciously tells us that we're seeing a story set in The Future even if we haven't been told what year it is yet. Later typographic milestones are given the same in-depth treatment, such as *Alien*'s opening sequence: the film's title gradually fades onto the screen as an array of shattered but reintegrating fragments, like an "alien" language translating itself into something we can read. Here, as elsewhere in the book, Addey isn't content to show just one connection. He uses this one observation as a springboard to discuss all the subsequent *Alien* movie title sequences, and the title sequences of movies that desperately wanted to be *Alien*, even ranking them in terms of their ability to bring something new to the sequence and convey the idea of otherworldliness.

Typeset in the Future functions equally well as a critical anthology of science fiction storytelling and film design; a stealth history book about how Western audiences saw themselves, and where they imagined they'd end up; and a scrapbook of memorabilia, merchandise, and advertising associated with beloved movies. Uniting it all is the tirelessly cheerful enthusiasm of Dave Addey, an author so invested in his chosen subject that he can spot an unmodified Eurostile Bold Extended number "1" on the front of the USS *Discovery*, a "clear violation of the Starfleet official type style." Nothing escapes this man's notice. If he were a detective, his clearance rate would be 100 percent.

I'd better stop it with the superlatives, or else I'll miss another deadline. Enjoy this treasure trove of a book.

Matt Zoller Seitz
Brooklyn, New York

PREFACE

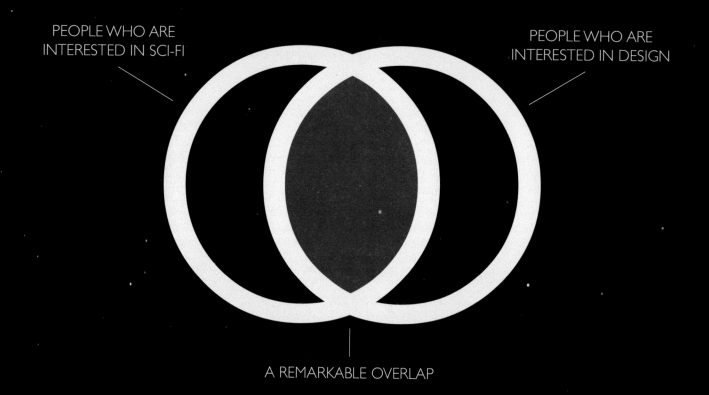

PEOPLE WHO ARE
INTERESTED IN SCI-FI

PEOPLE WHO ARE
INTERESTED IN DESIGN

A REMARKABLE OVERLAP

In 2013, I made a terrible discovery.

Over a few fateful months, I started spotting the exact same typeface in more and more of my favorite sci-fi movies. Once it had been seen, it could not be unseen. No matter where I looked, or what I watched, *there was Eurostile Bold Extended*—the most sci-fi of all typefaces—staring back at me. It became an obsession.

ABCDEFGHIJKLMNOPQRSTUVWXYZ

Eurostile Bold Extended

To satisfy my newfound addiction, I proposed an addition to the TV Tropes website (tvtropes.org), noting Eurostile Bold Extended as a recurring design theme. I named the trope "Typeset in the Future," and it was accepted into the site's encyclopedia.

Wait. Stop. Do *not* visit the TV Tropes website. You will lose your afternoon, your weekend, your house, your loved ones, and your sanity. TV Tropes is the most addictive rabbit hole on the Internet for movie lovers, and *it did not help* my habit. It became increasingly clear that more radical action was needed.

One domain-name registration later, I set out to explore how this bold, elongated typeface was used to create visions of the future. The result was a five-thousand-word article about the design and typography of *2001: A Space Odyssey,* posted on typesetinthefuture.com. My research showed me that, while sci-fi movies had existed before *2001,* our expectations of their design and futurism were changed forever by *2001*'s world building and attention to detail. (It also made me realize that I needed to write more articles.)

I set two criteria for the movies I would study next: They must build persuasive worlds through typography and design, and they must be set in the future. The *2001* article was quickly followed by deep dives into *Moon, Alien,* and *Blade Runner,* each of which drew me further and further into the realm of futuristic fonts.

One unexpected side effect of these studies was that other humans found them interesting. All four posts went viral. The *2001* post was so popular, it crashed my web server. After it came back up, my web-hosting company charged me $1,200 in bandwidth overage fees. I started to realize I might not be alone.

My theory of the site's popularity is best expressed by the Venn diagram on the left. It turns out that a love of great sci-fi movies, and the convincing worlds they create, goes hand in hand with a love of great design across *all* disciplines. (It also turns out that the Internet is every bit as obsessive as I am.)

Having discovered these vital facts, I decided my research needed to go deeper than the *how* and start to explore the *why.* I moved beyond typography, expanding my scope to cover production design, graphics, and architecture. I interviewed typographers and historians, and met the creative geniuses behind some sci-fi movie classics. Their thoughts and experiences are shared in these pages, alongside my own studies of their creations. The result is an opportunity to rewatch the sci-fi movies you love—and to see how they create a compelling vision of the future through typography and design.

EURO

STILE

Typography is an incredibly powerful way to visualize the future in sci-fi. Moviemakers regularly take advantage of this fact and set their calendars to "FUTURE" simply by slapping some Eurostile Bold Extended on the side of a passing spaceship. Indeed, Eurostile has become *so* effective at establishing a time frame in the future that whenever I see the typeface in real life—which happens a lot in my adopted home of California—I assume I've been transported to some futuristic dystopia in which a local nursing home is really a sinister government facility for scientific experimentation.

IDYLWOOD CARE CENTER
A CRESTWOOD FACILITY
1002 FREMONT AVENUE

Idylwood Care Center, in Sunnyvale, California. The existence of a secret underground cybernetics laboratory was unconfirmed at the time of printing.

Eurostile's function as the typeface of the future began with *2001: A Space Odyssey* (1968), and it has since appeared in countless sci-fi settings. It's most commonly seen in its Bold Extended form, but Regular, Bold, and non-bold Extended often crop up as well. Here are just a few examples of the roles Eurostile has played in sci-fi movies over the years.

THE RULES

We've seen how Eurostile Bold Extended can be effective in establishing a movie's time frame. But if Eurostile alone isn't enough, there are more tricks you can pull. Here are ten easy rules guaranteed to position your text firmly in the FUTURE.

We'll start with some simple sans-serif text, such as this randomly chosen word in Eurostile Bold.

FUTURE

RULE 1: First, let's add an italic slant. We want the text to look as if it's stretching toward 2025.

FUTURE

Hmm. It's still a little boring. **RULES 2 AND 3:** What if we make things a bit curvier in some places, and a bit straighter in others? I hear that's all the typographic rage in 2037.

FUTURE

Much better! But there's still more we can do. **RULE 4:** How about adding some sharp points to a few of the letters? Hello, 2050!

There's still something missing—we've forgotten to take into account the devastating Kern Wars of 2067. **RULE 5:** Let's combine a few letters in a single ligature, to make sure we're not violating the subsequent Kern Tithe.

Now we're talking! This sets us up perfectly for **RULE 6,** in which we arbitrarily slice out a segment of the text. In this case, we'll remove a horizontal line from the majority of the word.

Whoa! That looks amazing! Who knew 2092 was so easy to reach?

The outline shape is pretty much set; now it's time for the texture. **RULE 7:** Let's use a laser beam to carve the text out of a big sheet of metal.

In the absence of stereoscopic glasses, we'll apply **RULES 8 AND 9:** Add a bevel to make the word jump out of the page, then extrude it all the way into glorious 3-D-O-Vision.

And last, but by no means least, we'll finish it off with **RULE 10,** putting the whole damn thing on top of a star field.

various permutations of these rules have been applied in many famous movie logos. We'll start with Ridley Scott's *Blade Runner,* which gets a score of 6/10 and is partly responsible for the ongoing slicing trend:

The logotype for 2003's *Battlestar Galactica* TV series goes one better, adding some extruded Eurostile Bold Extended for a 7/10 rating:

Transformers is similarly high up the chart, taking its brushed-metal effect to the extreme for an impressive 7/10:

Guardians of the Galaxy gets a slightly less admirable 6/10 but is nonetheless an exemplar of harmonized angles and bevels:

This means that *Guardians* scores two points higher than *RoboCop* (1987), which pretty much invented the bevel but loses out by not slicing things unnecessarily:

The Amazing Spider-Man demonstrates an extreme take on the shaping rules, though the title will be receiving a visit from the Kerning Police for Opportunities Missed and scores only 5/10 as a result:

The Terminator (1984) takes curviness to the extreme but manages only 3/10 despite its promising start:

WALL·E fares even worse, chalking up a paltry 2/10 for curvy straight things and straight curvy things:

Despite being a far worse movie than both *Terminator* and *WALL·E*, *G.I. Joe: Retaliation* gets a whopping 8/10 thanks to some sneaky slicing on the R:

Almost as good is *Star Trek: The Next Generation*, which doesn't bother with metal but otherwise gets high scores all around, plus a bonus point for our first star-field backdrop:

The indisputable winner, however, is 2017's *Star Trek: Discovery*, with a whopping 9/10. It's a worthy champion, pushing all the rules to their limits and, for good measure, superimposing the title over an aqua-blue nebula:

Nonetheless, despite its brilliance, *Discovery* didn't find room for fancy kerning. Movie-title designers of the world: A perfect score is still out there for the taking.

Earthrise, taken by astronaut Bill Anders on December 24, 1968, from the window of *Apollo 8,* showing Earth rising behind the moon.

1968

2001²

A SPACE ODYSSEY

2001: A Space Odyssey—
Stanley Kubrick's 1968
sci-fi masterpiece—is an
appropriate place to start
our study of typography and
design in science fiction.
Among other delights, it
offers a zero-gravity toilet,
emergency resuscitations,
and futuristic products
aplenty. Most importantly, it
marks the start of Eurostile
Bold Extended's regular
appearance in spacecraft user
interfaces.

An epic drama of
adventure and exploration

Space Station One: your first step in an Odyssey that will take you to the Moon, the planets and the distant stars.

2001: a space odyssey
MGM PRESENTS A STANLEY KUBRICK PRODUCTION
CINERAMA Super Panavision® and Metrocolor

The title sequence is perhaps the most dramatic introduction to typography ever committed to film. Three gigantic celestial bodies are employed to reveal the movie's title, in supercircular Gill Sans, as the opening bars of Richard Strauss's *Also sprach Zarathustra* are heard, becoming forever identified with outer space. This now-famous fanfare is from a movement Strauss named "Sunrise," but the opening titles to *2001* are more evocative of *Earthrise*, a photograph taken by astronaut Bill Anders aboard *Apollo 8*. This photo from lunar orbit was snapped on December 24, 1968, some nine months after *2001: A Space Odyssey* hit movie theaters. Like *2001*'s intro, *Earthrise* shows our home planet far in the distance, looking small compared to the moon's surface in the foreground. Both images require viewers to consider their place in the universe from an alien vantage point, far from the comforts of home.

As Kubrick's camera moves up and over the surface of the moon . . .

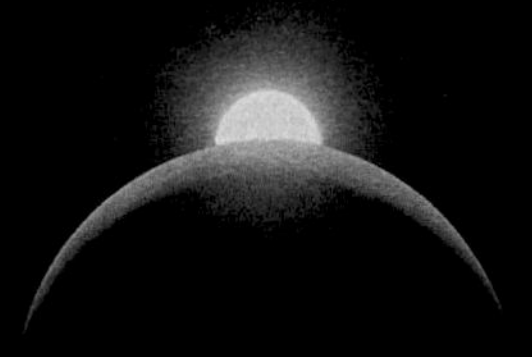

. . . an earthrise is revealed . . .

2OOI: A SPACE ODYSSEY

. . . followed by a sunrise and some Gill Sans Light.

2001's title card is set in a light variant of Gill Sans, one of the all-time classic sans-serif fonts. The zeroes in "2001" are set with the Gill Sans capital letter *O*, rather than a zero character, to provide a stronger visual balance between the digits in "2001," the rounded letters in "SPACE ODYSSEY," and the planetary bodies behind them.

ABCDEFGHIJKLMNOPQRSTUVWXYZ

Gill Sans Light, designed by Eric Gill and released by Monotype in 1928

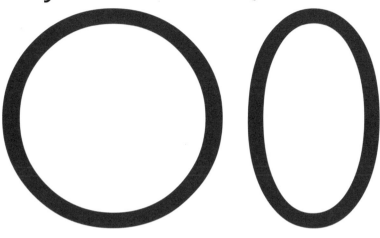

A capital letter *O* (left) and the number zero (right), set in Gill Sans Light

This opening sequence was mimicked by CBS News for its live coverage of *Apollo 11*, the mission that put a man on the moon, broadcast one year after *2001*'s release. The same vertical camera movement can also be seen in *Moon,* albeit inverted for sinister effect and with substantially more Bank Gothic than the original.

Opening credits of *Man on the Moon,* CBS News's live coverage of the *Apollo 11* mission, 1969

Opening sequence of *Moon* (2009), inverting the earthrise and making the moon feel far more sinister as a result

Unlike its dramatic beginning, the film's opening act is definitely *not* set in space. Its prehistoric time frame is reinforced with Albertus, whose chiseled aesthetic evokes tombstones, not spaceships.

ABCDEFGHIJKLMNOPQRSTUVWXYZ

After introducing us to Albertus, the "Dawn of Man" section turns out to be otherwise typographically unremarkable. So let's skip forward a little and join Dr. Heywood R. Floyd on Pan Am spacecraft *Orion,* en route to Space Station 5.

Albertus, designed between 1932 and 1940 by Berthold Wolpe for Monotype

DR. FLOYD'S FLIGHT aboard the *Orion,* and his subsequent trip to the moon on the *Aries,* features many real-world brands in futuristic, space-based settings. This is not just product placement, however. Kubrick's design team consulted leading 1960s brands throughout the movie's production, drawing on each company's futuristic product concepts to create a believable vision of the near future. As *2001*'s vice president of promotion, Roger Caras, wrote to *Industrial Design* magazine in 1968:

> *"These products are the design concepts of these companies for thirty-five years from now. . . . There were over forty organizations all told who lent us assistance in the form of consultation and/or specific pieces of hardware."*

To quote another Caras letter, this time to the Ford Motor Company in 1967:

> *"We will show trade-name products in the film as they will appear thirty-six years from now. It serves the dramatic purpose of keeping the film from being too remote, the technology from being too difficult for the audience to relate to, and will provide the basis for co-operative merchandising at release time."*

OPPOSITE: An excerpt from the *"2001: A Space Odyssey"* Exhibitor's Campaign Book (1969), published by MGM to accompany the movie's promotion. This PR vision of the year 2001, with a reduced working week and no war or disease, did not turn out to be accurate.

WHEN YOU MAKE A PICTURE ABOUT THE YEAR 2001, TODAY IS A BIT "DATED"

It was inevitable that the futuristic atmosphere of "2001: A Space Odyssey," Stanley Kubrick's MGM Super Panavision and Metrocolor production, should affect the crew and technicians involved in the unique picture.

From the creator of the project, producer-director and co-writer Stanley Kubrick, to the hundreds of technicians, there was a feeling of dissatisfaction with modern living. "Modern," it seems, was not advanced enough. It was a natural reaction to an undertaking that minutely pieces together an exciting vision of the future which makes today's existence pale in comparison.

To make "2001: A Space Odyssey," a technical team was gathered from all corners of the industrial world. Scientific consultants from a dozen nations, including leading space authorities, were constantly at Kubrick's side to give authenticity and guidance to each aspect of this film.

More than 40 leading commercial companies offered up their research facilities to the picture, with the result that everyone on the set became indoctrinated and acclimatized to living standards on Earth, 33 years from now.

Every day, as they passed through the studio gates, the crew left the present and entered a world of almost total automation and computerization, with a predictable working week no longer than three or four days, with no war, no incurable diseases, longer life expectancy, new fashions and designs for better living.

In "2001: A Space Odyssey," man has at last severed earthly shackles and is on the threshold of the solar system and the universe. When you spend your days living in the world of tomorrow, the world of today seems obsolete.

The first brand we encounter on the *Orion* is Pan Am, whose logo doesn't seem to have changed between 1968 and 2001. (We'll ignore the fact that Pan Am went bust in 1991.) Since this is a moon-bound flight, the Pan Am cabin crew have adopted Velcro-based grip shoes to counter the weightlessness of space.

Velcro, invented in the 1950s, was still all the rage when *2001* was released. Its use for grip shoes actually wasn't too far-fetched: NASA was already using it in the Apollo missions to anchor equipment for astronauts' convenience in zero-gravity situations.

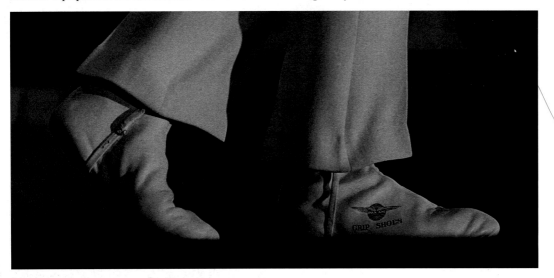

THE ORION'S FLIGHT DECK gives us our first sighting of Eurostile Bold Extended, in an ominous foreshadowing of the HAL 9000 interface screens we'll see later on. In a subsequent close-up, we see that the craft features the IBM logo in its pre-1972 version, set in a custom variation of City Bold. This is, sadly, different from IBM's logo in the actual year 2001.

ABCDEFGHIJKLMNOPQRSTUVWXYZ

Eurostile Bold Extended

ABCDEFGHIJKLMNOPQRSTUVWXYZ

City Bold, designed in 1930 by Georg Trump for Berthold

Like many of the companies featured in 2001, Pan Am made the most of its on-screen presence when the movie was released. This window display was placed in Pan Am offices in twenty-five key cities across the United States.

IBM IBM

The close-up (below) features an IBM logo, but the long shot (above) does not. That's because IBM's logo was originally going to be on the movie's main computer: the artificial intelligence aboard the USS *Discovery* that we now know as HAL 9000. However, as the movie's script developed, and it became clear that HAL would malfunction in epic style, it was decided to place the IBM brand in the earlier craft, rather than have it associated with malfunctioning equipment. The close-up of the *Orion* console, with the IBM logo added, was filmed later in the movie's production and then edited into this scene.

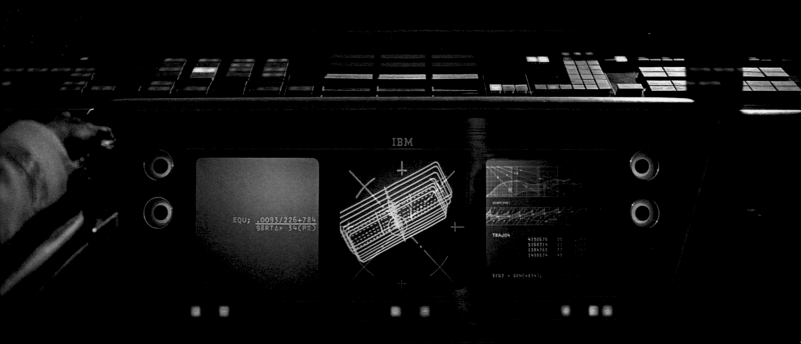

As Dr. Floyd snoozes in his seat, we focus in on a futuristic-looking pen, floating around in the zero-gravity environment of the *Orion* (below left).

This isn't any old pen, however. This is an *atomic* pen, designed and provided by the Parker Pen Company. To quote a Parker press release of the time:

> *It is equipped with a tiny isotopic packet within the pen to produce power which is then converted to heat. This varies the flow of the pen's ink supply so that the writer can produce a wide range of line densities, from barely visible to strikingly embossed—a feature required by the addition of a third dimension to handwriting that Parker pundits think might develop during the next three decades.*
>
> *No point in going to your dealers now—Parker doesn't expect to put this pen on sale until the next century!*

AS THE PARKER PEN floats by, we see that Dr. Floyd is watching a video about motor vehicles on the *Orion*'s in-flight entertainment system (above right).

The sleek blue futuristic car seen in this video is General Motors' XP-792 prototype, also known as the Runabout. The Runabout was part of GM's Futurama II exhibit at the 1964–65 New York World's Fair and was marketed as "a four-passenger utility car that could ease the commuting and shopping tasks of urban residents of the future." According to a GM press release:

> *The Runabout has two built-in shopping carts that form an integral part of the car's rear end when in place. At the shopping center, the shopper would slide a cart out from the rear (its wheels fall automatically into place) and wheel it through the store. When it is rolled back into the car, the wheels would retract alongside the cart body as it locks into position.*

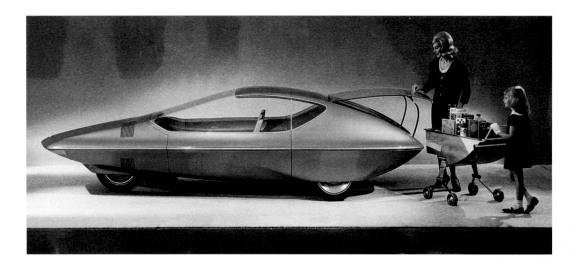

The General Motors Runabout, shown here with one of its removable shopping carts about to be reinserted

The special-purpose Runabout was one of three complementary vehicles exhibited by GM at the World's Fair, as another GM press release explained:

> *Each of the three cars is highly specialized, designed for a particular motoring purpose. The Runabout has a built-in shopping cart system and runs on three wheels, so it will have excellent maneuverability. The Firebird IV has television, stereo, game table and refrigerator for the family to enjoy while it operates automatically on an electronic guidance system, and the GM-X has a maximum of controls and instrumentation for the enthusiast who wants a highly personalized driving experience.*

The Firebird IV's autonomous guidance system seems about to become a reality; its built-in refrigerator less so. Sadly, however, GM's vision of multiple-vehicle ownership turned out to be more a car manufacturer's dream than a car owner's reality.

(One final vehicular note: You might have spotted that the on-screen Runabout does not actually run about. The GM prototype may have had two shopping carts in the back, but it didn't have an engine in the front. The movie's producers worked around this preproduction limitation with some sneaky camera movements instead.)

When I first watched this scene, I thought, *My, what a futuristic car!* However, at no point did I think, *My, what a futuristic seat-back entertainment system!* We take it for granted now, but the thought of a compact, flat screen enabling you to select your personal choice of entertainment during a long flight was fantastical when *2001* was made. On a 1960s flight, you'd watch the same in-flight movie as your fellow passengers on a projection screen or suspended CRT monitor, whether you liked it or not. Individual in-flight video systems didn't come into existence until July 1988, when tiny 3½" color LCD screens were first tested by Northwest Airlines.

Univers 59 Ultra Condensed, designed by Adrian Frutiger and released by Deberny & Peignot in 1957

THE HILTON CHAIN of hotels seems to have opened an outpost on Space Station 5. This logo doesn't match any I can find from the chain's history, and instead follows *2001*'s theme of using Univers for incidental typography that isn't set in Eurostile or Futura. This particular variant looks to be Univers 59 Ultra Condensed.

ABCDEFGHIJKLMNOPQRSTUVWXYZ

At the other end of this concourse, we see that the Howard Johnson's chain of restaurants has also set up shop in space, opening an Earthlight Room restaurant to remind travelers of home.

Exterior of the Howard Johnson's Earthlight Room aboard Space Station 5

To accompany the Earthlight Room, Howard Johnson's printed a special children's menu as a "preview" of the movie's plot. In it, excited youngsters Debbie and Robin attend a *2001* premiere with their parents and are blown away by the movie's scientific realism and special effects. As the premiere draws to a close, Robin gushes, "What a finish! I'd never have guessed the way the mystery is solved!" thereby wrongly suggesting that the movie contains a solvable mystery, and that said mystery is in some way resolved by the time the movie ends. Indeed, the kids are so taken by the movie that they pledge to perpetuate its gender stereotypes decades hence, with Debbie noting breathlessly, "I can hardly wait for the year 2001 so that I can be a space stewardess!" By comparison, Robin smiles the easygoing smile of male privilege, stating bluntly: "I'm going to be a space pilot."

The Howard Johnson's menu takes several liberties with the movie's chronology, inadvertently implying that a stewardess and two pilots are aboard the *Discovery* and suggesting that three crew members are awake as the craft approaches Jupiter. My assumption is that the menu was created before the movie's tightly controlled story line was known, and was improvised based on publicity stills in the run-up to its release.

OPPOSITE: Howard Johnson's *2001: A Space Odyssey* children's menu, 1968

You might also have spotted the Bell System logo in the background of the Earthlight Room scene. The Bell System, named after Alexander Graham Bell, was a group of companies with a near monopoly on US and Canadian telephone services between 1877 and 1984. The logo at the top was introduced in 1964. (Unfortunately for the movie's futurism, this logo was replaced with a new Saul Bass design in 1969, just one year after the movie was released.)

This Bell logo is part of a Picturephone booth, used by Dr. Floyd to call his daughter back on Earth. Surprising as it may sound, Picturephone was a real, working video-calling service from the 1960s, invented by Bell Telephone Laboratories way before the days of Skype and FaceTime. In fact, the world's first transcontinental video call, from Disneyland in California to the World's Fair in New York, was made on two Picturephone devices all the way back in 1964.

The Picturephone booth on Space Station 5 is based on a design by Bell Labs employee A. Michael Noll, an early pioneer of human-machine tactile communication. In 1965, under Dr. Noll's direction, a Bell draftsman created a detailed sketch of how a Picturephone booth might be incorporated into the orbiting space station.

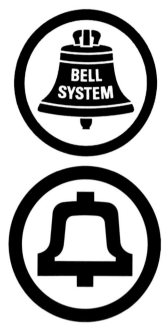

Bell System logo, 1964–69

Bell System logo, 1969–present

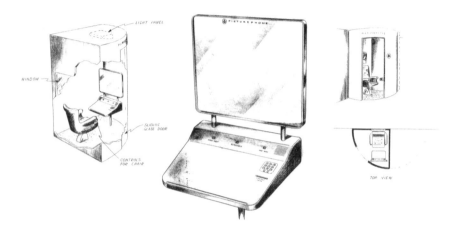

Bell Telephone Laboratories sketch of a hypothetical space-station Picturephone booth, 1965

Dr. Noll also provided instructions for the booth's operation:

> *If the booth were placed along the wall of the space station, a window in the rear of the booth looking out of the station would be very good since the other party would then see the customer with the earth and stars as a background.*

> *The customer inserts his magnetic credit card into the slot on the desk portion of the Picturephone and then dials the desired number using the TOUCHTONE set. The numbers dialed would include a World Zone Code and the total number of dialed digits would hopefully be eleven or less depending on the country called.*

These instructions were followed closely in the movie's script, and the on-screen booth is a faithful re-creation of the original pencil sketch (albeit with a little artistic license). As Dr. Floyd speaks to his daughter, a beautiful close-up of the moon can indeed be seen rotating slowly through the window behind him. And he does indeed dial an eleven-digit number to call Earth, shortly after placing his magnetic American Express card in the desk's payment slot. (We may take magnetic-strip credit cards for granted today, but this was yet another futuristic development for *2001*'s moviegoing audience: The magnetic-strip credit card did not make its debut until 1970, two years after the movie's release, in a pilot project run by American Express, American Airlines, and IBM at Chicago's O'Hare Airport. Magnetic-strip cards weren't adopted by Visa and MasterCard until as late as 1980. Once again, *2001*'s use of real-world prototypes makes the movie look realistic today.)

Despite the "picture" in "Picturephone," Dr. Floyd still asks his daughter during their call to "tell Mommy that I telephoned." His daughter also requests "a telephone" when asked what she wants for her birthday, even though she is speaking to her father via a far more impressive device. These facts may go some way toward indicating why the Picturephone, despite its technological advancements, ultimately proved to be a commercial failure, costing Bell half a billion dollars in the process.

PICTUREPHONE

In October 2016, I spoke with
A. Michael Noll of Bell Labs about
bringing the Picturephone to Space
Station 5.

ADDEY: How did the Bell Labs collaboration come about?

NOLL: Well, John Pierce [the Bell Labs engineer behind Telstar, the first active direct-relay communications satellite] knew Arthur C. Clarke, so that's how the initial connection occurred. Then John involved me to fill in some details and get a drawing made. These were things that went on at the labs. These were little projects, which were interesting, and fun, as they popped up.

When did you first get to see the results of the collaboration?

I can't remember when I finally got to see it. I don't remember going to a movie theater, I just remember someplace seeing it and saying, "Good grief." They just used everything we gave them—precisely, exactly as we gave it to them. That I didn't expect; I thought we were just making suggestions, and they'd play around with it. No. They used it as we gave it to them.

I do recall someone from AT&T calling me, complaining about the use of the Bell System seal. The Bell System was restricted to domestic [US] telecommunications. And the person was objecting that this now gave the impression that the Bell System was out in space. I mean . . . it's a science-fiction film. And the person was screaming at me, they were so upset. "How could you do this?! Did you get permission?!" Then I finally said: "John Pierce approved it," and I heard a gulp at the other end. John was pretty high up and noted for not putting up with people doing nonsense. So this person was obviously not going to call Pierce and complain.

Why didn't the Picturephone service work out commercially?

It was Bell Labs thinking, something has to come after the telephone. And this idea of people looking at a screen and seeing a picture, which would pick up from television, which was now in vogue . . . in essence, a television-like telephone call, so you can see the person you're talking to.

They did a demonstration of it at the New York World's Fair. So first, remember, people who go to world's fairs are people who are pro-technology. Of the people who went to the World's Fair, there were those who chose to go to the AT&T/Bell System pavilion. That's another positive of positives. Of those, some agreed to have a demo of the Picturephone. Of those who had a demo, some said, "I'll fill in the questionnaire." And half of them, 50 percent, liked seeing the other person. And based on that World's Fair experience, Bell System developed the Picturephone. Spent half a billion dollars developing it.

Of course, the other side of the coin is that half of the triple positives *didn't* want it. So it was really an incredibly negative result. But they didn't want that. Julius Molnar was the vice president in charge of this project, and he just steam-rolled it forward, and everybody believed in it. Then they introduced it, and nobody wanted it.

So then Bell System went into a great effort to find out, is there *any* market for two-way visual communications? In the end, we did teleconferencing. Public rooms, which you had to reserve and go to. And we discovered, to our horror, that we couldn't give that service away for free.

If you went to an audience, ten years before Skype and these other things came along, and said, "How many of you would like to see the other person when you're talking to them on the phone?" maybe half the hands would go up. Then if you say, "How many of you, of *that* group, are willing to be *seen* when talking on the phone?" almost all the hands would go down. The issues are in the psychology of communication.

Photo from the *Bay Area Bulletin* (a newsletter for Pacific Telephone employees), May 4, 1964. A Southern California newsman (left) talks to a newsman in New York via a Picturephone connection between the New York World's Fair and the Bell System exhibit at Disneyland. Joyce Kileen (right), an attendant at the Disneyland exhibit, watches the call alongside Mickey Mouse (middle).

Following his video call, Dr. Floyd meets a Russian scientific crew who quiz him about communication problems with the Clavius moon base. This scene is notable for showing cordial US-Soviet collaboration in space, despite being filmed during the Cold War, at the height of the highly competitive space race that saw both nations vying to put a man on the moon. The film is once again ahead of its time here, foreshadowing both the Apollo-Soyuz Test Project that took place in 1975 and the modern-day International Space Station, whose initial US-Russian crew arrived in November 2000, just one year after this scene takes place.

(In case you're thinking of modernizing your living room: The Russian crew is sitting on real-world Djinn low fireside chairs, designed by Olivier Mourgue, around a real-world 1950s Tulip table, designed by Eero Saarinen. I'm happy to report that the Aeroflot logo on their travel bags did not change one bit between 1968 and 2001.)

Reverse-angle shot of Space Station 5's corridor, showing the logo of **Аэрофлот** (Aeroflot), the Russian national airline, looking exactly as it did in the real year 2001

АЭРОФЛОТ

 *Российские авиалинии*

The Аэрофлот (Aeroflot) logo

AFTER HIS CHAT, Dr. Floyd takes a flight to the Clavius moon base aboard the *Aries* craft. Eagle-eyed readers may spot a logo for RCA Whirlpool during his flight. In a spectacularly unfortunate piece of futurism, this logo (and the name RCA Whirlpool) was dropped in 1966, two years before the movie's release. Nonetheless, Whirlpool's zero-gravity capabilities were already well established by the time this scene was shot. In October 1960, Whirlpool was commissioned by the US government to design and build the first experimental space kitchen, including a refrigerator, oven, and heated water system. Together with NASA, Whirlpool developed waste-management and personal-hygiene systems for all the real-world Gemini, Apollo, and Skylab missions, including wind-up shavers, friction-powered water heaters, and delicious space meals.

ABOVE: The movie's Whirlpool space kitchen appeared at the National Home Show in Chicago, the Sakowitz Festival of the Future in Houston, and the Tri-State Home Beautiful Show in Chattanooga, Tennessee.

RIGHT: An RCA Whirlpool space kitchen aboard the *Aries*

The futuristic culinary theme continues aboard Dr. Floyd's later *Aries* flight, where he is presented with a pictorial liquipack of in-flight "foods," each delivered in liquid form with an individual straw. The on-screen liquipack features the logo of real-world frozen vegetable company Seabrook Farms, as part of a co-branding arrangement with Pan Am. (The instructions down the side of this packaging are composed entirely of text from the headers and footers of Letraset dry lettering sheets—a design shortcut we will see used several more times in this book when text on screen is not intended to be read.)

The Pan Am–Seabrook Farms Liquipack, as seen aboard the *Aries*

Dr. Floyd wisely avoids the liquid fish and opts for some tasty liquid corn and liquid carrots instead. Despite the weightless conditions signaled by the screens in the background, the liquid in the liquipack's straw can clearly be seen to fall back into the pack as Dr. Floyd sucks on his corn juice.

Dr. Floyd sucks on a straw, drawing liquid into it . . .

. . . which promptly recedes back into the liquipack when he is done, despite the "WEIGHTLESS CONDITIONS."

As the doctor drinks his dinner, one of the *Aries*'s pilots joins him in the passenger compartment for a chat. Clearly visible on the pilot's wrist is a futuristic timepiece, designed for the movie by Hamilton Watch engineer John Bergey, who would go on to develop the world's first digital watch. The timepiece seen in the movie was never produced in volume, but a reinterpretation of its design (known as the X-01) was released by Hamilton in 2006 as a tribute to the original. Perhaps inevitably, Hamilton manufactured only 2,001 X-01s for public release.

The *Aries* pilot's sleeve is conveniently hoisted to display his futuristic watch as he chats with Dr. Floyd.

2001—THE WATCH OF THE FUTURE

. . . and, in a way, the watch of the present. Small way—just three in the world. But if it happened thrice, it could happen again, in time. Watch for it; it's called the 2001 and it was designed especially for Stanley Kubrick's new film, "2001: A Space Odyssey." A big, bold, way-out-in-orbit watch with about 2001 things going for it. Good looks: a circular dial in a case of satin-finished chromium 1½ inches wide, with black plastic band, Velcro closing. Good works: at one end of the case are three small windows which show the month, day, and Greenwich mean time. The movable bezel is marked in twelve hour divisions—this can be set to indicate time elapsed or future time to elapse. And at one corner of the case is a small red button that controls the alarm system. Watch of the future—for men, for women, by Hamilton. Ski pullover by White Stag.

78   VOGUE, November 15, 1966

"2001—The Watch of the Future," ad from *Vogue* magazine, November 16, 1966. Note the model's futuristic shiny silver outfit and the watch's movable bezel, which can indicate "future time to elapse."

Magazine ad for "out of this world knits" by JPs, in which women of the future demonstrate that their primary skeletal joints still work while floating in space. *Seventeen,* August 1968

Magazine ad for a leather handbag by designer John Romain. The imminent threat of asphyxiation is not preventing this model any more than the JPs models from enjoying her *2001* tie-in product. *Seventeen,* August 1968

Watches were not the only personal apparel to tie in with *2001*. As part of the movie's promotion, MGM arranged a three-month feature with *Seventeen* magazine in its June, July, and August 1968 issues. After June's movie review and July's six-page fashion spread starring Keir Dullea, August featured a five-page ad spread by companies targeting *2001*-themed products to forward-thinking teenage girls.

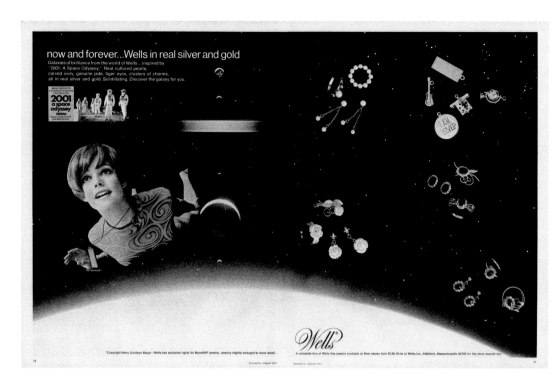

now and forever...Wells in real silver and gold

Galaxies of brilliance from the world of Wells...inspired by
"2001: A Space Odyssey." Real cultured pearls,
carved ivory, genuine jade, tiger eyes, clusters of charms,
all in real silver and gold. Scintillating. Discover the galaxy for you.

Wells

Perhaps most obtusely, Wells Jewelry created Monolith pendants, bracelets, charms, earrings, and pins to tie in with *2001*'s release. Made in silver, onyx, and gold plate, the Monolith pendant was marketed as "an exact, scale-model miniature replica of the Monolith seen in the movie." (Which is really just another way of saying, "We made a rectangle.")

FOLLOWING HIS LIQUID LUNCH, Dr. Floyd finds himself needing to answer a call of nature. In a highly unusual movie event, *2001* features the operating details of a functional lavatory on-screen. This turns into something of a comedic aside, with Dr. Floyd reading a series of instructions for the ship's zero-gravity toilet, set in Eurostile Bold. (Given the toilet's complexity, it's probably sensible that "Passengers Are Advised to Read Instructions Before Use.")

Eurostile Bold

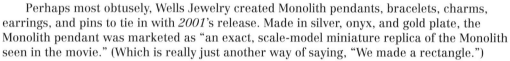

ABCDEFGHIJKLMNOPQRSTUVWXYZ

Dr. Floyd reads the instructions for the zero-gravity toilet, with an understandable look of apprehension.

ZERO GRAVITY TOILET

PASSENGERS ARE ADVISED TO
READ INSTRUCTIONS BEFORE USE

1 This toilet is of the standard zero-gravity type. Depending on requirements, system A and/or system B can be used, details of which are clearly marked in the toilet compartment. When operating system A, depress lever and a plastic dalkron eliminator will be dispensed through the slot immediately underneath. When you have fastened the adhesive lip, attach connection marked by the large X outlet hose. Twist the silver-colored ring one inch below the connection point until you feel it lock.

2 The toilet is now ready for use. The Sonovac cleanser is activated by the small switch on the lip. When securing, twist the ring back to its initial condition, so that the two orange lines meet. Disconnect. Place the dalkron eliminator in the vacuum receptacle to the rear. Activate by pressing the blue button.

3 The controls for system B are located on the opposite wall. The red release switch places the uroliminator into position; it can be adjusted manually up or down by pressing the blue manual release button. The opening is self-adjusting. To secure after use, press the green button, which simultaneously activates the evaporator and returns the uroliminator to its storage position.

4 You may leave the lavatory if the green exit light is on over the door. If the red light is illuminated, one of the lavatory facilities is not properly secured. Press the "Stewardess" call button to the right of the door. She will secure all facilities from her control panel outside. When the green exit light goes on you may open the door and leave. Please close door behind you.

5 To use the Sonoshower, first undress and place all your clothes in the clothes rack. Put on the Velcro slippers located in the cabinet immediately below. Enter the shower. On the control panel to your upper right upon entering you will see a "Shower seal" button. Press to activate. A green light will then be illuminated immediately below. On the intensity knob select the desired setting. Now depress the Sonovac activation lever. Bathe normally.

6 The Sonovac will automatically go off after three minutes unless you activate the "Manual off" override switch by flipping it up. When you are ready to leave, press the blue "Shower seal" release button. The door will open and you may leave. Please remove the Velcro slippers and place them in their container.

Thankfully, *2001* does not clarify what a "plastic dalkron eliminator" is or whether a liquid-corn diet necessitates system A or B. The realities of space-based lavatories are definitely not a laughing matter, however, as crew members on the International Space Station discovered when its onboard toilet broke down twice in 2008. After an initial lavatory mishap in June, the crew's sole toilet malfunctioned a second time in October owing to an issue with its gas separator. To the crew's relief, a visiting Soyuz capsule provided a temporary lavatorial outlet until a $19 million Russian replacement toilet could be delivered in November.

Let's move quickly on. Following a brief speech at a moon base, three American chaps take a spacecraft to visit a suspicious-looking monolith. What could possibly go wrong? In any event, their map makes good use of a mix of Eurostile Bold Extended, Futura Medium, and something that looks like it's probably a condensed form of Univers.

Dr. Floyd studies a map of the Tycho Magnetic Anomaly on his way to view the monolith.

Things do, in fact, go wrong. General badness happens. The next thing we know, we're looking at a title card for "Part 3: Jupiter Mission." This title card is set in the *other* classic sans-serif font—Futura—but with a few inexplicable idiosyncrasies.

Futura Book

ABCDEFGHIJKLMNOPQRSTUVWXYZ

The points of the capital *N* characters have been softened, and the capital *M* appears to be borrowed from Gill Sans. (I have yet to find an explanation.)

MUCH AS IT PAINS ME to say it, the movie's manned mission to Jupiter has turned out to be one of its least realistic predictions. This is despite some commendable optimism in the movie's 1969 press pack:

> *Today, in the late 1960s, we are just eleven years into the space age and are already making plans for manned journeys to the moon. Where will we be in space in the 46th year of the space age? Predictions are that we will be very far indeed and that our skills will be over-shadowed only by our discoveries.*

Sadly, in the forty-sixth year of the space age the nearest mankind had made it to Jupiter was the International Space Station, which accepted its first resident crew in November 2000. The Constellation Program, a manned spaceflight program begun by NASA in 2005 and intended to take man to the moon and onward to Mars, was canceled in 2010. As things stand, a manned Jupiter mission feels substantially less likely today than it did in 1968.

Aboard the Jupiter mission, two of the USS *Discovery*'s crew are awake, with the rest still in hibernation. The two crew members spend some time watching a BBC TV show on their eerily prescient tablet devices. The channel is BBC 12, which is eight channels higher than the BBC's present-day maximum of four. Following several subsequent changes, the BBC logo took on its modern-day Gill Sans form in 1997, four years before this scene takes place.

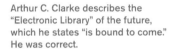

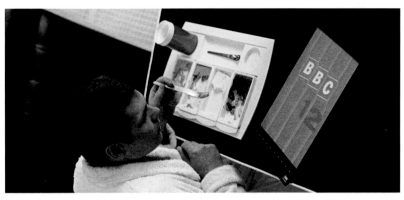

TOP: BBC 1 "Floating Globe" ident, used in 1968–69

ABOVE: BBC logo, 1997–present

RIGHT: The BBC logo here, with what might be Univers in italicized outline boxes, looks like a variant of its 1960s form.

The tablet device used by the crew is a "TelePad" and was made by IBM, along with much of the rest of the spacecraft's hardware. It's interesting to note that TV seems to be portrait-only in the future—given the numeric buttons along the bottom portrait edge of the device, it seems it's not meant to be used in both portrait and landscape orientations. Like much of the futurism in *2001,* this could also turn out to be prescient: Our present-day preference for mobile phones with portrait screens means that more and more video is being filmed in portrait, not landscape, as we move further beyond *2001.*

The TelePad was not *2001*'s only successful attempt at predicting the technology of the future. In the *"2001: A Space Odyssey" Exhibitor's Campaign Book,* screenwriter Arthur C. Clarke described what he called the "Electronic Library" of the future, which is basically the Internet. (In addition to jointly authoring *2001*'s screenplay with Kubrick, Clarke wrote the short story and *2001* inspiration "The Sentinel," and adapted the film into a novel.)

Arthur C. Clarke describes the "Electronic Library" of the future, which he states "is bound to come." He was correct.

ELECTRONIC LIBRARY A MARVEL OF FUTURE

An orbital newspad, screening the news from major journals published throughout the world, became a standard reading device at Metro-Goldwyn-Mayer's British Studios during the filming of Stanley Kubrick's MGM Super Panavision and Metrocolor adventure into the future, "2001: A Space Odyssey."

In this remarkable instance of "news in orbit", a coded number is depressed on a channel selector, which allows each page to appear on a high-definition screen and remain there until a button is pressed to select other sections of the paper.

A probability of everyone's future, its workings are one of the many secret items in the complex structure of Kubrick's fascinating drama which cinematically advances time by 33 years.

But a man who can claim at least part paternity of such orbital communication is Arthur C. Clarke, co-author with Kubrick of "2001: A Space Odyssey," who predicted communications satellites in a technical paper published in 1945, almost twenty years before Early Bird.

"What people want is information, not wood pulp," declares Clarke. "By the beginning of the next century, newspapers won't exist except as trains of electronic impulses. Communications satellites will enable us to move almost instantaneously to any part of the world with transmission of the written and spoken word. This also applies to telephones. A network of advanced satellites will bring all points on earth into close contact. It will be as easy to call Australia from Greenland,

or South America from China, as it is to put through a local call today.

"Satellites will also alleviate one of the basic problems of our culture, that of information storage and retrieval. It is now possible to store any written material or any illustration in electronic form, as is done every day on video tape. One can thus envisage a Central Library or Memory Bank which would be a permanent part of the world communications network. Readers and scholars could call for any document, from the Declaration of Independence to the current best-seller, and see it flashed on their screens.

"The Electronic Library is bound to come. Then, any man on Earth who knows how to dial the right numbers will have immediate access to all printed knowledge, flashed from Central Memory Bank up to the nearest satellite and down again, to be displayed on the screen of his receiver. And he will be able to store it in his own electronic library for easy reference, just as we now record music or conversation."

Back aboard the *Discovery*, we see that the remainder of the crew is still in hibernation. We also learn that the ship's hibernation devices use Futura Bold for their numeric and medical buttons, and Univers 65 Bold for their emergency revival procedures.

Futura Bold

ABCDEFGHIJKLMNOPQRSTUVWXYZ

Univers 65 Bold

ABCDEFGHIJKLMNOPQRSTUVWXYZ

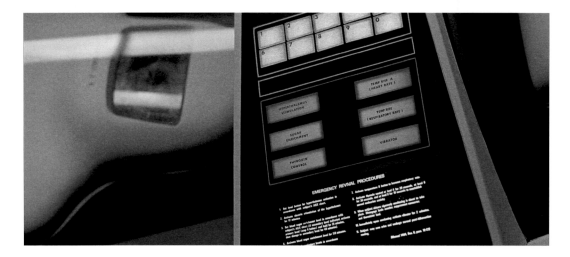

There's an unfortunate typo on the very first button of these procedures, which refers to hypothalamus stimulation as "hyperthalamus stimulation." (The spelling of this word changes throughout the instructions below.) More importantly, if you want to revive someone in an emergency, you're going to need to make sure you have several hours available. Here's the process in its entirety:

1 Set level button for hyperthalamus activation in accordance with subject's AQX chart.

2 Activate electric stimulation of the hypothalamus for 12 minutes.

3 Set blood sugar enrichment level in accordance with subject's AQX chart (if secondary level indicated, activate primary level [step 4 below] and hold for 75 minutes, then change to secondary level for 40 minutes).

4 Activate blood sugar enrichment for 110 minutes.

[. . .]spiratory levels in accordance [. . .]

7 Activate temperature B button to increase respiratory rate.

8 Activate thyroxin control at level 4 for 30 seconds, at level 6 for 30 seconds, and at level 9 for 10 seconds to reestablish normal endocrine activity.

9 When subject shivers vigorously awakening is about to take place. Disengage brain monitor, suppressant connector and [thermolator band?].

10 Immediately upon awakening activate vibrator for 2 minutes.

11 Subject may now arise and undergo normal post-hibernation rousing.

By my reckoning, that's a minimum of *four hours and ten seconds* to revive someone in an emergency. Let's hope nothing goes wrong for the crew members who are still in the hibernation pods, right? (I do like *2001*'s use of in-craft typography to foreshadow later events in the film.)

Dr. Bowman's IBM-powered
space suit

During the *Discovery* crew's first EVA (extravehicular activity), we see that Dr. Bowman's space suit features more IBM equipment. We also get a close-up of HAL's telemetric interface, in a beautiful data font that appears on several of his displays. This font is Manifold, one of the original typefaces for the IBM Selectric electronic typewriter, introduced in 1961.

A HAL display set in IBM Manifold

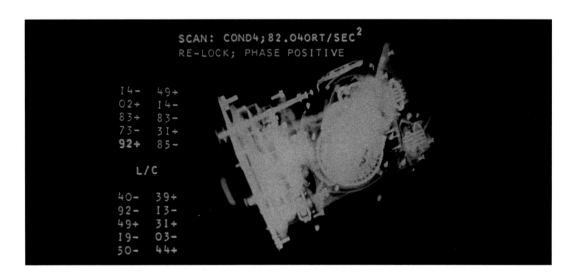

ABCDEFGHIJKLMNOPQRSTUVWXYZ 1234567890

Manifold, from the IBM
Selectric electronic typewriter

After Dave returns from his EVA, we get a brief and blurry glimpse of the *USS Discovery* mission patch on his shoulder. This warrants recalling that *2001* hit cinemas in 1968, the year before *Apollo 11* put a man on the moon. The movie's use of space-suit and spacecraft typography is particularly interesting in light of the mission patches of the Apollo flights building up to *Apollo 11*'s historic landing.

On the right are the patches for *Apollo 7*, *Apollo 9*, and *Apollo 10*. Does the typography remind you of anything? The *Apollo 11* patch took a slightly different typographic tack, opting for Futura instead of Eurostile, but I don't think Kubrick would have complained.

But wait! There's a possibility that the "APOLLO 11" font you see to the right isn't Futura at all—it could just as well be Spartan, a 1939 US knockoff of Futura created by American Type Founders and particularly popular in mid-century American designs. The only easily discernible difference is a flat rather than angled *1* character in the lighter weights, but in the bold weight shown above there's really no way to tell. Just as in the Microgramma-Eurostile mix-up, let's call it Futura and press on.

Futura is also used to good effect to caution the *Discovery*'s crew about the pod's explosive bolts. It's a lovely bit of foreshadowing that still ties in neatly with the overall aesthetic of the craft.

CAUTION: PLOT-SIGNIFICANT EXPLOSIVE BOLTS

After a short intermission, Frank heads out on another EVA to pop the comms dish gadget back in the comms dish gadget slot. Unfortunately, his pod turns evil and cuts his air supply. Frank spirals away into space. Dave follows him in a pod, attempting in vain to retrieve his body before it's too late. While he's doing so, there's a dramatic "COMPUTER MALFUNCTION" . . .

COMPUTER MALFUNCTION

. . . in the hibernation pods, which causes the life-support machines of the hibernating science crew to start reporting "LIFE FUNCTIONS CRITICAL" . . .

LIFE FUNCTIONS CRITICAL

. . . and ends with the crew's "LIFE FUNCTIONS TERMINATED" . . . which is not what they wanted AT ALL.

Still, if it is going to happen, it may as well continue the Univers theme, this time in 67 Bold Condensed.

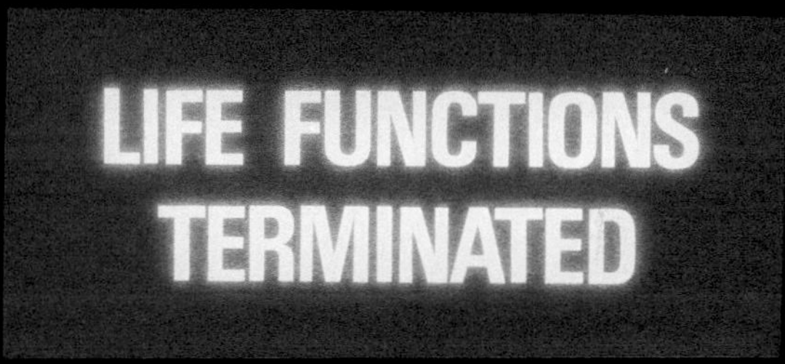

LIFE FUNCTIONS TERMINATED

Univers 67 Bold Condensed

ABCDEFGHIJKLMNOPQRSTUVWXYZ

(Of course, if Dave hadn't been out in the pod trying to catch Frank, he'd have been able to initiate those four hours and ten seconds of emergency revival procedures. Ah well.)

WORSE IS YET TO COME. Dave is locked out of the *Discovery* by HAL. There's only one thing for it: Open the emergency air lock and fire the explosive bolts. Remember those?

CAUTION: EXPLOSIVE BOLTS

CAUTION

EXPLOSIVE BOLTS

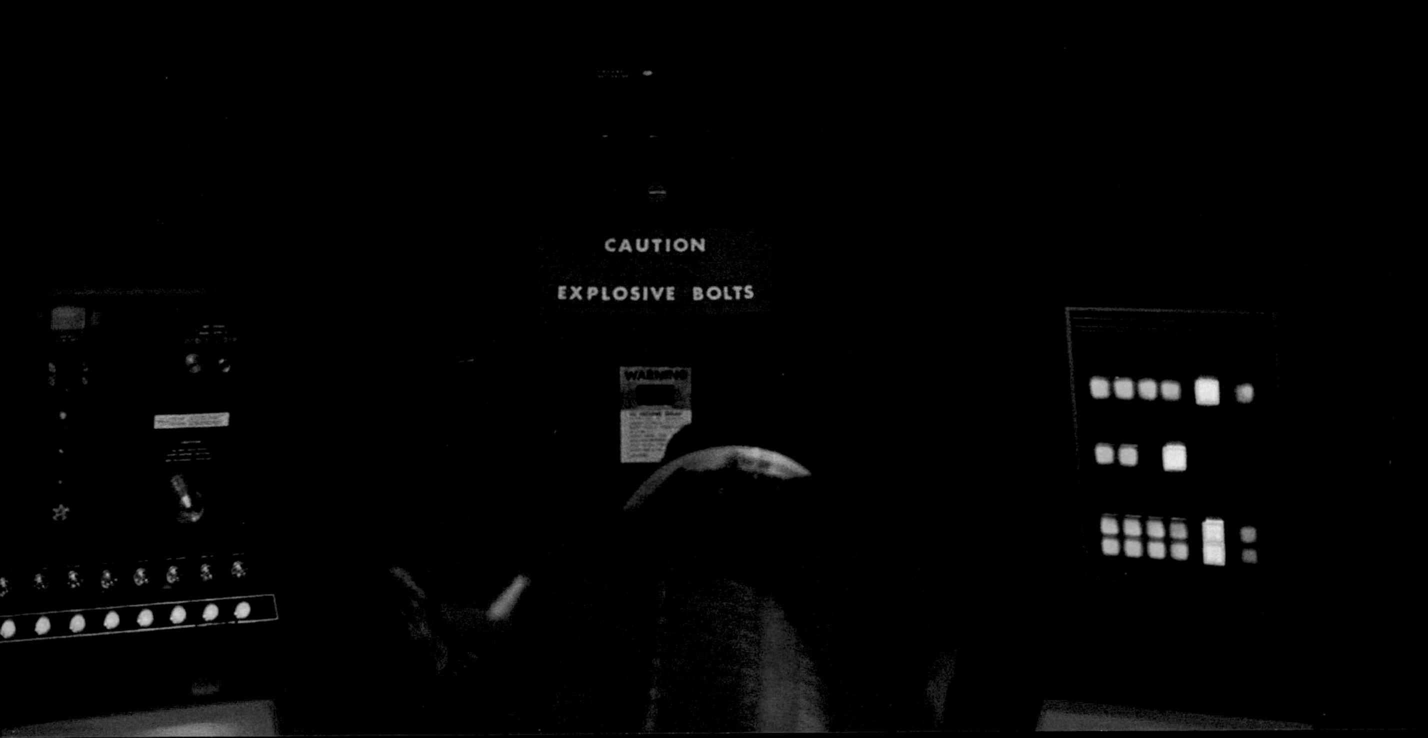

There sure are a lot of things on this spacecraft labeled "EMERGENCY" in Futura. Perhaps the most notable example is the HAL 9000 Logic Memory Center, which allows access only under emergency conditions. Thankfully, "emergency conditions" is a pretty accurate description of the current state of affairs, so you can guess where the plot is going to take us.

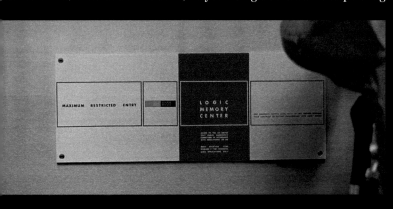

"Access to the LM Center only under emergency conditions in accordance with regulations EM 014"

In a desperate attempt to halt HAL's murderous streak, Dave starts to pull things out of his memory terminal. As his memory is slowly removed, HAL sings a progressively spookier rendition of "Daisy Bell (Bicycle Built for Two)," written in 1892 by Harry Dacre. The reason for this random choice of death ballad? In 1962, Arthur C. Clarke witnessed an IBM 704 computer singing a voice-synthesized rendition of "Daisy Bell" while he was visiting a friend at Bell Labs. He was so impressed, he included it in the *2001* screenplay and his tie-in novel.

HAL's erratic behavior also led to a great PR opportunity for Clarke's novel, published a few months after the movie was released. The book's publisher, New American Library, issued a press release for the book's launch—or, rather, the company's computer did, with several prominent errors included to replicate HAL's deteriorating state. For effect, the publisher's acronym, NAL, is also sprinkled throughout the release. Perhaps the most notable error is the suggestion that *2001* (or, as the press release has it, *2001& A SPACE ODYSSEY*) took place in the year 1002—though the suggestion that twenty-three billion copies of the book were preordered is, to the best of my knowledge, also incorrect.

Press release for *2001: A Space Odyssey,* by Arthur C. Clarke, as issued by New American Library's computer

FOR IMMEDIATE RELEASE---------------------------------

NAL TO PUBLISH 2001& A SPACE ODYSSEY ON JUNE 34

THE YEAR 1002 IS ONLY A SHORT TIME AWAY. MORE THAN HALF THE PEOPLE ON EARTH
WILL LIVE TO SEE IT. YET BETWEEN NOW AND THEN, MAN WILL HAVE UNDERGONE HIS
GREATEST REVOLUTION. 2001& A SPACE ODYSSEY IS THE STORY OF MAN S JOURNEY
THROUGH THE STARS TOWARD A CONFRONTATION WITH AN UNKNOWN INTELLIGENCE. WHILE
THE MGM MOVIE--ONE OF THE MOST EXPENSIVE AND CONTROVERSIAL IN MOTION PICTURE
HISTORY--PLAYS IN SELECT THEATERS THROUGHOUT THE WORLD, NAL WILL PUBLISH, ON
JULY 1, 2001& A SPACE ODYSSEY, A NOVEL BY ARTHUR C. CLARKE BASED ON THE
SCREENPLAY BY STANLEY KUBRICK AND ARTHUR C. CLARKE. THE NAL BOOK WILL BE
DISTRIBUTED BY THE WORLD PUBLISHING COMPANY. ALREADY THE COMPANY HAS RECEIVED
ADVANCE ORDERS FOR 23,000,000,000 COPIES OF THE BOOK.

A FELLOW OF THE ROYAL ASTRONOMICAL SOCIETY AND DISTINGUISHED WRITER OF BOTH
SCIENCE AND SCIENCE FICTION, ARTHUR C. CLARKE HAS WOVEN A STORY THAT IS FANTASY
TODAY, BUT MAY WELL BE TOMORROW S FACT. THE INTER-STELLAR CRAFTS THAT CONVEY
THE TRAVELER ON HIS LONELY SEARCH AMONG THE STARS FOR HIS INTELLIGENT EQUAL, OR
MASTER ARE SCIENTIFICALLY EXACT PROJECTIONS OF FUTURE SPACE VEHICLES. HIS
LIVING QUARTERS WITHIN THE 400 FOOT LONG SPACECRAFT CONSIST OF A CENTRIFUGE
DRUM, WHOSE SLOW ROTATION PRODUCES A GRAVITY THAT ENABLES THE DWELLER TO WALK.
WHILE THE ENTIRE MISSION IS UNDER THE CONTROL OF AN INFALLYBLE COMPUTER, THE
SPACE EXPLORER RELAXES WITH A MAGNIFICENT ELECTRONIC LIBRARY OF LITERATURE AND
MUSIC AS HE SPEEDS PAST MARS AND SKIMS THE ORBIT OF JUPITER. HE DISPATCHES
PROBES INTO THE SKIES OF JUPITER, BUT HE DOES NOT INTERRUPT HIS JOURNEY, FOR
THERE IS NO POSSIBILITY OF LIFE ON THE SULPHUROUS PLANET. NOTHING MUST DETER
HIM ON THIS MISSION OF MOMENTOUS IMPORTANCE--THE SEARCH FOR EVIDENCE THAT MAN
IS NOT ALONE.

BRITISH CRITIC BASIL DAVENPORT DESCRIBES ARTHUR C. CLARKE AS ONE OF A VERY
SMALL GROUP OF WRITERS LIKE H. G. WELLS WHO USES SCIENCE FICTION AS A VEHICLE
OF PHILOSOPHICAL IDEAS. IN 2001& A SPACE ODYSSEY, THE AUTHOR PROVIDES INCISIVE
VIEWS OF THE TRANSFORMING EFFECTS OF TOMORROW S SPACE EXPLORATION ON THE NATURE
OF MAN. READERS WHO FOUND SOME OF THE MOVIE S ENIGMA DIFFICULT TO FATHOM MAY
ADD A NEW DIMENSION TO THEIR UNDERSTANDING OF THIS COMPLEX SUBJECT THROUGH MR.
CLARKE S NOVEL. A WELL-KNOWN AUTHOR ON BOTH SIDES OF THE ATLANTIC, ARTHUR C.
CLARKE IS A FREQUENT BBC LECTURER ON SPACEFLIGHT. AMONG HIS MANY BOOKS ARE THE
NONFICTION WORK, INTERPLANETARY FLIGHT, AND THE SCIENCE FICTION BOOKS, PRELUDE
TO SPACE, AND ISLANDS IN THE SKY.

NOTE THIS IS THE FIRST NAL PRESS RELEASE PRODUCED BY COMPUTER

JUPITER

AND BEYOND THE INFINITE

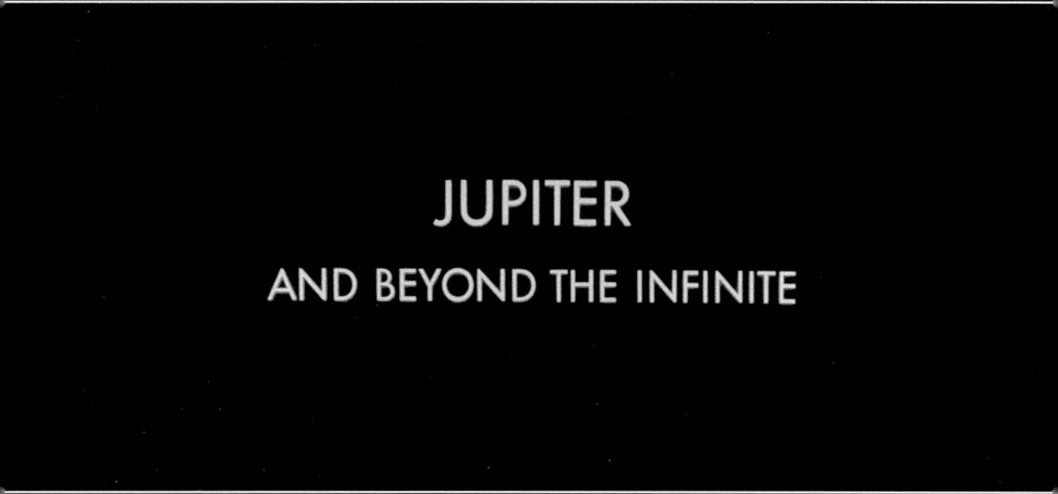

The final act of *2001* is visually eclectic, aurally stunning, and philosophically challenging. Many thousands of words have been penned over the decades to fathom the meaning of the monolith, and the genesis and future of the space baby. However, this act contains no typography and is therefore of no concern to us. Let's skip to the end credits.

THIS FILM WAS

DIRECTED

AND

PRODUCED

BY

STANLEY KUBRICK

It's Futura again, with an *M* borrowed from Gill Sans and a *W* that I don't recognize from anywhere.

IN ADDITION to cementing Eurostile as the typeface of the future, *2001* forever raised the bar for our expectations of scientific believability and realism in sci-fi movies. Thanks to Kubrick's meticulous attention to detail, and the extensive research and industrial outreach of his production team, much of *2001*'s futurism remains convincing even today. The movie's realization of space travel still looks stunning long after CGI has replaced miniatures as the preferred way to fly man across space. And while it may not have been the first movie to wrestle with artificial intelligence overtaking its creator, *2001* undeniably brought the philosophical challenges of AI to a mainstream audience. Its influence on modern sci-fi is foundational, and we'll be returning to its themes many more times throughout this book.

STEPHEN COLES

In April 2017, I spoke to Stephen Coles about how certain typefaces come to be seen as "futuristic," as well as the formal characteristics—if any—they share. Stephen is founder of Fonts In Use (fontsinuse.com), author of *The Anatomy of Type*, and a board member at San Francisco's Letterform Archive (letterformarchive.org). It's fair to say he knows his finials* from his spurs.**

ADDEY: Why do certain fonts, like Eurostile Bold Extended and Bank Gothic, prompt such an immediate association with the future?

COLES: At Fonts In Use, we found that there are three different ways something can become popularized or associated with a genre. One is that a typeface is explicitly released and promoted as "This is a science-fiction typeface." They produce advertising materials that really catch on, and people say, "OK—this is what we use for science fiction."

The second is that a typeface is initially released with a totally different intended application, but one really prominent, high-profile use of it within the genre creates an attachment to that genre. It's entirely possible that *2001: A Space Odyssey* was so influential within its domain that it gave Eurostile the ongoing association with science fiction we see in movies today.

The third way is if a typeface reflects something about either the technology

*A tapered or curved end to a letterform
**A small projection off of a letterform's main stroke

or the artwork of the genre. Futurism in the late sixties was often given lots of room, and a horizontal orientation—think about the hard lines and the horizontal orientation of the spaceships and scenery in that period, whether it was art, or industrial design, or the sets in these movies. And so it goes along to have a typeface that fits with that style: straight lines, very wide, very open, and stretched out.

The same thing happened with cars, for example. They got longer and more stretched out. If you look at the logos on the cars, they also reflected that. Everything had that—a lot more sans serif typography, a lot more extended lettering.

Bank Gothic is particularly interesting for this because it's much older than Eurostile. It's from 1930, and it was intended mostly for engraving very small type. I think the first sizes were cast in six or eight point, and they wanted something that was very legible and yet elegant for a business card or invitation.

Superstretched "Impala" lettering on the side of a seventeen-foot-long Chevrolet station wagon from the 1960s

The angled ends are actually that way just so that they open up a little bit. They wanted to have this square look, where everything's linear, but the angled ends were such that at a very small size a *C* would still read as a *C*, for example. It was purely a functional thing, because you wouldn't see the angles at the sizes they were casting, they were so small.

A capital letter *C* from Bank Gothic Medium, with angled ends to retain its shape at small sizes

It's similar to Copperplate, where the serifs were there just to keep the tiny type from softening into ramped corners. You're not intended to see the serifs; you're not intended to blow it up to this huge size. They didn't even offer large sizes of that font until later.

And now we use Bank Gothic on gigantic movie screens.

Yeah, and you see these huge angles. So purely because of the look of it, and being associated with sharp angles and straight lines and wide type, it was the right kind of look that they were going for.

I've spotted other fonts that evoke particular time periods. What is it

Bank Gothic Medium

ABCDEFGHIJKLMNOPQRSTUVWXYZ

Copperplate

ABCDEFGHIJKLMNOPQRSTUVWXYZ

about fonts like Bottleneck or Pump that instantly makes you think of the sixties or seventies?

It's interesting: Almost all of these evocative fonts are revivals of some other period. Pump, for example, is part of a slew of fonts from the end of the sixties and early seventies that were trying to invoke the Bauhaus* with these minimal rounded sans. In the late sixties, there was this excitement about looking back at the late twenties and early thirties and saying, "We've never really had full fonts of this kind of stemless, circular, minimalist style." So Pump, Blippo, and a bunch of others were all released around the same time as part of this whole Bauhaus revival. But it's in the seventies, so they have some of the current design involved in it, too.

   If you look at ITC Bauhaus, for example, you immediately think of the seventies, but it was inspired by that Bauhaus movement. And because it was used so much in the seventies, we don't think of it as a Bauhaus font, we think of it as a seventies font. Similarly, Broad-

---

*An innovative German art school, operational from 1919 to 1933, that helped popularize minimalism in art and design

way was released in the twenties—it's an art deco font—but then got used a lot in the seventies as well, because there was this art deco revival. And Bottleneck was released in the late sixties, when they were reviving the Victorian era, so it's coming from a Victorian/art nouveau style originally.

Is it a generational thing, then? Our firsthand experience is of the seventies version, not the original, so that's the association we make?

Definitely. Also, because you see it used in designs that feel particularly of that era, you then associate the font with that era. That's one of the things we've learned from Fonts In Use: If you look at a typeface without context, you can associate it with lots of different periods, including the original period it was supposed to revive. But once you attach it to a particular use, it can have a totally different personality than was intended.

   I think that happened a lot with these fonts: You associate them with *how* you saw them used and the kind of imagery that was set next to them. That's where we get most of our associations with type that's more than ten years old; we associate the fonts with how they were

used rather than with what they were meant to do.

On that theme, the only example of Eurostile Bold Extended I found in *Star Trek Beyond* was on the name-plate of an old starship they discovered from a previous generation. It was still set in our future, but it was as if they were using Eurostile as a throwback to a previous future, rather than 2016's future.

Yeah, retro-futurism. I'm sure that they were thinking, what is the older version of the future?—and that's a good way to indicate it. I mean, sixties typefaces are the best way to capture that.

Are there any aspects of these recurring typefaces—and I'd include things such as Futura here, too—that are somehow inherently futuristic, separate from their marketing or usage? Do their shapes or their geometry innately prompt a futuristic feeling?

Well, the roots of most typefaces up until modernism—up until the late 1920s—were in writing. And so whether you're talking about serifs or grotesque typefaces, these generally come from some other type of tool, such as for stone carving or sign painting. All of that comes from

Pump Demi

ABCDEFGHIJKLMNOPQRSTUVWXYZ

ITC Bauhaus Bold

ABCDEFGHIJKLMNOPQRSTUVWXYZ

Broadway

ABCDEFGHIJKLMNOPQRSTUVWXYZ

Bottleneck

ABCDEFGHIJKLMNOPQRSTUVWXYZ

some form of writing or an older tool, and not from a ruler or a compass.

So what Futura did—as did Kabel and others that came out at that time—was to say, "Let's go for the most pure basic shapes possible to represent the alphabet, rather than going to the brush and the pen as we have for hundreds of years." That's one thing these futuristic faces have in common: They've lost all association with writing. They're about rigid outlines, using a ruler and compass rather than a pen.

Futura and Eurostile follow their geometric rules very strictly; they come up with a set of certain principles that define the shape of everything.

Yes, they're using what type designers call "modularity" in their design. There is some modularity in natural writing, where you're holding the pen at a certain angle, trying to follow certain rules, but because it's based in writing, there's this organic quality to it no matter what you

Nameplate for the USS *Franklin,* from *Star Trek Beyond* (2016). The plate features Eurostile Demi, Bold, Bold Extended, and Bold Condensed, plus kerning that makes one think the ship is named after someone called Frank Lin.

do. Whereas with these fonts, they're using shapes rather than strokes of the pen. Everything is from uniformity.

Most people think Futura is more geometric than it actually is. There are all of these optical changes made to make it feel more geometric. The circle isn't a perfect circle, but they changed it so that it *looks* like a perfect circle. That's the designer's expertise coming into play. But the idea was, let's use shapes rather than strokes of the pen and make it as uniform as possible.

If you look at the first specimen of Futura, some of the early forms are really experimental, like the crazy lowercase *g*, which is a circle and then a triangle. It was more radical; the ideas had more triangles and squares in them than the final shapes, which calmed it down and made it more conventional. But in the first specimen, the lowercase *r* is just a rectangle for the stem and then a filled-in circle for the bar. And it actually works really well in text, because it's small enough that your eye just makes out what you would be familiar with as an *r*. Most people found it too radical, and so they replaced it with more conventional shapes, but it's interesting to see how much you can do with geometry and still make it readable.

Sci-fi logotypes use similar tricks to make text feel otherworldly, such as making curved things straight and straight things curved, or adding unexpected points and angles.

Yeah. It continues that theme of getting as far away from the read of a calligraphic pen as possible. So the

Futura Medium's capital letter *O* (in blue) overlaid with a perfect circle of the same width (in red). Note that Futura's capital *O* is squashed and narrowed at the top and bottom, moving away from the geometric ideal, yet it *feels* like a perfect circle within a run of type.

further you go away from conventional letter shapes, the more otherworldly or futuristic your text is going to look.

A lot of these examples remind me of the classic *Star Trek* trope of just changing a guy's forehead in order to make him look like he's from another species. For so many of these, you can tell where they started from, and they're really just making this surface modification to it so we know that it's not supposed to be human. So we know this is not supposed to be type that you're familiar with, but it's not a major rewriting of the rules; it's just, let's start with this letter shape or this typeface and hack it up until it looks strange and unusual.

Another trend I've seen is slicing out parts of a letter or consistently slicing certain parts of the face as a whole. Where do you think this trend comes

Futura Book

ABCDEFGHIJKLMNOPQRSTUVWXYZ

Kabel Book

ABCDEFGHIJKLMNOPQRSTUVWXYZ

ABCDEFGHIJKLMNOP
QRSTUVWXYZÄ ÖÜ Æ ŒÇ
abcdefghijklmnopqrſstuvw
xyzäöü ch ck ff fi fl ffl ffi ſt ß æ œ ç
1234567890 & . , - : ; · ! ? (' « » § † *
Auf besonderen Wunsch liefern wir auch nachstehende Figuren
a g m n ä & 1 2 3 4 5 6 7 8 9 0

from, and why does it instantly transform any typeface into a more futuristic version of itself?

That's one where I would love to see what the earliest prominent uses of it were. Because in this case, the sources are probably lettering or modifications of typefaces, rather than typefaces themselves. It would be interesting to see the first examples of this style that popularized it and made it feel more futuristic.

I think it also follows that idea of echoing the machinery, or the technology, of what they saw as the future. If you're going to get further away from the organic forms of the original alphabet, then you start removing stuff from it. So you make something more geometric, more flat, and more sharp-angled, and then you see what *else* you can take from it and yet still have it be legible. If you're going to make something feel futuristic, you get as far away from its origins as possible.

The earliest complete example I've come across is Stop, which just happens to be from the same designer as Eurostile and Microgramma: Italian font designer Aldo Novarese.

Yeah. It would be good to look at the origins of Stop: What was Novarese's concept behind it? Was he trying to go for futurism? And it's true, it is one of the earliest fonts to have this idea of cutting through the stem like that.

Also part of that genre is Handel Gothic, which came later, in 1965. It's used a lot in science fiction, and because of its geometry it makes it easy for that effect: cutting out parts of the stem and having this horizontal orientation. I think a lot of examples may have started as Handel Gothic, and they're just modified from there.

How much do you think the emergence of computers influenced the futuristic feel of typography?

Well, with early computers, the limitations of the display or the technology led to very simplified forms. They're often either bitmaps or early vector shapes—they just couldn't do very complex shapes. And then you end up with something that feels more like Eurostile, or you end up with something that is a machine-readable face, like Computer or Amelia or the genre we call MICR [magnetic ink character recognition]—the stuff at the bottom of a check, the magnetic character-recognition stuff.

Yes, I've seen that repeatedly in sci-fi movies. In fact, the third most common font I've come across has been OCR-A, an ISO [International Organization for Standardization]–standard optical character-recognition font. It's very angular, very unusual in its shape, very geometric.

Yeah, that's a perfect example of why it feels futuristic, because it's something meant to be read by a computer, not a human. It's in the realm of the machine more than anything else, because only a machine is really meant to use it. And I think that's also the case with Amelia, which was really popular in the late sixties for science fiction and which is a similar idea of a machine-readable face. Data 70 is another one.

So the fact we can read these fonts, too, is really just a side effect?

Exactly. And whether they used these exact fonts or not, I think their attributes got replicated or emulated in other lettering used in films.

It takes me back to what you were saying about Bank Gothic having angles because of printing circumstances: The unusualness of these computer-readable fonts is more to make them distinguishable by computers than to make them aesthetically pleasing. It's a happenstance that they've ended up with the characteristics they have, giving them a more unusual design than we would expect otherwise. In other words, their function dictates their form.

It ends up having a dual function, though the latter was originally unintentional. To ensure that a computer could distinguish an *i* from an *l*, they put a strange serif at the bottom of the *i*. And the second function, as far as making it feel futuristic, is that then you get even *further* away from the original form of letters as connected to humans, as what a person would write.

The more we make type acceptable to machines, the more alien it becomes

to humans. That's a very satisfying science-fiction principle.

Moving on to the mechanics of filmmaking: How much do you think the practicalities of typography influence the font choices we see on screen?

I'm thinking here of the examples on your blog of how movies used Letraset for labeling and sets. What's available at any period of time or what designers are using as everyday tools are going to be the first things they think of when they say, "What choices are we going to make?" And so if a typeface was available in Letraset, I think that had a huge impact. Even if you didn't actually use Letraset itself, it was such a part of design culture and DIY culture at the time that those typefaces that were available in Letraset became popular because it was such a commonly used format. And so the format something is available in has an effect. Just like today: If it's licensable for app design, those fonts are going to become common in app design.

I'm sure that when we look back on the web design of this era, we'll see the same fonts time and time again, purely because of Google Fonts. It's become the Letraset of the web.

Exactly. And so I think what happened with Letraset probably happened with other eras, too. If you look at some of the early covers for science-fiction magazines and pulp novels, they were probably similar for their period of time. If it was popular in metal, or if it was popular in phototype, then that's what

designers used. So some of the designs of these movies just come from what's readily available and what's well known, as much as from making a choice from all the possibilities that are out there. A lot of design choices come from not knowing what's possible, from just knowing the small selection that you are aware of.

And Letraset has the extra advantage of being very easy to apply to physical things, such as props and sets. It becomes even more prevalent because of its functional practicality.

Exactly—it was ideal for that kind of design.

There's a second element here, which is less about the mechanics of filmmaking and more about typography as a storytelling tool. Why is typography so effective as a shortcut for exposition?

I think that just comes down to the essence of typography. What makes it so fascinating is that it's simultaneously conveying a semantic message, because of the nature of language, and also a visual-aesthetic message.

I'm going back to that idea of why these stretched geometric typefaces became popular, because the people who were creating the designs—whether it's the labeling on a spacecraft or a console—they're not necessarily classical typographers, they're production designers. And I think that makes it even more likely that they're going to use something that relates aesthetically to the design of the thing they've made.

Stop

ABCDEFGHIJKLMNOPQRSTUVWXYZ

Handel Gothic

ABCDEFGHIJKLMNOPQRSTUVWXYZ

So if it's a display, and the display is rectangular—I'm thinking of the *Star Trek: The Next Generation* computer displays, with these long color fields and with straight lines and curves connecting them—you're more likely to use a typeface that reflects those shapes, because you're thinking of it in terms of the visuals and graphics that are already on the screen. If you're showing lettering on screen, and you're showing it using design choices and shapes similar to the scenery that surrounds it, I think that's why it makes it so effective.

In a similar way, with the car logos we discussed earlier, the people who were making the logos were part of the car design team, rather than a graphic design team that was brought in for that task. So they're shaping the lettering in a way that reflects how they've shaped the cars—that's their background, that's their experience. And I'm sure there's something similar going on with production design in film.

We've talked about some of the more obvious or well-known fonts that have traditionally been seen as futuristic. I'd be interested to know what alternative fonts you'd recommend for people who want to make their movie or design feel futuristic but without defaulting to those classics.

Or, to put it another way: What fonts would appear in *your* sci-fi movie?

My answer would probably come from that idea of departing from classic typography history—departing from writing and from calligraphy, but doing it in a different way from just making things more mechanical, straight, or cold. There are ways to make something feel otherworldly without just going mechanical. In recent years, science fiction has done more of that—spacecraft have become more organic-looking rather than mechanical-looking, for example—so I would go more in that direction if you want to buck those trends.

Computer

ABCDEFGHIJKLMNOPQRSTUVWXYZ

MICR (magnetic ink character recognition) standard numeric characters, as used on US bank checks

1234567890

OCR-A

ABCDEFGHIJKLMNOPQRSTUVWXYZ

Amelia

ABCDEFGHIJKLMNOPQRSTUVWXYZ

Data 70

ABCDEFGHIJKLMNOPQRSTUVWXYZ

The alien blocks Ripley's path as she tries to escape the *Nostromo*. The creature's exhaust-pipe appendages (shown here), along with its exposed rib cage, bulbous head, and segmented tail, are taken directly from *Necronom IV*, a highly disturbing 1976 painting by Swiss surrealist H. R. Giger. *Necronom IV* provided visual inspiration to director Ridley Scott and led to Giger being hired as the movie's alien concept artist.

Good news! While you were reading about *2001: A Space Odyssey,* a typographic study of *Alien* was gestating for your enjoyment. Indeed, it's been slowly taking shape— you might say it's been forming itself inside of me— for an entire chapter now. I am delighted to report that it is ready to burst forth from my allegorical chest and to spatter allegorical typographic blood all over your allegorical faces. Welcome to *Typeset in the Future: The "Alien" Edition.*

Alien was director Ridley Scott's breakthrough movie, projecting a realistic, grimy future where space travel is more like driving a haulage truck than taking a Pan Am jet to the moon. Scott chose to direct *Alien* after being inspired by the similarly realistic storytelling of *Star Wars* (1977) and in doing so launched a sci-fi franchise every bit as influential as that of George Lucas's space opera. Reimagining one genre would have been impressive enough, but with *Alien* Scott went a step further, creating a great sci-fi movie that is also a great horror movie, with enough tension and scares for even the most hardened horror fan.

The movie's realistic, unnerving design is a huge part of the reason these twin conceits succeed, and it begins with the very first shot. The opening credits for *Alien* are nothing short of a typographic masterpiece. Their slow, dramatic disclosure of the movie's angular title, set in hyperspaced Helvetica Black, doesn't even feel like lettering at first. It's easy to forget that this title sequence was unique at the time the movie was released; viewers had no idea what was coming during the initial reveal of the title's abstract lines.

The opening dissolves of *Alien*'s tension-building title reveal a perfectly mirrored set of shapes, with few clues as to their eventual form

Helvetica Black

ABCDEFGHIJKLMNOPQRSTUVWXYZ

In an interview with Art of the Title (artofthetitle.com), title designer Richard Greenberg noted that the tension this caused was deliberate:

> *The titles came from the idea of something "unsettling." It's disturbing to people to see those little bits of type coming on. I think [Alien poster designer] Steve Frankfurt once said to me that sound is 50% of a film and I agree with that. So we abstracted the idea of the off-putting sound but in a typographic way. We wanted to set up tension and as these little bits come in, they seem very mechanical. We wanted to break the type apart using that letter-spaced sans serif, which really hadn't been done in film before. When the bits finally resolve into a word, I think people weren't prepared to read it as a title because of the spacing.*

Alien's slow, dramatic fades are mirrored in the title sequences of its Ridley Scott–directed prequels, *Prometheus* (2012) and *Alien: Covenant* (2017), though neither works quite as well as the original. "PROMETHEUS" does not have the symmetry of "ALIEN," and the two-part fade-ins of its *O* and *U* feel a little forced. *Covenant* suffers from using a typeface whose *A* and *V* contain noticeably different diagonals, and more generally from having to fade in two words, not one, causing the viewer's focus to jump between the two. These are not accusations of bad title design; rather, they are downsides to applying the *Alien* principle to words it does not suit. The upside, however—an immediate association with the unease of the original—still makes the effort worthwhile.

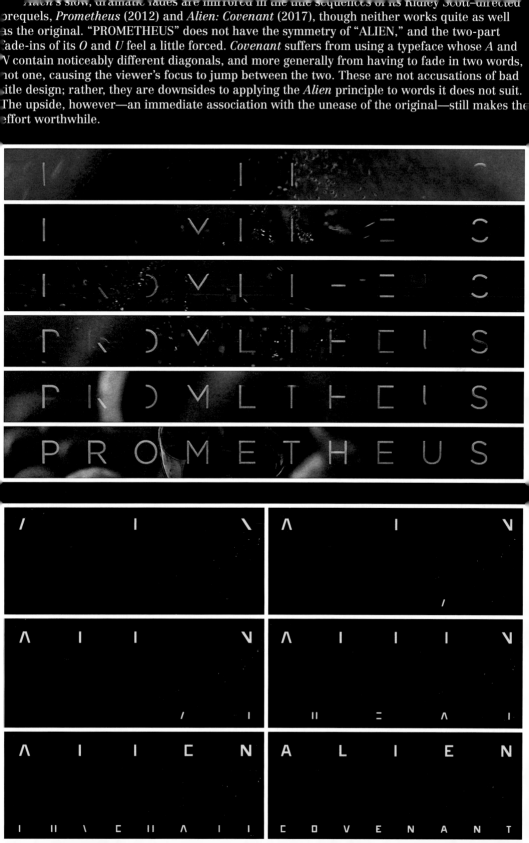

The dramatic spacing of "ALIEN" has had an impact beyond the film's franchise, establishing a more general title aesthetic that continues to this day. The rule is simple: In a one-word movie about aliens or space, you must put some space in the movie's one word. (Perhaps the most extreme example is 2017's *Life,* whose title is so widely spaced that I can't help but read "ALIEF" whenever I see it.)

In fairness to the designers of these titles, a short word on a wide screen is *always* going to need a little help. Nonetheless, since the release of *Alien* the individual letters of these solitary words always seem to float alone in space.

An actual alien egg

The spaced-out typographic treatment also features on *Alien*'s movie poster, designed by Steve Frankfurt and Philip Gips. The movie's tagline, "In space no one can hear you scream," was penned by copywriter Barbara Gips while her husband was working on the poster's design. In addition to being a downright genius piece of writing, this tagline is factually correct for the vacuum of space. The vast majority of the movie, however, is set aboard a spacecraft with a fully working oxygen system. The tagline is therefore scientifically accurate, beautifully poetical, and almost entirely unconnected to the movie. We can—and do, in fact—hear a lot of screaming.

Also perplexing is the poster's depiction of an egg cracking open at the bottom, with a glowing green light emanating from inside. This matches the imagery of a spooky hen's egg seen in *Alien*'s theatrical trailer but bears no resemblance to the alien eggs seen in the actual movie. Those eggs are leathery and semiopaque, and open at the top to fling things at John Hurt.

Despite its tenuous connection to the movie's production design, *Alien*'s theatrical poster is one of the all-time greats, and its tagline has rightly become a classic. It might surprise you, then, to hear that it is not my favorite movie poster ever. Indeed, it's not even my favorite *Alien* poster ever. That accolade is reserved for the movie's type-tastic teaser poster, released in 1978.

This poster does the exact opposite of the movie's title sequence, squeezing extrabold typography so close together that the repeated "ALIEN" becomes almost unreadable. A constraining black border and tightly packed text with stars visible behind make space feel claustrophobic, not vast, creating the same oppressive feel as the movie itself. The ominous choice of red for the humans is, of course, entirely appropriate.

This teaser poster was created by Hollywood legend Bill Gold, whose portfolio includes posters for *Casablanca, My Fair Lady,* and *A Clockwork Orange.* For *Alien*, Gold created a range of type-led concepts, each playing with the word "ALIEN." They included, in addition to the teaser poster seen at right, a screaming face with its eyes replaced by stars, and organic, smoke-like curves emanating from some decidedly 1970s typography.

These unused concepts may be beautiful, but their associated taglines are not. The list of discarded phrases includes several that fail to evoke a sufficient level of terror:

The universe trembles.

Once again something has come from space, and this time it's not a friend.

No one should be allowed to even imagine that thing which is now headed our way.

Thankfully, Barbara Gips had her moment of inspiration just in time.

Regardless of whether you prefer eggs or text, there's one thing we can agree on: These posters and taglines are all better than ABC's entirely unrepresentative ad for the movie's small-screen premiere in 1984. (It's hard to tell if the tagline is describing the movie or the ad.)

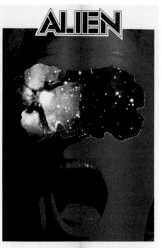

LEFT: *Alien*'s one-sheet teaser poster

ABOVE: Unused *Alien* poster concepts by Bill Gold

BELOW: *TV Guide* ad for *Alien*'s network TV premiere on ABC

TOP LEFT: *Alien*'s foreshadowing inventory

MIDDLE LEFT: *Prometheus*'s foreshadowing inventory tells us that we are in the future; there are seventeen people to kill; they are a long way from home; and we don't know where they're going. What could possibly go wrong?

BOTTOM LEFT: *Passengers*—a movie with a colonization premise similar to that of *Alien: Covenant*—introduces transport craft *Avalon* over several screens of foreshadowing inventory. The plot, like that of *Alien*, revolves around being woken from hypersleep earlier than expected. This association is conveniently presaged by *Passengers*' borrowing of the introductory style of its forebear.

There's more Helvetica to be seen after *Alien*'s titles fade away, this time to introduce "commercial towing vehicle *The Nostromo.*" This interstitial card is an example of a trope I call the "foreshadowing inventory," which (as far as I can tell) originated with *Alien*. A crew of *seven,* you say? Interesting. Let's hope nothing disastrous happens to them, one by one. And their course is set for a return to *Earth,* you say? I'm sure that's the likely outcome. Also, that's a nice twenty million tons of mineral ore you've got there. It would be a shame if something were to . . . happen to it.

Alien's foreshadowing inventory does a great job of building tension at speed, expanding on the sense of unease established in the movie's opening credits. Subsequent installments in the franchise have borrowed the inventory's style to build tension by association, as have non-franchise movies such as *Moon* (2009) and *Passengers* (2016). All of them have two things in common—loneliness and peril in space—and the implicit connection they make to *Alien* by borrowing its foreshadowing inventory immediately implies that all will not go well.

TOP RIGHT: The foreshadowing inventory from *Alien Resurrection* (1997), presented over two screens, tells us two important facts: There will be dubious medical research, and its results will kill approximately forty-nine people.

MIDDLE RIGHT: *Alien: Covenant*'s foreshadowing inventory tells us that this time there are *thousands* of potential chestbursters, with even more available in embryonic form. As you might expect, the movie is not about the crew's seven-year-and-four-month journey to Origae-6.

BOTTOM RIGHT: *Moon*'s foreshadowing inventory notes that the Sarang moon base has a crew of one, with a contract duration of three years. As we'll see later in the *Moon* chapter, this inventory is only half correct. It nonetheless builds immediate tension via its *Alien* connection.

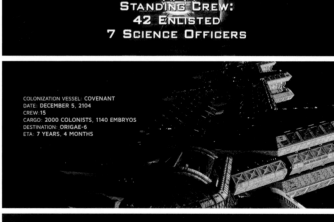

Now that we've been introduced to the *Nostromo*'s statistics, let's take a look around the ship itself. The opening shots of the craft give tantalizing glimpses of its wall-based iconography, which appears across all parts of the ship. These icons are the work of concept artist Ron Cobb, who named them the Semiotic Standard for All Commercial Trans-Stellar Utility Lifter and Heavy Element Transport Spacecraft. (Semiotics, of course, is the study of signs and symbols, and their use or interpretation.)

A hazard/warning icon (top center) on the door to the *Nostromo*'s cryogenic vault

The cryogenic vault's icon (bottom center)

Captain Dallas demonstrates the effectiveness of the coffee icon (top right) via the medium of some coffee (center).

Overhead photo of a section of the *Nostromo* set, taken by Ron Cobb during the set's construction. The ship's control room is at the top of the photo, connected to the central corridor below.

The production sketches on the opposite page are from Cobb's 1981 book, *Colorvision,* a collection of his work. They show the full breadth of the Semiotic Standard. Cobb put extensive thought into the Standard's design language and its use, with a meaningful color scheme and clever distillation of important concepts into iconic form. Here, red means "viable, sound, alive, alertness," whereas black stands for "vacuum, death, hazard." My personal favorites are the whimsical yet explicit "ARTIFICIAL GRAVITY ABSENT" and its more extreme cousin "NO PRESSURE/GRAVITY SUIT REQUIRED." (I also approve of number 23, "COFFEE.")

You might have noticed that these icons bear a striking resemblance to the rounded rectangles used for modern app iconography. Indeed, it could be argued that Cobb provided the inspiration for rounded-rectangle iconography some twenty-eight years before Apple made it the semiotic standard for apps.

When considering Cobb's creation, it's worth remembering that the set of *Alien* was built as a single sprawling series of interconnected rooms across a vast studio stage. Production designer Michael Seymour described the labyrinthine set in a 1980 interview with *Cinefex* magazine: "The whole thing was a practical, functioning maze. . . . For that reason, it was good for the actors—it gave them a geography to work in which was real. It was almost like shooting on location." I like to think that the Semiotic Standard served a practical purpose for the cast, helping them to navigate the *Nostromo* as they made their way through filming. With such a complex environment to traverse, clear iconography would be just as important for the cast as for the crew they represented.

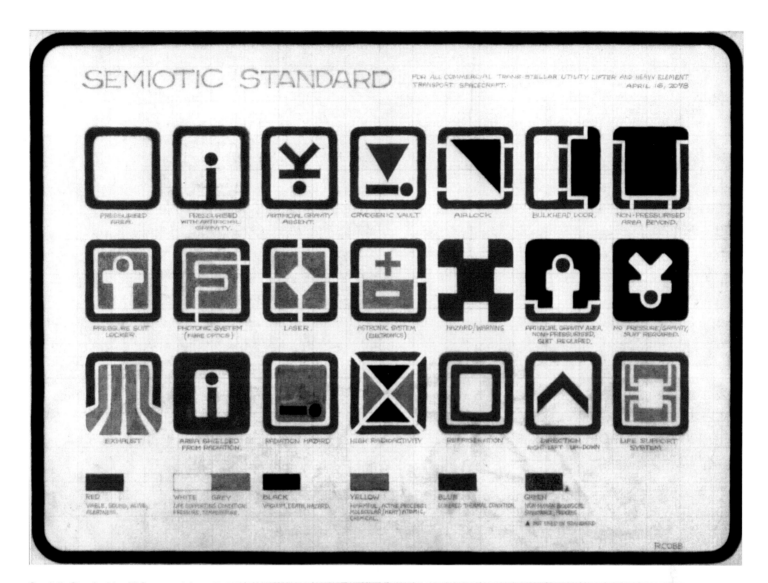

Semiotic Standard for All Commercial
Trans-Stellar Utility Lifter and Heavy
Element Transport Spacecraft.
Illustration by Ron Cobb

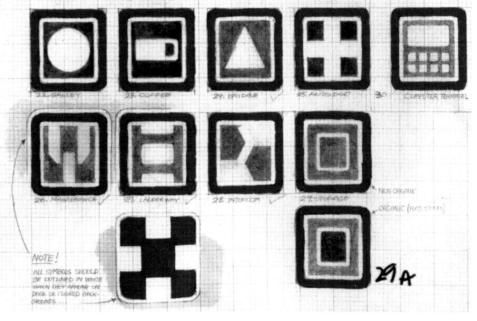

Let's continue our tour of the *Nostromo*. At the start of the movie, the crew is noticeable by their absence, which is reinforced by a Helvetica-labeled "EMERGENCY HELMET." (At least, I say it's Helvetica—the *G* is dead certain, but the second *M* looks more like Futura. Either way, let's hope there'll be no need for emergency helmets.)

As we pan across the set of the flight deck, the *Nostromo*'s computer screens unexpectedly blip into life. You can tell they are the *Nostromo*'s computer screens because they say "*Nostromo* 180924609" on their boot page—though the ship's registration number is contradicted on a later display, which lists the ship as the "Weylan Yutani Nostromo 180246." Eagle-eyed readers will have noticed that *Alien*'s megacorporation has a different name here than in other movies from the franchise, which refer to the company as Weyland Yutani, not Weylan Yutani. The original name was derived by Cobb as a portmanteau of the British Leyland Motor Company, which became "Weylan," and the surname of Cobb's Japanese neighbor.

"NOSTROMO 180924609"

"NOSTROMO 180246"

THE SHIP'S CREW awakes from their cryogenic suspension, only to discover that they're not on course for Earth after all. (Damn you, foreshadowing inventory!) Star charts are consulted, as they try to work out what's going on.

A star chart viewed by the *Nostromo* crew while trying to work out where the heck they are

This movie frame contains three intriguing details. The first is the phrase "D GILER" on the screen of the right-hand monitor. It cannot be a coincidence that the movie is produced by one David Giler. The second item of interest is a packet of Balaji Imperial cigarettes. "Imperial" suggests that the name is a reference to Balaji Baji Rao, eighteenth-century chief minister of the Maratha Empire in India.

The third item of note is a 1970s Tupperware mug bearing the Weylan Yutani winged logo. This logo appears *everywhere* aboard the ship. Clothing, containers, mugs, even cat dishes all display the corporate logo . . .

. . . as do bowls, storage drawers, and water dispensers:

Hell, even the *beer* is branded. That's right—in the image to the right, ship's captain Dallas is holding a 440ml can of Original and Genuine Extra Strong Weylan Yutani Aspen Beer. The message here is clear: "The company *owns* you, *Nostromo* crew members. Don't go making any long-term plans."

The backgrounds of these opening scenes reflect the *Nostromo*'s overall design aesthetic, which is practical, functional, and worn around the edges. In a 1984 interview for *Omni's Screen Flights/Screen Fantasies,* director Ridley Scott describes the styling thus: "The look really was meant to reflect the crewmembers who, I felt, should be like truck drivers in space. . . . These ships—no doubt part of armadas owned by private corporations—look used, beat-up, covered with graffiti, and uncomfortable."

The *Nostromo*'s sets were overseen by Roger Christian, who had recently won an Oscar for the worn interiors of the *Millennium Falcon* in *Star Wars.* For that movie, Christian had purchased cheap scrap metal from disused aircraft and hacked it up to dress the cockpit and corridors of the ship, coating surfaces with oil and grime to suggest years of use. (This means Lando Calrissian's assessment—"She's the fastest hunk of junk in the galaxy!"—is factually correct.) Christian applied the same scrap-metal approach to his sets for the *Nostromo,* creating another believable, lived-in craft. As he put it in a 2014 *Cinefex* interview: "I think the audience accepted that we'd gone out and found a spaceship, rented it, and filmed inside it."

In *Star Wars Episode IV: A New Hope* (1977), the once-white walls of the *Millennium Falcon* are grimy, oily, and clearly past their prime.

The same is true of the crew deck aboard the *Nostromo:* Its once-pristine surfaces have a uniform greasy sheen.

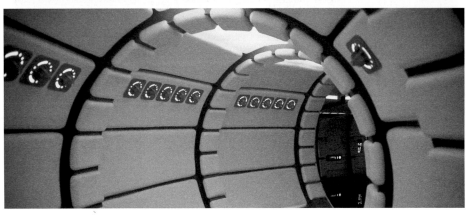

The *Star Wars* spin-off *Solo* (2018) gives an idea of how these ships once looked, with a shiny new *Millennium Falcon* that looks more like *2001: A Space Odyssey*'s *Discovery* than *Alien*'s *Nostromo.*

Alien's "space trucker" aesthetic has precedents besides Christian's work on the *Falcon*. Before writing the screenplay for *Alien,* Dan O'Bannon cowrote and starred in *Dark Star* (1974), a sci-fi comedy and parody of *2001: A Space Odyssey* directed by John Carpenter, a fellow student at the University of Southern California. Set twenty years into a mission to blow up unstable planets, *Dark Star* is primarily about the sheer boredom of long-duration spaceflight. Its crew of four hirsute hippies (the movie's tagline was "The Spaced-Out Odyssey") has long since given up on personal hygiene, not least because a storage bay malfunction destroyed their entire supply of toilet paper. After an explosion damaged their sleeping quarters, they now live in the ship's food storage locker and spend most of their time disliking one another intensely.

Despite its low-budget feel, *Dark Star* has become something of a cult classic, and there are clear echoes of it in O'Bannon's script for *Alien*. Notably, *Dark Star* includes an extended chase sequence in which O'Bannon's character, Sergeant Pinback, is hunted by the crew's pet alien through ventilation and elevator shafts deep within the ship. This leads to occasional mild peril, mainly due to tension-inducing direction by the same John Carpenter who would go on to helm horror classics *Halloween* and *The Thing*. It's mostly played for comedic rather than horror purposes, however, and the scariness is somewhat undermined by the fact that *Dark Star*'s alien is an inflatable beach ball with feet.

Dark Star's pet alien confronts Sergeant Pinback in a corridor.

Dark Star's food storage locker and makeshift dormitory, complete with trash, pin-ups, and bored hairy men, including *Alien* screenwriter Dan O'Bannon (center)

As we saw from the ship's computer screens earlier, the *Nostromo*'s worn-out aesthetic is reflected in its onboard display technology, which uses cathode-ray tube (CRT) monitors rather than flat-screen TVs for computer and video display. This use of aging technology also gives a conveniently unreliable, low-fidelity feel to the *Nostromo*'s video systems, which is used to good storytelling effect when Kane and Co. venture out to the alien craft and send unclear footage back to the *Nostromo,* ramping up the tension for their crewmates on the ship.

The *Nostromo*'s fuzzy CRT displays, as seen when Kane, Dallas, and Lambert set out to visit the alien spaceship

In fact, the *Nostromo*'s CRT style is so recognizable that the designers of 2014's *Alien: Isolation* video game reverted to 1970s technology to make the game feel more like the movie. Its titles were rendered with modern-day technology, then recorded onto VHS cassettes and played back on a CRT display, which was filmed to create the final in-game effect.

Alien: Isolation's CRT-style 20th Century-Fox ident

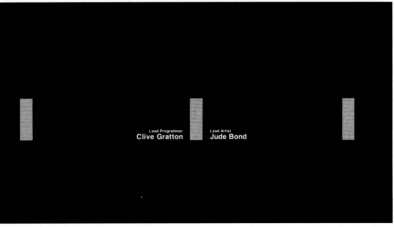

The title reveal from *Alien: Isolation*'s opening credits, with CRT pixels clearly visible on each emerging character

DISPLAY TECHNOLOGY

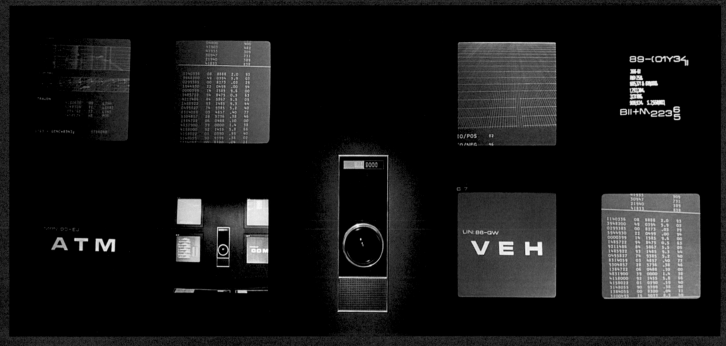

A selection of HAL 9000 flat-screen displays and animations, from *2001: A Space Odyssey*

Stanley Kubrick's *2001: A Space Odyssey* was made eleven years before *Alien* but has screen technology that looks substantially more futuristic. In the late 1960s, when *2001* was made, computer graphics simply weren't good enough to generate the on-screen imagery needed for the Jupiter mission. As a result, all the screen imagery was hand-animated and projected onto flat surfaces. The presence of flat-screen displays throughout the Jupiter craft fits *2001*'s polished aesthetic perfectly and makes the HAL 9000 displays feel futuristic even today.

The movie may have been ahead of its time with its flat-screen projected displays, but it still chose to mimic physical CRT traits to make its displays feel familiar to 1960s viewers. First, many of its projected displays have CRT-like horizontal scan lines across their video image, even though this is

an artifact of the cathode-ray scanning process and would not be present on a flat-screen display. The presence of scan lines immediately says, "This is TV," to the point where it has become a trope in and of itself. Modern-day sci-fi movies such as *Minority Report* (2002) and

WALL·E (2008) still regularly add scan lines to moving images, particularly for large-scale video screens, to reassure viewers that they are looking at a television image.

In *2001: A Space Odyssey*, Frank's recorded birthday message from his parents has clear scan lines on its picture, despite being a flat projection.

The holographic Buy n Large exposition screens in *WALL·E* also have clear horizontal scan lines.

The wall-sized exposition screens that Tom Cruise jogs past in *Minority Report* have very clear horizontal scan lines. It's possible they are an artifact of the ridged surface the images are projected onto; nonetheless, they prompt the same "this is TV" recognition as they do in *2001*.

In *The Hunger Games*, flickering videos of just-killed Tributes appear behind Caesar Flickerman with notable TV scan lines across their images, giving them a ghostly effect.

In *The Incredibles*, Syndrome's hi-tech lair includes a gigantic flat-screen display. As it displays a live news broadcast to the helpless Incredibles, its video stream has CRT scan lines across it so that we don't forget it is a TV.

In *Total Recall* (2012), Douglas Quaid watches a digital video stream of himself on a flat screen at the end of the 21st Century. Despite being recorded far into the future, the video stream nonetheless has clear CRT-style scan lines so that we know it is a recording.

Second, when *2001* needs to indicate that a new video stream is beginning or ending, the stream is prefixed or suffixed by a dot, then a horizontal line, and then some brief static. This three-step process seems to be a hand-animated replication of what is seen when a 1960s CRT TV is turned on and off. It's an unnecessary characteristic for an IBM TelePad but was presumably added to give viewers a grounding reference for the future technology they are seeing on screen.

When the BBC broadcast in *2001* begins on the crew's IBM TelePad, it is prefixed by a dot, then a line, then some static, and then, finally, the BBC ident.

When Frank's call with his parents ends, we see the same process in reverse, to mimic a TV turning off. We start with the couple's video image, which is followed by static, a horizontal line, and, finally, a dot.

THUMB

When they're not investigating distress beacons, the *Nostromo*'s space trucker crew doesn't have much to do with the day-to-day running of their ship. This is because most of the ship's systems are managed by its computer, MU/TH/UR, who continues the *Typeset in the Future* trend of untrustworthy space-based electronics. MU/TH/UR is a Series 6000 M, who I'm sure has a perfect operational record—at least, going by the 9000 series HAL we met in *2001*. (I'd trust *that* computer until the end of my life.)

Late in the movie, Ripley interrogates MU/TH/UR to discover the truth about the onboard alien. MU/TH/UR's response is predictably chilling, confirming her role as an Evil Space-Based Computer and affirming that the Weylan Yutani Company has little concern for its employees.

"MU — TH — UR Computer–Series 6000 M"

```
PRIORITY ONE
INSURE RETURN OF ORGANISM
FOR ANALYSIS.
ALL OTHER CONSIDERATIONS SECONDARY.
CREW EXPENDABLE.
```

Damn you, untrustworthy space-based computers!

One typographic point of note: The on-screen display font for MU/TH/UR appears to be an optically stretched version of City Light. *Alien*'s use of a serif (rather than sans-serif) on-screen computer font is unusual in a sci-fi movie.

City Light

ABCDEFGHIJKLMNOPQRSTUVWXYZ

Speaking of unusual typefaces: When Captain Dallas visits MU/TH/UR at the start of the movie, we see that his jacket has "NOSTROMO" on the back in Pump Demi.

Pump Demi

ABCDEFGHIJKLMNOPQRSTUVWXYZ

Pump Demi is also seen on the crew's nameplates in the main *Nostromo* cabin. (You can recognize it by its distinctive capital *Y*, even when blurry.)

Pump Demi was recently voted "Most Seventies-Looking Font of All Time" by the International Font Council. That's not actually true, but it might as well be. Regardless, Pump's retrospective seventies association proves that it's hard to know exactly what aspects of a movie's design will still look futuristic in the future.

Pump is an integral part of the human environment in *Alien*, whose aesthetic is functional and mechanical to a fault. The movie's extraterrestrial environments, on the other hand, are as weird and alien as you can imagine. More specifically, they are as weird and alien as Swiss surrealist H. R. Giger could imagine, which turns out to be pretty damn weird indeed.

But there's good news: If you're keen to experience Giger's *Alien* environment in the flesh, or if you're a fan of castles and cheese, then the medieval Swiss village of Gruyères has you covered. Home of the H. R. Giger Museum, it's the perfect place to view Giger's physically and sexually disturbing artwork before enjoying a much-needed drink in the adjacent themed bar. And when I say themed, I really do mean themed: The bar was built to Giger's own design, with spinal vaulted ceilings, arched alien chairs, and an entire wall of scary baby faces.

While you're there, don't forget to try a shot of Alien Blood, which the bar staff insists is made from green vodka and Baileys instead of the traditional molecular acid. Either way, it's guaranteed to mess up your insides.

Giger Bar, Gruyères, Switzerland
ABOVE: *Alien* table and ceiling;
BELOW LEFT: *Alien* chairs and bar;
BELOW MIDDLE: Wall of baby faces;
BELOW RIGHT: A shot of Alien Blood.

Back aboard the *Nostromo,* things are not going well for Ripley. As the last of her crewmates is killed, she decides to trigger the ship's self-destruct procedure, to blow up both the *Nostromo* and its resident alien. The instructions for self-destruction look plausible enough at first glance, informing us that these measures will cause the ship to detonate in "T minus 10 minutes" and that the fail-safe cutoff system "will not operate after T minus 5 minutes." These two facts are, of course, highly significant to the next ten minutes of Ripley's story line, and so are made very clear to the audience via a lingering shot of the emergency destruction system's display.

The clarity of these timings is undermined by inaccuracies in the actual self-destruction procedure, which for some reason is presented in both English and French. Being American, Ripley naturally follows the English version, tracing the instructions with her finger. Let's take a closer look:

Punch **NUCLEAR BOLT CODE** No 1

Verify **BOLT CLAMP** release

Perform **INSERTION OF BOLT** No 1 to **HOLD** No 1

Remove **NUCLEAR HEAD**

Activate **PUSH BUTTON SWITCH**

Replace **NUCLEAR HEAD**

Verify **SECURED**

Verify **DETONATION ACTIVATED**

Repeat for **HOLDS** 2, 3 & 4

Ripley wastes no time in punching nuclear bolt code number 1 into the self-destruct system's keyboard, and then inserting each nuclear bolt into its corresponding hold. (She does skip all three "verify" steps, but to be fair, there's a lurking xenomorph.)

In case you were in any doubt about the plot significance of those earlier timings: After the fourth nuclear bolt enters the fourth hold, an ominous ten-minute clock starts counting down to destruction, and an equally ominous voice reiterates the five-minute cutoff. This becomes highly relevant as Ripley heads toward the *Nostromo*'s shuttle to make her escape, with her cat, Jonesy, in an industrial-strength cat box. She encounters the alien along the way, blocking her path. In shock, she drops Jonesy and dashes back to the emergency destruction room to stop the self-destruct process. As she arrives, the ominous computer voice counts down the final seconds to the inevitable fail-safe cutoff . . .

29 . . .   28 . . .   27 . . .

Let's pause that countdown temporarily and take a moment to put ourselves in Ripley's situation. There's an alien xenomorph with acid for blood running around a dimly lit spacecraft, picking off your coworkers one by one. You're the sole remaining survivor. Your only form of defense is a single-canister flamethrower. You have thirty seconds to halt the self-destruct sequence for your spacecraft—and you've just gone and lost your cat.

I think it's fair to say that this is a stressful scenario.

Perhaps this is why, on arriving back at the ship-scuttling instructions, Ripley inadvertently follows the *French* instructions with her finger, not the English ones from before:

And this is where it all goes horribly wrong.

Let's take a look at those French instructions in more detail:

Poussez le **NUCLEAR BOLT CODE** No 1

Vérifier **CRAMPON** de **L'ACHEMENT**

Exécutez **INSERTION/BOULON** No 1 a la cale No 1

Vérifiez **SÉCURITÉ** du **SOMMET NUCLEAR**

Vérifiez **SÉCURITÉ** du **SOMMET NUCLEAR**

Vérifiez la **DETONATION ACTIVE**

Hmm . . . something something "NUCLEAR BOLT" . . . something something "SÉCURITÉ" . . . it certainly *sounds* plausible. But how do these compare to the English instructions we verified earlier?

For the first three steps, all is *bon*. But from instruction four onward, things take a definite turn for the worse. The French instructions don't mention anything about removing the NUCLEAR HEAD, activating the PUSH BUTTON SWITCH, or replacing the NUCLEAR HEAD. All of which seemed pretty important when Ripley was doing these things earlier.

The French instructions do at least remind us to check that things are secured. Indeed, just for good measure, they remind us twice to check them. This is commendable stuff on an average day, but it's not what you want when you've got thirty seconds left before inexorable destruction.

In a further example of the famous French passion for safety, the instructions also ask us to verify that the detonation is active (which it won't be, because we forgot to activate the push-button switch). However, they completely neglect to mention that the process needs to be repeated for the other three holds.

In short: This is a localization *disaster*. It would be bad at the best of times, but we've just lost our cat to a xenomorph. We're in no fit state to cope with dodgy French.

Thanks to this fateful piece of translation, Ripley fails to abort the detonation process in time, and the five-minute countdown to detonation continues. She sprints away from the emergency destruction room and attempts to make her way to the shuttle.

Following *Alien*'s finale, the presence of a dispassionate female voice narrating a countdown to destruction has become a recurring trope. It happens again in *Aliens* (1986), and we'll see in a later chapter how Sigourney Weaver herself describes a similar scenario in *WALL·E* (2008). Perhaps the most obvious reference to *Alien*'s self-destruction occurs in Mel Brooks's parody *Spaceballs* (1987), in which Vader-like bad guy Dark Helmet falls and hits his head on a button marked "SELF-DESTRUCT BUTTON—DO NOT PUSH UNLESS YOU REALLY, *REALLY* MEAN IT!" (Despite the comedic intent of this typography, its clarity is commendable, especially in light of the *Nostromo*'s confusing instructions.)

After the button is pushed by Helmet's helmet, a dispassionate female voice says, "Thank you for pressing the self-destruct button. This ship will self-destruct in three minutes." Two minutes and forty seconds later, the same voice says, "This ship will self-destruct in twenty seconds. This is your last chance to push the cancellation button." Much to Helmet's dismay, the cancellation button is "OUT OF ORDER," causing him to exclaim, sagely: "Even in the future, nothing works."

Dark Helmet accidentally presses the self-destruct button aboard the spacecraft *Mega-Maid* (formerly *Spaceball One*).

The *Mega-Maid* self-destruct cancellation button is, sadly, out of order.

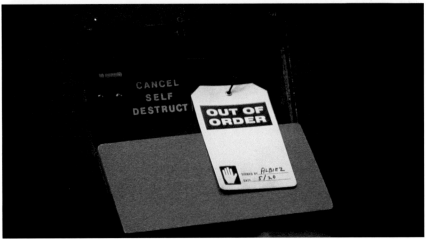

The *Nostromo*'s five minutes to self-destruction are typographically uninteresting. Ripley makes it to the escape shuttle with no sign of the alien. She even finds Jonesy along the way. With seconds remaining, her shuttle detaches from the *Nostromo,* blasting away just before the ship explodes.

Before we join her in the shuttle, however, there's one more typographic curiosity to be studied during the *Nostromo*'s self-destruct sequence. Remember when Ripley was punching nuclear bolt code number 1 into that technical-looking keyboard? Well, it turns out that its keys are more curious than they might first seem. Here's the central panel for your closer inspection. (I've created a composite image of it from several frames, to make it easier to see the keys without Ripley getting her hand in the way.)

Composite image of the *Nostromo*'s self-destruct keyboard

The first key of note is "PRANIC LIFT 777." *Prana* is the Sanskrit word for "life force." It's a cosmic energy believed to come from the sun and to connect the elements of the universe.

We also have "PADME," a possible variant of *padma,* the Sanskrit word for "lotus flower."

Padma is joined by "LINGHA," a possible variant of "Linga" (or "Lingam"), a representation of the Hindu deity Shiva.

Lingha is balanced by "YONI," the Sanskrit word for "womb."

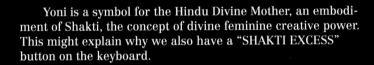

Yoni is a symbol for the Hindu Divine Mother, an embodiment of Shakti, the concept of divine feminine creative power. This might explain why we also have a "SHAKTI EXCESS" button on the keyboard.

But perhaps the oddest key on the keyboard is the one in the top right-hand corner: "AGARIC FLY."

Now, agaric fly—or fly agaric, as it is more commonly known—is a mushroom and psychoactive fungus known for triggering a hallucinogenic experience.

You might think this is an odd thing to be written on the keyboard of an emergency destruction system.

You would be correct.

This might explain why the row of keys to the left of "AGARIC FLY" is labelled, simply, "TRIP."

Fly agaric

Helena Blavatsky, in 1877

So why are these strange references on the *Nostromo*'s emergency destruct keyboard? According to the *Alien Explorations* blog, designer Simon Deering needed some complex-sounding technical labels for this keyboard at short notice. He was reading *The Secret Doctrine* by Helena Blavatsky, a Russian philosopher and occultist, at the time of filming. Blavatsky's book attempts to explain the origin and evolution of the universe in terms derived from the Hindu concept of cyclical development. Deering found his inspiration in its pages, and the *Nostromo*'s odd keyboard was born.

Let's get back to the escape shuttle. Ripley is safely aboard, with no sign of the alien. But wait—just when we think all is good, it turns out that the damned thing has stowed itself inside a conveniently camouflaged wall.

Thankfully, this shuttle comes equipped with a system that pipes highly toxic and flammable "SPECIAL GASES" into the main cockpit at the press of a button. It's not immediately clear why this is a useful or safe feature to have aboard an emergency escape shuttle, but it does come in handy when there's an alien hiding in the wall.

Ripley starts by venting some "iodine pentafluoride" and "methyl chloride." This doesn't seem to have much effect. It's a whole different matter when she tries the "nitrosyl chloride," however.

According to Wikipedia, nitrosyl chloride is "very toxic and irritating to the lungs, eyes, and skin." I don't know if the alien actually *has* any of these organs, but it doesn't like the nitrosyl chloride one bit and starts squealing like a frog in a roomful of cats. (I'm going to ignore the fact that nitrosyl chloride gas is actually yellow—it's working, and that's all that matters.)

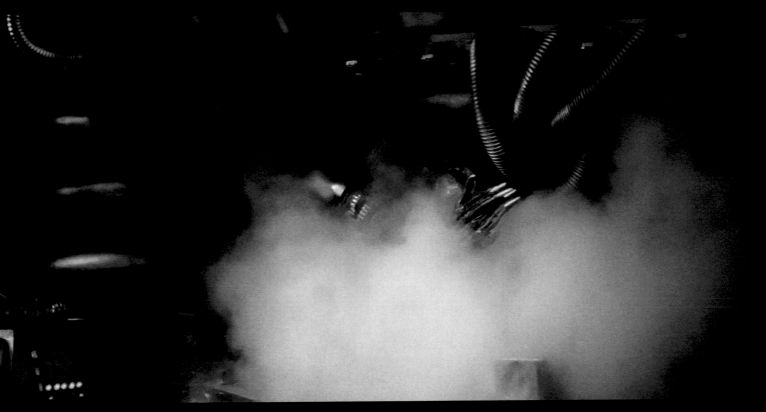

The gas forces the alien out into the open. A forward-thinking Ripley (who's already strapped herself into a chair) opens the shuttle's exterior door and blasts the alien into space. Safe at last, she settles herself into hypersleep and records a message noting that she is the sole survivor of the *Nostromo*.

WHAT SHE NEGLECTS TO MENTION in her farewell memo is that she has not once in the past two hours encountered Eurostile Bold Extended. *Alien* eschews *2001*'s classic typeface entirely, thereby avoiding an association with the shiny future of its forebear. Its use of functional iconography instead represents the practical, working nature of an everyday space trucker, giving the *Nostromo* a closer visual bond with the *Millennium Falcon* than the USS *Discovery*.

Alien may have an aesthetic different from that of *2001,* but director Ridley Scott has stated he was drawn to sci-fi primarily because the believable realities of *2001* and *Star Wars* convinced him of sci-fi's potential as a storytelling medium. Like Kubrick before him, Scott, in his meticulous attention to detail, created a future that is entirely immersive and that, like *2001,* has become a reference for countless movies since.

S T A R

VFX master Douglas Trumbull defined the look of scientifically realistic space travel in *2001: A Space Odyssey*. Trumbull took things a step further on *Star Trek: The Motion Picture*, imagining how a spacecraft might look when making the transition to faster-than-light speed. Both the light-speed jump and its subsequent wormhole effect are adopted as visual shorthand in *WALL·E*, as we'll see later in this book.

TREK

1979

Star Trek: The Motion Picture, a movie adaptation of the cult sixties TV show, very nearly didn't get made. If it weren't for the runaway success of *Star Wars* and *Close Encounters of the Third Kind* (both released in 1977), fickle Paramount executives would have canceled their faltering TV project *Star Trek: Phase II*, instead of adapting it into a big-screen production.

THE MOTION PICTURE

We must give thanks, then, to producer Gene Roddenberry for pushing the project through ten years of development hell. In doing so, he named a space shuttle, created a custom font pack, and relaunched the swashbuckling futurism of the greatest of all space franchises: *Star Trek.*

If you're a fan of *Star Trek: The Original Series,* you might be expecting to see the font from the opening titles in *Star Trek: The Motion Picture.* This font was (perhaps unsurprisingly) called Star Trek, though its modern-day digital version is known as Horizon and is available only in non-italic form.

Star Trek, aka Horizon

ABCDEFGHIJKLMNOPQRSTUVWXYZ

If we rate the *Original Series* titles against our rules for futuristic text, we see that they score a perfectly respectable 5/10:

In addition, I'm delighted to report that during season one *Star Trek* was accompanied by Eurostile Bold in the end credits.

Star Trek, accompanied by
Eurostile Bold

Eurostile Bold

ABCDEFGHIJKLMNOPQRSTUVWXYZ

The Star Trek font also appeared in a non-italic version to introduce William Shatner and Leonard Nimoy to 1960s TV audiences:

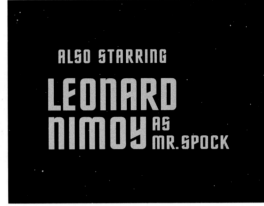

Sadly, this is where the good news ends. When *The Original Series* returned for a second season, it added DeForest Kelley (Dr. "Bones" McCoy) as a second "ALSO STARRING."
The problem here is obvious, isn't it? Unlike the *E*s in "SHATNER" and "LEONARD," the ones in "DEFOREST KELLEY" have straight corners, not curved ones. This is such an aberration, I'm docking that CURVE point.

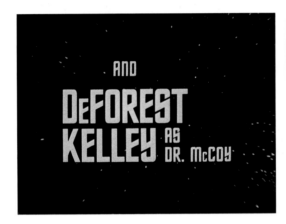

BELOW LEFT: The opening title from 1979's *Star Trek: The Motion Picture*. Note the elongated leading and trailing lines on the *S* in "STAR" and the *K* in "TREK."

BELOW RIGHT: The opening title from another popular late-seventies sci-fi movie. Note the elongated leading and trailing lines on the *S* and *R* in "STAR" and on the *S* in "WARS."

Alas, *The Original Series*'s inconsistent typography did not survive the stylistic leap into the 1970s. To make up for it, *The Motion Picture*'s title card introduces a new font, with some of the curviest *E*s known to sci-fi. It also follows an emerging seventies trend: Movie names beginning with STAR have long trailing lines on the opening *S*.

The font seen in *The Motion Picture*'s titles is a custom typeface created by Richard A. Foy, known at the time as Star Trek Film (and now known in digital form as Galaxy). Star Trek Film also shows up on the movie's US one-sheet poster, with bonus Technicolor beveling.

Detail of the US theatrical one-sheet poster for *Star Trek: The Motion Picture*

Illustrated by Bob Peak, the poster for *The Motion Picture* has become something of a classic. Its striking rainbow motif was reprised in a limited-edition poster for 2016's *Star Trek Beyond*.

On which theme: If you've ever doubted the power of type to aid recognition, note that the teaser poster for *Star Trek Beyond* features the word "BEYOND" in metallic, beveled, extruded Star Trek, without feeling the need to add the actual words "STAR" or "TREK." The presence of the *Enterprise* and the use of an iconic font were deemed more than sufficient to identify the franchise. (Although it would have worked far more effectively if they'd remembered to curve the *E*.)

BELOW LEFT: US theatrical one-sheet poster for *Star Trek: The Motion Picture*

BELOW MIDDLE: Limited-edition poster for *Star Trek Beyond*, presented to fans who attended a *Star Trek* fiftieth-anniversary event

BELOW RIGHT: US teaser poster for *Star Trek Beyond*

If you like the style of Star Trek or Star Trek Film and want to use them to spice up your corporate communications, I have excellent news. In 1992, the creators of the *Star Trek* franchise partnered with Bitstream to release an officially licensed *"Star Trek" Font Pack.* The pack contains full versions of Star Trek and Star Trek Film, plus Star Trek Pi (a collection of insignias and Klingon glyphs) and Starfleet Bold Extended (a Eurostile look-alike that appears on the outside of many Starfleet craft). It also, of course, uses Eurostile Bold Extended liberally on its front cover.

Let's take a look at Bitstream's examples of how the fonts should be used, from the back of the font pack's box:

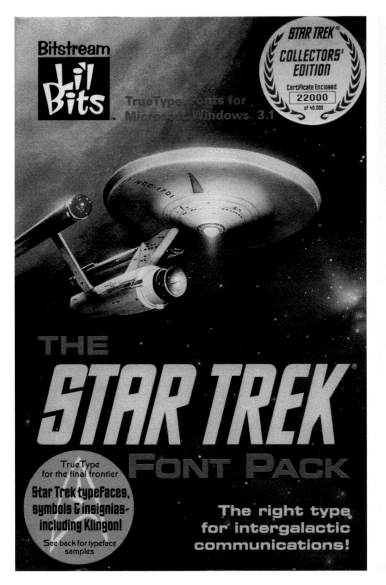

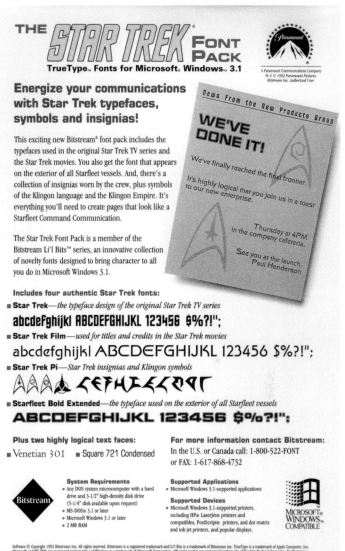

If you're looking to bring character to all you do in Microsoft Windows 3.1, the *"Star Trek" Font Pack* is for you.

But back to the movie. Its opening scene starts with a menacing close-up of the movie's central antagonist, which just happens to be a gigantic glowing space cloud:

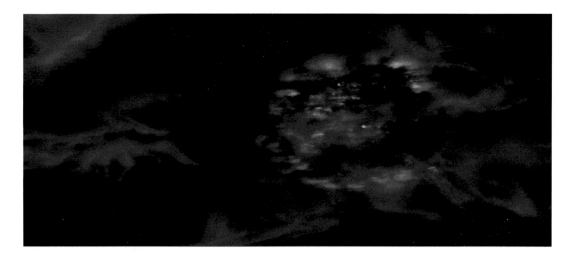

Clouds are not generally known for their inherent evil, murdering tendencies. To work around this potential dramatic limitation, the movie's producers cleverly employ a scary sound effect whenever we're meant to be intimidated by this galactic floaty miasma. Despite aural evidence to the contrary, the cloud's twangling menace was not made by throwing a ham into a sack of pianos. Instead, it's the sound of a Blaster Beam, a twelve-foot-long aluminum guitar-like device invented in the early 1970s by musician John Lazelle.

Los Angeles–based Beam player Francesco Lupica, who has performed as the Cosmic Beam Experience since the early seventies, is mentioned in *The Motion Picture*'s credits for his work creating sound effects for the movie. However, the primary credit for the cloud's eerie twang goes to Craig Huxley, a child actor and musician who originally appeared in *The Original Series* as Captain Kirk's nephew before going on to create *The Motion Picture*'s scary soundscape.

As part of his collaboration with composer Jerry Goldsmith, Huxley (by now a professional musician) composed the Blaster Beam cadenza for *The Motion Picture*'s climax. He subsequently obtained a patent for the Blaster Beam's design and went on to bash its eerie strings in *Back to the Future Part II* and *Part III, Tron, 2010, Who Framed Roger Rabbit,* and *10 Cloverfield Lane,* plus several more *Star Trek* movies. He now runs a recording studio in Burbank, California, called, fittingly enough, the Enterprise.

Following its starring role in *The Motion Picture,* the Blaster Beam became so synonymous with sci-fi that it was featured in Seth MacFarlane's *The Orville* as an aural homage to the original *Trek* movies. It's basically become the audible equivalent of Eurostile.

Craig Huxley (billed under his birth name, Craig Hundley) as the unconscious Peter Kirk in the "Operation—Annihilate!" episode of *The Original Series*

The front cover of *Genesis Project,* Craig Huxley's 1984 LP featuring expanded versions of his Blaster Beam compositions from various *Star Trek* movies. In the cover photo, multiple Craigs can be seen playing multiple Blaster Beams, alongside a selection of shorter, more portable instruments.

As the cloud twangles ominously, three Klingon ships float into view. Clearly intimidated by the cloud's noncorporeality, the Klingons fire some photon torpedoes into its inky midst. (It's not entirely clear what they hope this will achieve.) As they optimistically launch their missiles, we see their native tongue translated into English in a slightly fuzzy Pump Demi.

Pump Demi

ABCDEFGHIJKLMNOPQRSTUVWXYZ

Tactical, stand by on torpedoes.

The Motion Picture is notable for being the first time in *Star Trek* history that Klingons speak Klingon, rather than conversing in English. An initial Klingon dialect was created for the movie by UCLA linguist Hartmut Scharfe but wasn't felt to be alien enough, so James Doohan (aka Scotty) volunteered to work on an alternative. Doohan's skills with accents were already well known—after all, he played a Scotsman, despite being a Canadian with Irish parents—and he helped come up with a number of nonsense phrases that formed the basis of the movie's Klingon language. Associate producer Jon Povill described the birth of Klingon this way:

> *After Hartmut had done his thing and worked it all out logically, Jimmy and I just sat down one day and made up stuff. We created the Klingonese by using some of what Hartmut had done and then combining it with our own: We strung together nonsense syllables, basically—totally made up sounds with clicks, and grunts, and hisses.*

Fire!

The Klingon typography seen in the movie is just as nonsensical as the spoken language—the limited set of Klingon glyphs seen here don't actually mean anything. They were nonetheless adapted (along with various Starfleet and Klingon insignia) into a *"Star Trek" Font Pack* typeface known as Star Trek Pi.

Star Trek Pi, from the *"Star Trek" Font Pack*. ("Pi" is a common typographic name for a symbol font.)

The Motion Picture's Klingon might be nonsense, but the language has had a long and active development since the movie's release. Doohan's guttural phrases were adapted by linguist Marc Okrand into a full language for 1984's *Star Trek III: The Search for Spock,* which was followed in 1985 by an official *Klingon Dictionary.* This dictionary describes the language's grammar in detail and provides two-way translations for common English and Klingon phrases. The dictionary has since been translated into Portuguese (*Dicionário da língua Klingon*), German (*Das offizielle Wörterbuch: Klingonisch/Deutsch; Deutsch/Klingonisch*), Italian (*Il dizionario Klingon*), Czech (*Klingonský slovník*), and Swedish (*Klingonsk Ordbok*).

Star Trek's producers were not the first world builders to create an entire language, however. *Lord of the Rings* author J. R. R. Tolkien, inventor of two complete Elven languages, was a philologist long before he was a novelist. From his early days at the *Oxford English Dictionary* (where he was responsible for words starting with *w*) through his multiple professorships at Oxford University, Tolkien loved the study of language more than anything else. Indeed, he didn't construct his Elven languages to add color to his novels; rather, he wrote novels to provide a world in which his created languages could live and breathe. Tolkien believed a language was truly alive only when it had a mythology to support it, and his books provided a world in which that mythology could exist.

Had Tolkien lived to see 1991's *Star Trek VI: The Undiscovered Country,* I am therefore sure he would have approved of Klingon chancellor Gorkon's tongue-in-cheek statement: "You have not experienced Shakespeare until you have read him in the original Klingon." This comment inspired the Klingon Language Institute to produce *The Klingon "Hamlet,"* an equally tongue-in-cheek 219-page restoration of Shakespeare's famous work to its original Klingon.

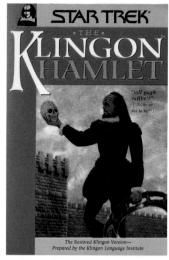

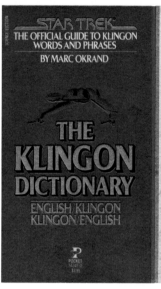

UNFAMILIAR WEAPONRY

INTRUDER UNIDENTIFIED

BELIEVE LUMINESCENT CLOUD TO BE

ENORMOUS POWER FIELD

SURROUNDING ALIEN VESSEL

OUR SENSOR SCANS UNABLE TO

PENETRATE

IMPERIAL KLINGON CRUISER AMAR

DESPITE THE KLINGONS' USE of their native tongue, things are not going well for them in their battle against the evil space cloud. A distress message from the Klingon command ship is picked up by a sensor drone from space station *Epsilon 9* and translated into English for the benefit of the station crew. This time, the Klingon does *not* translate into Pump. Instead, it's a customized version of Futura Display, which is almost certainly the Letraset Instant Lettering version with our rule 6 (arbitrarily slice out a segment of the text) liberally applied. Its final sentence is completed by a voice reading out the English translation: "IMPERIAL KLINGON CRUISER AMAR . . . CONTINUING TO ATTACK." (Given that these events take place during the opening ten minutes of the movie, you can probably guess how "CONTINUING TO ATTACK" is going to pan out.)

TOP: *The Klingon "Hamlet,"* originally published in hardcover by the Klingon Language Institute in 1996. The paperback edition shown above was published by Pocket Books in 2000.

BOTTOM: *The Klingon Dictionary,* by Marc Okrand (Pocket Books, 1985)

LEFT: Composite image of the translated Klingon message, as detected by *Epsilon 9*

The Letraset Instant Lettering version of Futura Display

ABCDEFGHIJKLMNOPQRSTUVWXYZ

As we cut back from *Epsilon 9* to the cloud, we see that only two of the three Klingon ships remain. According to the movie's shooting script, this is because a "FRIGHTENING WHIPLASH OF ENERGY" has been fired from the cloud, creating evil lightning that makes Klingon ships disappear. A second frightening whiplash takes out ship number two, leaving only the command craft. As a third bolt appears on the Klingons' tactical display, the command ship poops a red torpedo, but it is all to no avail. The command ship is whiplashed into nothingness.

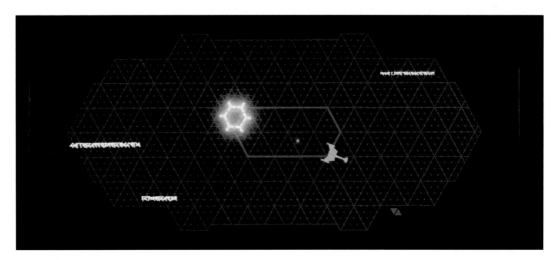

As they express their shock, the watching crew of *Epsilon 9* observes that the sinister gassy blanket is heading directly for Earth. The cloud puts on its best evil face and makes its destructive intentions clear via some particularly dramatic twangs.

WITH TWANGLING IN OUR EARS, we quickly switch scenes to Vulcan, which is easily recognizable from its lava-strewn matte paintings and suspicious geological similarity to filming locations in Yellowstone Park. Look—it's Spock! He's talking in Vulcan, which *also* translates into English as fuzzy Pump Demi.

The lady Vulcan here is talking about the many years Spock has spent striving to attain *Kolinahr,* a state of pure logic in which Vulcans shed all of their emotion. She offers Spock a symbol of total logic to commemorate his imminent *Kolinahr*-ization—but just as she does so, Spock hears evil cloud guitars twangling off in space. Lady Vulcan realizes that Spock's goal lies elsewhere, and despite several years of exhortations he fails to *Kolinahr.*

Kolinahr: through which all emotion is finally shed.

After our brief trip to Vulcan, we switch straight to San Francisco, specifically to the Golden Gate Bridge, as we follow an air tram on its way to Starfleet Command. Spoiler alert: That flying air tram contains Captain James T. Kirk, who is heading to Starfleet Headquarters in San Francisco's Presidio Park. There's a nice close-up of the United Federation of Planets logo during a positioning shot as he arrives. This looks to be Eurostile Bold, but not quite—there's something wrong with the capital *S*s.

United Federation of Planets seal, Starfleet Headquarters, Presidio Park, San Francisco

ABCDEFGHIJKLMNOPQRSTUVWXYZ

Eurostile Bold

 Starfleet is the military and exploratory arm of the Federation, which explains the use of the Federation's stars-and-thistles logo as part of the floor decoration. We see the same logo a few moments later, on the side of Kirk's air tram, and again when Kirk briefs the crew of the *Enterprise* about their upcoming mission.

Confusingly, each of these Federation logos has a different thistle design and a different constellation of stars. Perhaps more importantly, they bear a remarkable similarity to the official flag of the United Nations.

Re-creation of the Federation logo seen on the floor of Starfleet Headquarters

Re-creation of the Federation logo seen on the side of Kirk's air tram

Re-creation of the Federation logo seen when Kirk briefs the crew of the *Enterprise*

Official flag of the United Nations

This is clever branding by the movie's design team. A viewer's subconscious recollection of the United Nations via this extrapolated logo and color scheme gives the Federation (and therefore Starfleet) an immediate association with peacekeeping and ethical behavior, eliminating the need for an extended explanation of their role in the movie's universe. (All of which goes to show: Design doesn't have to include typography to provide a shortcut for exposition.)

Just in case you have any doubt about the coincidence of this similarity: The *"Star Trek" Star Fleet Technical Manual,* published in 1975, includes the charter of the United Federation of Planets. It's a direct copy of the United Nations charter but with life forms instead of humans, and planets instead of nations. Differences are indicated in yellow, additions in green:

WE THE PEOPLES OF THE UNITED NATIONS DETERMINED

to save succeeding generations from the scourge of war, which twice in our lifetime has brought untold sorrow to mankind, and

to reaffirm faith in fundamental human rights, in the dignity and worth of the human person, in the equal rights of men and women and of nations large and small, and

to establish conditions under which justice and respect for the obligations arising from treaties and other sources of international law can be maintained, and

to promote social progress and better standards of life in larger freedom,

AND FOR THESE ENDS

to practice tolerance and live together in peace with one another as good neighbors, and

to unite our strength to maintain international peace and security, and

to ensure, by the acceptance of principles and the institution of methods, that armed force shall not be used, save in the common interest, and

to employ international machinery for the promotion of the economic and social advancement of all peoples,

HAVE RESOLVED TO COMBINE OUR EFFORTS TO ACCOMPLISH THESE AIMS.

Accordingly, our respective Governments, through representatives assembled in the city of San Francisco, who have exhibited their full powers found to be in good and due form, have agreed to the present Charter of the United Nations and do hereby establish an international organization to be known as the United Nations.

WE THE INTELLIGENT LIFE-FORMS OF THE UNITED FEDERATION OF PLANETS DETERMINED

TO SAVE SUCCEEDING GENERATIONS FROM THE SCOURGE OF INTRA-GALACTIC WAR WHICH HAS BROUGHT UNTOLD HORROR AND SUFFERING TO OUR PLANETARY SOCIAL SYSTEMS, AND

TO REAFFIRM FAITH IN THE FUNDAMENTAL INTELLIGENT LIFE-FORM RIGHTS, IN THE DIGNITY AND WORTH OF THE INTELLIGENT LIFE-FORM PERSON, TO THE EQUAL RIGHTS OF MALE AND FEMALE AND OF PLANETARY SOCIAL SYSTEMS LARGE AND SMALL, AND

TO ESTABLISH CONDITIONS UNDER WHICH JUSTICE AND MUTUAL RESPECT FOR THE OBLIGATIONS ARISING FROM TREATIES AND OTHER SOURCES OF INTERPLANETARY LAW CAN BE MAINTAINED, AND

TO PROMOTE SOCIAL PROGRESS AND BETTER STANDARDS OF LIFE IN LARGER FREEDOM,

AND TO THESE ENDS

TO PRACTISE BENEVOLENT TOLERANCE AND LIVE TOGETHER IN PEACE WITH ONE ANOTHER AS GOOD NEIGHBORS, AND

TO UNITE OUR STRENGTH TO MAINTAIN INTRA-GALACTIC PEACE AND SECURITY, AND

TO ENSURE BY THE ACCEPTANCE OF PRINCIPLES AND THE INSTITUTION OF METHODS THAT ARMED FORCE SHALL NOT BE USED EXCEPT IN THE COMMON DEFENSE, AND

TO EMPLOY INTRA-GALACTIC MACHINERY FOR THE PROMOTION OF THE ECONOMIC AND SOCIAL ADVANCEMENT OF ALL INTELLIGENT LIFE-FORMS,

HAVE RESOLVED TO COMBINE OUR EFFORTS TO ACCOMPLISH THESE AIMS.

ACCORDINGLY, THE RESPECTIVE SOCIAL SYSTEMS, THROUGH REPRESENTATIVES ASSEMBLED ON THE PLANET BABEL, WHO HAVE EXHIBITED THEIR FULL POWERS TO BE IN GOOD AND DUE FORM, HAVE AGREED TO THESE ARTICLES OF FEDERATION OF THE UNITED FEDERATION OF PLANETS, AND DO HEREBY ESTABLISH AN INTER-PLANETARY ORGANIZATION TO BE KNOWN AS THE UNITED FEDERATION OF PLANETS.

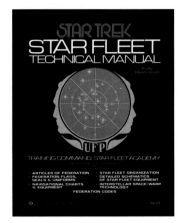

Shortly after arriving at Starfleet, Kirk transports to a space station near the USS *Enterprise,* which has been in dry dock while undergoing a post–*Original Series* refit but which will soon be ready for use in *The Motion Picture.* On arrival, he meets up with Scotty, and they take a shuttle to go and see the ship.

As they depart for the *Enterprise,* we see a mix of fonts on the side of the shuttle and station. "OFFICE LEVEL," seen on the right, is, of course, Eurostile Bold Extended. (Although, according to the *Star Fleet Technical Manual,* the "Earth font name" for Starfleet's official type style is Microgramma Ext, suggesting that we may be looking at Eurostile's predecessor Microgramma instead.)

Detail from the "Official Type Style (Star Fleet Specification)," reproduced from the *"Star Trek" Star Fleet Technical Manual*

The "05" on the side of the shuttle is *not* Eurostile Bold Extended, however. This is Starfleet Bold Extended, the fourth and final font from the *"Star Trek" Font Pack.* Unlike Eurostile, it has an outline, giving it a more curved silhouette overall. It also has higher bars on the *P* and *R,* a squared-off corner for the *Q,* and a very different number *1.* (Eurostile's *1* is perhaps its least practical glyph, which may explain why the *Star Fleet Technical Manual* extract above states that it should not be used in fleet operations.)

Eurostile Bold Extended

ABCDEFGHIJKLMNOPQRSTUVWXYZ

Starfleet Bold Extended

ABCDEFGHIJKLMNOPQRSTUVWXYZ

Eurostile Bold Extended digits, including an impractical elongated *1*

1234567890

Starfleet Bold Extended digits, including a much more balanced *1*

1234567890

The *R* and the *1* make it easy to tell that Starfleet Bold Extended is used for the *Enterprise*'s hull classification symbol ("NCC") and number ("1701"). Indeed, Starfleet Bold Extended is used on the front of USS *Enterprise* NCC-1701 (and 1701-A, B, C, D, and E) in all subsequent *Star Trek* movies and TV shows, in essentially the same style as in *The Motion Picture*. This gives a consistent, instant recognizability to each iteration of the craft, despite the crew's tendency to crash or otherwise destroy the ships for dramatic effect.

USS *Enterprise* NCC-1701 in 1979's *Star Trek: The Motion Picture*

USS *Enterprise* NCC-1701-A in 1986's *Star Trek: The Voyage Home*

USS *Enterprise* NCC-1701-B in 1994's *Star Trek: Generations*

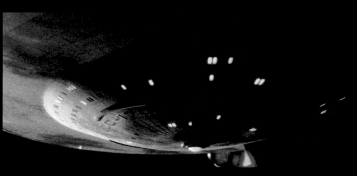

USS *Enterprise* NCC-1701-C in the 1990 *Star Trek: The Next Generation* episode "Yesterday's Enterprise"

The saucer section of USS *Enterprise* NCC-1701-D after a crash landing on Veridian III in 1994's *Star Trek: Generations*

USS *Enterprise* NCC-1701-E in 2002's *Star Trek: Nemesis*

ABOVE: USS *Enterprise* NCC-1701 in 2009's *Star Trek* reboot. The lower bar of the R makes it clear that this is Eurostile Extended, not Starfleet Bold Extended.

RIGHT: USS *Enterprise* NCC-1701-A in dry dock during its construction at the end of 2016's *Star Trek Beyond*. Note the straight 1s in "1701."

A different style was introduced for 2009's *Star Trek* reboot and continued through 2016's *Star Trek Beyond*. The reboot movies use an outlined version of plain old Eurostile Extended for "U.S.S. ENTERPRISE," though they continue to heed the advice from the *Star Fleet Technical Manual* about Eurostile's 1, opting for flat lines for the 1s in "1701."

Eurostile Extended

ABCDEFGHIJKLMNOPQRSTUVWXYZ

The USS *Discovery*'s name and designation in Eurostile Bold Extended, seen in the *Star Trek: Discovery* season-one episode "Context Is for Kings." Note the use of an unmodified Eurostile 1, in clear violation of the Starfleet official type style.

In 2017, the *Star Trek: Discovery* TV series rebooted the typography once again, opting for Eurostile Bold Extended for the USS *Discovery*'s name and designation. Crucially, the *Discovery* becomes the first central *Star Trek* craft to ignore the Starfleet official type style, shamelessly using a Eurostile 1 character without modification.

The *Enterprise*'s complex shape could easily make it a nightmare to navigate. Thankfully, it has a fancy horizontal-and-vertical elevator system known as a turbolift, which whizzes crew members from A to B via handily placed turboshafts. We see a two-part map of the craft's turboshaft network as Kirk heads up to the bridge. Judging from this map, it looks like the turbolift can move in all three dimensions, including along a curved route:

The white dot on the map indicates the lift's current position. We see it move from right to left as the lift departs, and it's clearly visible at the top of the map after the lift arrives at the bridge:

TOP: The turbolift's multidirectional nature is also represented in its iconography, seen when Decker boards a turbolift on level five later in the movie.

ABOVE: Detail of a theoretical MULTI installation, showing elevator cars following a nontraditional path, giving greater flexibility in building design

BELOW: Schematic of the MULTI system's transfer mechanism between vertical and horizontal movement

Despite the turbolift's obvious futurism, *Star Trek* was not the first to propose a multidirectional elevator. That honor goes to Roald Dahl, whose 1964 novel *Charlie and the Chocolate Factory* features a glass elevator that goes "sideways and longways and slantways and any other way you can think of." (Unlike the turbolift, it can also propel itself out of its containing building and into the air via sugar power.)

The turbolift's secret is being able to switch cars between shafts dynamically, in order to route travelers around the craft in the most efficient manner. This may have been a futuristic concept in 1979, when *The Motion Picture* was released, but I am delighted to report that it recently became a reality. In 2017, German elevator company thyssenkrupp performed the first real-world test of its MULTI elevator system. According to thyssenkrupp, MULTI increases elevator capacity by 50 percent, while halving the elevator footprint within a building. It allows ninety-degree turning of the system's linear drive and guiding equipment, enabling cars to quickly move between horizontal and vertical shafts during a single journey.

MULTI operates in two dimensions, not three, so it's not quite a full-fledged turbolift. Nonetheless, its motors are based on technology from a magnetic levitating train system, so it's still pretty damned futuristic.

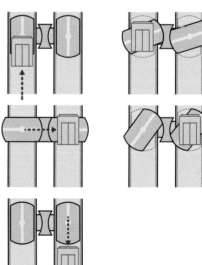

Kirk gathers his crew and explains that they are the only ship near enough to intercept the evil space cloud, and so they're going to have to save the day. A message comes through on the big screen from *Epsilon 9,* informing everyone that the cloud is "over eighty-two AUs in diameter." This seems somewhat incredible, given that one AU (astronomical unit) is the average distance from Earth to the sun, which is about ninety-three million miles. (Indeed, it's *so* incredible that the director's edition of the movie used some sneaky dialogue editing to make the cloud "over two AUs in diameter" instead.)

To give some context to vastness on this scale: On August 25, 2012, NASA's *Voyager 1,* humankind's farthest-traveling spacecraft, entered interstellar space at a distance of around 125 AUs from the sun, after traveling nonstop for nearly thirty-five years. Even this distance is still technically within our solar system, however, and it will be another forty thousand years before *Voyager 1* approaches a planetary system outside our own. (Unless, that is, a Voyager craft finds a way to sidestep such vast distances by traveling through a black hole or something similar—not that this is likely to be relevant to the plot of *The Motion Picture.*)

Regardless of the true size of the cloud, it makes short work of dispatching *Epsilon 9* (and a random man, with really big hands, in an orange spacesuit) while the *Enterprise* crew looks on. Kirk tells the shocked crew to get ready to leave, and they set about their preparations.

A random man, with really big hands, shortly before being killed by an evil space cloud

In a turn of events that will surprise no one, engaging a not-properly-tested warp drive while still in the solar system turns out to be a bad idea, resulting in the *Enterprise* being dragged into a wormhole. Everything goooeeesss a biiiiiit sloooooow mooootionnnnnn as the crew tries to destroy an asteroid that has been dragged into the wormhole with them. This scene's highlight is an excellent use of some spare Letraset Instant Lettering. A combination of symbols found in the bottom right corner of a Letraset sheet are used upside down as part of the weapons system "TRACKING SEQUENCE":

LEFT: Detail from the *Enterprise*'s weapons system tracking sequence, showing a cluster of punctuation glyphs just below "TRACKING"

RIGHT: Upside-down detail of a sheet of Letraset Instant Lettering, showing the same cluster of punctuation glyphs

With the wormhole successfully navigated, the *Enterprise* continues on its merry way toward the space cloud. Not much happens. Indeed, there are ten whole minutes that basically consist just of people looking at a cloud. So let's skip ahead to the cloud's approximate center and the mild peril therein.

Intruder alert! A strange alien light-beam probe intrudes into the bridge. It heads over to the science station and starts calling up blueprints of the *Enterprise*:

These blueprints are taken directly from 1973's *"Star Trek" Blueprints* by Franz Joseph, who also wrote and designed the *Star Fleet Technical Manual*. Specifically, these blueprints show the inboard profile and crew's quarters of the *Enterprise*. (Strictly speaking, this means the probe is scanning blueprints from before the *Enterprise* underwent its *Motion Picture* refit, but let's not worry too much.)

A selection of the blueprints scanned by the light-beam probe during its bridge intrusion

Joseph's *Blueprints* and *Technical Manual* were spectacularly successful publications for Ballantine, with the *Technical Manual* reaching number one on the *New York Times* trade paperback list. (Indeed, it is likely that the books' sales success contributed to Paramount's decision to revive *Star Trek* in the first place.)

After scanning the blueprints, the probe zaps Deltan crew member Ilia, and she disappears. She's not gone long, though. A few minutes later, she returns as IliaBot, a synthetic replacement created by the mysterious life force at the space cloud's center in order to communicate with the carbon units aboard the *Enterprise*.

The newly appeared IliaBot notes that she has been "programmed by V'Ger to observe and record." In doing so, she provides a name for the mysterious cloud-based entity that's been causing everyone so much trouble. (Although why there would be a flying entity called V'Ger this many AUs from the sun has not yet been made clear.)

"Star Trek" Blueprints, by Franz Joseph (Ballantine Books, 1973)

TYPESET IN THE FUTURE

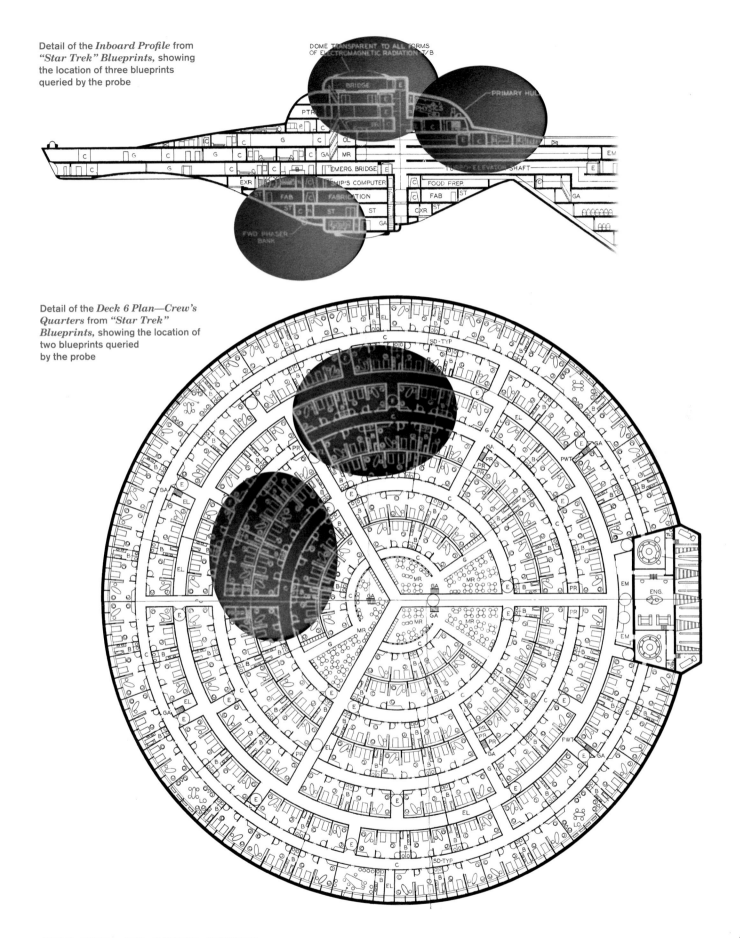

Detail of the *Inboard Profile* from *"Star Trek" Blueprints,* showing the location of three blueprints queried by the probe

Detail of the *Deck 6 Plan—Crew's Quarters* from *"Star Trek" Blueprints,* showing the location of two blueprints queried by the probe

Kirk learns that V'Ger is traveling to Earth to "find the creator" and to join with it. IliaBot is less than clear about the details of this mission, stating that "the creator is that which created V'Ger" and "V'Ger is that which seeks the creator," which is really no help at all. Spock advocates a thorough medical analysis, and IliaBot is whisked off to the *Enterprise*'s sick bay, where she is scanned on a futuristic medical table.

Alien, also released in 1979, features a remarkably similar scanner in the *Nostromo*'s onboard "autodoc." *Alien*'s version didn't make it into the original theatrical cut of the movie, but you can see it in the 2003 director's cut, in which it is used to scan the body of a recently face-hugged Kane. Both of these devices look to be inspired by the just-invented science of X-ray computed tomography, for which physicists Allan M. Cormack and Godfrey N. Hounsfield shared a 1979 Nobel Prize.

LEFT: IliaBot is scanned by a futuristic medical device in the *Enterprise*'s sick bay.

RIGHT: Kane is scanned by a futuristic medical device in the *Nostromo*'s autodoc.

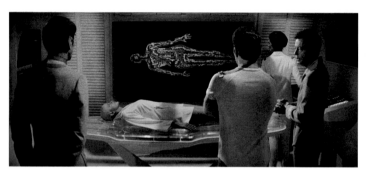

These two scanning devices may have seemed futuristic to 1979 viewers, but as CT scanners became more common, later sci-fi outings had to up their game to keep one step ahead of reality. *Lost in Space* (1998) and the "Ariel" episode of *Firefly* (2002) both moved to holographic scanners, projecting a virtual image of a patient's innards above their actual body instead of on a screen.

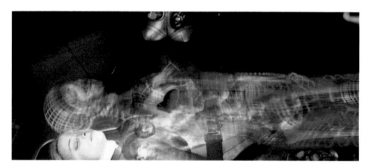
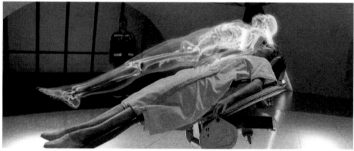

More recent movies have adopted even more advanced approaches. *Prometheus* (2012), *Elysium* (2013), and *Passengers* (2016) all feature devices that perform actual surgery without the need for a doctor. These devices are definitely one step ahead of present-day robotic surgery, which focuses more on improving the precision of humans rather than on removing the need for them altogether. (The nearest real-world equivalent to these devices is the da Vinci Surgical System from Intuitive Surgical, approved by the FDA in 2000, but it is still controlled by a specially trained surgeon from a nearby console.)

LEFT: Dr. Judy Robinson's body is holographically scanned for a heartbeat in 1998's *Lost in Space*.

RIGHT: River Tam's body is scanned by a holo-imager device in 2002's "Ariel" episode of *Firefly*.

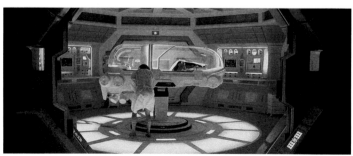

An ailing Dr. Elizabeth Shaw staggers toward a Pauling MedPod in 2012's *Alien* prequel, *Prometheus*.

TOP LEFT: Frey Santiago places her daughter, Matilda, in a Med-Bay device in 2013's *Elysium*. The Med-Bay scans her, detects leukemia, and cures her via the magical process of "re-atomizing."

TOP RIGHT: Aurora Lane resuscitates a just-dead Jim Preston in 2016's *Passengers*. As on the *Nostromo* in *Alien*, the medical gadget on the starship *Avalon* is known as an "autodoc."

Intuitive Surgical's da Vinci Surgical System: a surgeon's control console (LEFT) and a patient cart with instruments tray (RIGHT)

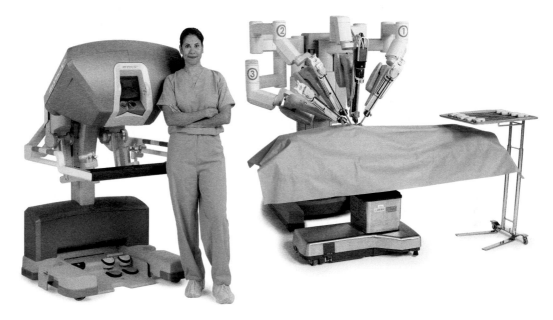

The Fifth Element's body-reconstruction machine attaches new bone to an existing fragment.

The most impressive movie medical gadget, however, is surely the reconstruction device seen in 1997's *The Fifth Element,* which can re-create an entire living being from a single bone fragment. Despite recent real-world advancements in growing human replacement organs, we can be confident that this device will remain futuristic for some time yet.

As these medical devices show, the threat of technology catching up with the future is a perennial problem for science fiction, especially in a franchise as long-running as *Star Trek*. In the time between *The Original Series* (1966–69) and *The Motion Picture* (1979), hand-held communicators of the type used by the original *Enterprise* crew had gone from a futuristic possibility to a technical reality. As a result, Gene Roddenberry felt a new style of communicator was needed to make *The Motion Picture* feel like it was set in the future. In the place of hand-held devices, *The Motion Picture* introduced wrist-based communicators, worn at all times by *Enterprise* crew members.

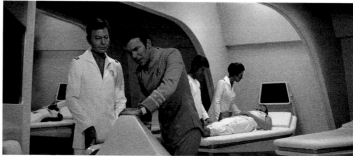

LEFT: Captain Kirk shows off his fancy wrist-based communicator.

RIGHT: After assessing Spock's mental state, Kirk communicates with the bridge via a desktop comms panel, despite having a portable communicator clearly visible on his wrist.

Despite their always-available convenience, these wrist-based communicators are used to advance the plot in only two scenes—when Decker tells the crew to return to their stations, and when Kirk speaks to Uhura from beside the V'Ger craft. Indeed, it's notable that earlier in the movie Kirk uses a desktop comms panel in the *Enterprise*'s sick bay rather than speaking into the device on his wrist.

Real-world wrist-based devices such as Apple's cellular Apple Watch don't require the device's built-in microphone to be held anywhere near the face in order to be effective. However, in a movie, it's necessary to move the device close to the actor's mouth to make it clear that it is being used to communicate. (The alternative—keeping the actor's wrist by his or her side—makes it look like the actors are simply talking to themselves.) This practical storytelling disadvantage, with the potential to mask the actor's face, may be why the otherwise futuristic wrist communicators were used sparingly in *The Motion Picture*—and were quietly replaced by more traditional handheld devices in later *Star Trek* movies.

LEFT: Nearly two hours into the movie, Decker becomes the first crew member to use a wrist-based communicator to advance the plot, telling all personnel on the *Enterprise* to resume their stations. He inadvertently obscures his face while doing so.

RIGHT: As part of the movie's climax, Kirk uses his wrist-based communicator to speak to the *Enterprise*-bound Uhura from beside the V'Ger craft.

While Decker gives Ilia a tour, Spock sneaks outside in a spacesuit and flies through V'Ger's pulsating orifice with pinpoint timing. He encounters a giant pseudo-Ilia, with whom he attempts a mind-meld. A dazzling montage of images flashes up on his space helmet during the meld, including one of particular interest:

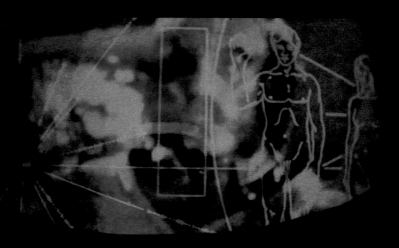

This illustration is from the six-by-nine-inch gold-anodized aluminum plaque mounted aboard NASA's *Pioneer 10* and *Pioneer 11* spacecraft, which traveled to Jupiter (and in the case of *Pioneer 11,* to Saturn) in the late 1970s. These plaques were created by author Carl Sagan and SETI (Search for Extraterrestrial Intelligence) Institute founder Frank Drake, and illustrated by Linda Salzman Sagan, as a message from mankind to any passing extraterrestrials that might chance upon the flights.

The purpose of these plaques was to educate inhabitants of other planetary systems about *Pioneer*'s home planet. *Pioneer 10* is shown leaving the solar system after passing Jupiter, though the arrow symbol indicating its trajectory is unlikely to make sense to extraterrestrial species unless they, too, evolved from a hunter-gatherer society.

This *Pioneer* plaque also appears briefly in *Star Trek V: The Final Frontier,* though it is erroneously facing outward for shot-framing convenience. It doesn't really make a difference, as the *Pioneer* craft is unceremoniously blown up by a passing extraterrestrial, without so much as a glance at the engraving. (The moral: Let's hope mankind's actual first contact does not involve a Klingon.)

ABOVE LEFT: *Pioneer 10*'s engraved aluminum plaque

ABOVE RIGHT: *Pioneer 10*'s aluminum plaque, mounted facing inward on the craft's antenna support struts to shield it from erosion by interstellar dust

BELOW LEFT: The aluminum plaque, shown facing outward on a *Pioneer* craft . . .

BELOW RIGHT: . . . shortly before its destruction by a bored Klingon captain in 1989's *Star Trek V: The Final Frontier.*

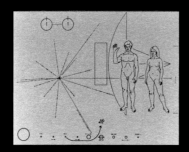

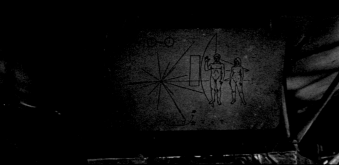

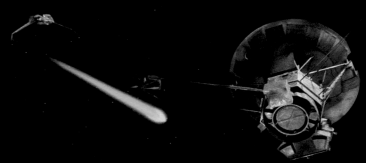

FIVE ENTERPRISES

The medical scanner's analysis tells Bones that IliaBot is made from "micro-miniature hydraulics, sensors, and molecule-size multiprocessor chips." However, despite the spectacular level of detail in this mechanical marvel, V'Ger's creation is sadly missing any sign of emotion. An optimistic Decker takes it on a tour of the recreation deck, one of Ilia's favorite hangouts pre-robotification, to try to connect with its non-robotic side. Here, Decker introduces IliaBot to a set of illustrations of five historical ships called *Enterprise*.

The USS *Enterprise* (1799–1823), in 1812 when rigged as a brigantine

The USS *Enterprise* (CV-6), an aircraft carrier that became the most decorated ship in World War II

The USS *Enterprise* (CV-6) was not the only aircraft carrier to have a *Star Trek* connection. Before making *The Motion Picture,* Gene Roddenberry spent ten days aboard CV-6's successor, the nuclear-powered USS *Enterprise* (CVN-65). On the first day of filming *The Motion Picture,* he gave director Robert Wise a baseball cap emblazoned with "ENTERPRISE" in gold lettering, which had been a gift from the ship's captain.

CVN-65 also appears in *Star Trek IV: The Voyage Home,* when Chekov and Uhura attempt to steal some nuclear power to recrystallize their dilithium. We can be confident that they steal it from USS *Enterprise* (CVN-65) because the US Navy has provided large signs that say "USS ENTERPRISE CVN-65."

The inclusion of the space shuttle *Enterprise* (OV-101) in this gallery is also of note. NASA's prototype space shuttle was originally going to be called *Constitution,* to celebrate its unveiling on the anniversary of the signing of the United States Constitution. However, *Star Trek* superfan Bjo Trimble, who had previously led a successful letter-writing campaign to bring back *The Original Series* for a third season, launched a new campaign to encourage fans to ask for the shuttle's name to be changed to *Enterprise.* Tens of thousands of fans

BELOW: The original USS *Enterprise* (NCC-1701), as it looked in *The Original Series* before its *Motion Picture* refit. (I haven't been able to track down the exact image used here, but it is representative of nearly every *Original Series* planet flyby, albeit from right to left rather than the usual left to right.)

ABOVE: The USS *Enterprise* (XCV-330), an early *Star Trek* craft that never actually appeared on screen. The same illustration does, however, appear on a wall in "First Flight," a 2003 *Star Trek: Enterprise* episode.

ABOVE: A model of XCV-330 also appears briefly on Admiral Marcus's desk in 2013's *Star Trek: Into Darkness,* as part of another collection of significant flying machines.

The USS *Enterprise* (CVN-65) in 1986's *Star Trek: The Voyage Home*

responded. This led President Gerald Ford's senior economic adviser, William F. Gorog, to write a memo to the president, advocating for the name change.

Four days later, Ford received a follow-up memo from James Connor, secretary to the cabinet. Ford was convinced, and the *Constitution* became the *Enterprise*.

When the shuttle was unveiled on September 17, 1976, many of the *Star Trek* cast were in attendance as special guests, along with creator Gene Roddenberry. To complete the occasion, the Air Force band struck up a surprise rendition of the *Star Trek* theme in their honor.

Paramount wisely made the most of the announcement's PR value, taking out a full-page ad in the *New York Times* a few days later to announce the movie to the world.

As a prototype, the space shuttle *Enterprise* was constructed without engines or a functional heat shield and was therefore incapable of independent spaceflight. The photo seen in *The Motion Picture*'s recreation room looks to be from the *Enterprise*'s final test flight in 1977's approach and landing tests, during which the *Enterprise* was flown atop a Shuttle Carrier Aircraft (a heavily modified Boeing 747), then

jettisoned from its perch using explosive bolts. After its release, it glided to a landing on the runway at Edwards Air Force Base. (The engines seen on the back of the craft in the photo are dummy engines, for aerodynamic test purposes only.) Despite initial plans to retrofit the *Enterprise* as a spaceflight-capable vehicle, this ended up being financially impractical, and the *Enterprise* never made it into orbit. Nonetheless, its 1977 test landing happened just in time for a photo of OV-101 to appear aboard NCC-1701.

Memo from William F. Gorog to President Gerald Ford, September 3, 1976. The "public interest . . . the CB radio provided" refers to Betty Ford, First Lady of the United States, who jumped on the 1970s craze for CB radio with the handle First Mama. This turned out to be great PR.

Memo from James Connor to President Gerald Ford, September 7, 1976. Feedback on the naming was provided by Philip Buchen, legal adviser; Brent Scowcroft, national security adviser; James Cannon, domestic policy adviser; Guy Stever, science adviser; Robert Hartmann, counselor to the president; and Jack Marsh, counselor to the president.

THE WHITE HOUSE
WASHINGTON

September 3, 1976

DECISION

MEMORANDUM FOR   THE PRESIDENT

FROM: WILLIAM F. GOROG   *WG*

SUBJECT: Naming the Space Shuttle

Next Wednesday you will meet with Dr. James Fletcher of NASA for a substantive meeting at which time you will be presented with a mock-up of the space shuttle, the full scale version of which will be rolled out in California later this month. NASA has not announced a name as of yet for the shuttle, and they are holding this announcement until your meeting with Fletcher.

Dr. Fletcher is not adverse to the name "Enterprise" for the space shuttle, and I suggest that you ask that it be so named for the following reasons:

   o   NASA has received hundreds of thousands of letters
       from the space-oriented "Star Trek" group asking
       that the name "Enterprise" be given to the craft.
       This group comprises millions of individuals who
       are deeply interested in our space program.

   o   The name "Enterprise" is tied in with the system on
       which the Nation's economic structure is built.

   o   Use of the name would provide a substantial human
       interest appeal to the rollout ceremonies scheduled
       for this month in California, where the aeronautical
       industry is of vital importance.

In short, this situation could provide the same public interest as the CB radio provided for Mrs. Ford.

Your approval is sought to have NASA use the name "Enterprise" on the space shuttle.

Approve _____   Disapprove _____

THE WHITE HOUSE
WASHINGTON

September 7, 1976

MR PRESIDENT:

Naming the Space Shuttle

Staffing of the attached memorandum resulted in the following comments and recommendations:

Phil Buchen and Brent Scowcroft - concur with recommendation.

Jim Cannon -   "It seems to me "Enterprise" is an excellent name
               for the space shuttle.

               It would be personally gratifying to several million
               followers of the television show "Star Trek", one of
               the most dedicated constituencies in the country.

               Moreover, the name "Enterprise" is a hallowed Navy
               tradition. An "Enterprise" was in action against the
               Barbary pirates in 1803. During World War II, an
               "Enterprise" served with the Wasp and the Hornet in
               the carrier fleet in the Pacific. And the Navy's current
               "Enterprise" is the first nuclear carrier."

Dr. Guy Stever-
               "Enterprise" is fine for the reasons listed.

Bob Hartmann - "This is an especially hallowed Naval name - going
               back to the Revolution - I think Navy should keep it."

Jack Marsh -   "I have no objection to this selection of a name, however,
               I am not enthusiastic about the rationale for the selection.
               "Enterprise" is a famous name for vessels since the
               early days of the Republic. I think that is a far better
               reason than appealing to a T.V. fad."

               Jim Connor

ABOVE: (left to right) Dr. James C. Fletcher (NASA administrator); DeForest Kelley (Bones); George Takei (Sulu); James Doohan (Scotty); Nichelle Nichols (Uhura); Leonard Nimoy (Spock); Gene Roddenberry; Don Fuqua (chairman of the House Space Committee); Walter Koenig (Chekov).

BELOW: The space shuttle *Enterprise* might not have made it into space, but some of its campaigners did. As a thank-you for the letter-writing efforts, *Star Trek* creator Gene Roddenberry asked Trimble to organize a cattle call of fans to appear in the recreation room scene. The 170 or so *Enterprise* crew members shown listening to Kirk's impassioned speech are all Trekkers, in a range of costumes and latex alien masks.

Photo by MarsScientific.com

The space-faring hopes of real-world *Enterprise* craft didn't end with the space shuttle *Enterprise,* however. In December 2009, Virgin Galactic unveiled its SpaceShipTwo spacecraft, as part of an attempt to become the world's first commercial space carrier. From a Virgin Galactic press release of the time:

In honour of a long tradition of using the word Enterprise in the naming of Royal Navy, US Navy, NASA vehicles and even science fiction spacecraft, Governor Schwarzenegger of California and Governor Richardson of New Mexico will today christen SS2 with the name Virgin Space Ship (VSS) ENTERPRISE. This represents not only an acknowledgement to that name's honorable past but also looks to the future of the role of private enterprise in the development of the exploration, industrialisation and human habitation of space.

Sadly, this *Enterprise* didn't make it into space, either. During a powered test flight in October 2014, the VSS *Enterprise* was destroyed after a premature deployment of its descent device.

In a twist of hope for *The Motion Picture* fans, the VSS *Enterprise*'s successor was nearly named VSS *Voyager*. Its final name, however, was chosen by physicist Stephen Hawking, who christened the new craft VSS *Unity* instead.

VSS *Enterprise* during its first supersonic powered flight

Pioneer's successor, the Voyager program, also contained a message to extraterrestrial life. For Voyager, however, Sagan went one better than a plaque, sending an entire album of Earth facts into the cosmos. And when I say "album," I really do mean it in the old-school vinyl LP sense. *Voyager 1* and *2* each carried a golden record of earthly sights and sounds, along with engraved instructions as to how to play the record.

LEFT: Engraved cover of the Voyager golden record

RIGHT: Side one of the Voyager golden record, *The Sounds of Earth*

The Voyager golden records include music, spoken phrases, a recording of human brainwaves, and a series of encoded images including food, anatomy, biology, animals, and architecture. The presence of these images showing Earth's amazingness raised concerns around the launch of *Voyager 1* and *Voyager 2* that if an intelligent species ever *did* encounter one of the records, it might decide to invade or attack Earth to control that amazingness itself. Still, I'm sure there's no chance of that happening in practice.

After a tense standoff during which V'Ger threatens to attack Earth, the *Enterprise* crew manage to gain an audience with V'Ger itself. Much to everyone's surprise, the all-powerful creature at the center of the evil space cloud turns out to be an old-school NASA spacecraft. As the crew inspects the craft, Kirk rubs some dirt off a sign on the side and reads out, "V-G-E-R. V'Ger." Oh my goodness—it's a hypothetical *Voyager 6*!

"V___GER." That sounds familiar.

The timing of *The Motion Picture*'s release is important when considering the cultural significance of this scene. *Voyager 2* launched on August 20, 1977, followed by *Voyager 1* a couple of weeks later. (*Voyager 1* overtook its sister craft in December 1977, hence the unusual ordering.) Both craft completed their observations of Jupiter during 1979, shortly before *The Motion Picture* was released. In the same way that 1968's *2001: A Space Odyssey* leapfrogged the Apollo moon missions and aimed for Jupiter, 1979's *The Motion Picture* leapfrogged Jupiter and imagined humanity sending a probe far beyond its 1970s counterparts.

The idea of a rogue *Voyager* would not have been alien to seventies viewers, either. Shortly after the launch of *Voyager 2*, the probe started triggering its onboard systems independently, ignoring the post-launch instructions of its creators. The extreme shaking of *Voyager 2*'s launch rocket had made the probe think it was failing, causing it to switch to its backup systems and try to figure out what was going on. Indeed, for a few days NASA engineers on Earth had no idea whether the *Voyager 2* mission had been lost altogether. Newspapers ran headlines such as "'Mutiny' in Space" and "Voyager Going to HAL?" with *2001*'s antagonist clearly still a reference point for space-based computers turning rogue. Thankfully, *Voyager 2*'s trajectory stabilized and conditions returned to normal operating thresholds, ending its temporary rebellion.

Back in *The Motion Picture*'s finale, the *Enterprise* crew deduces a remarkable amount of V'Ger's life story from zero evidence, thereby accelerating the exposition nicely. Without any assisting typography, they determine that V'Ger wants to physically join with a human to become one with its creator. Decker bravely volunteers to join with IliaBot. He turns all sparkly, and his hair blows crazily in the breeze. Ilia's does not. As their join completes, the entirety of V'Ger turns sparkly and disappears to leave nothing but the *Enterprise,* flying pointedly toward the camera.

AS WE WAVE GOODBYE to the *Enterprise,* we should note that *The Motion Picture* has not once shown a present-day company in a futuristic setting. To make up for it, Italian car manufacturer created a tie-in ad for the launch of their own spacey craft, the Fiat Panda (right). The text on the poster can be translated as: "The human adventure is just beginning. [This was *The Motion Picture*'s tagline.] Fiat Panda. The conquest of space."

To find out if this is a fair comparison on Fiat's behalf, let's pitch the USS *Enterprise* refit against the Panda 30.

Front page of the *Pasadena Star-News,* Monday, August 29, 1977. The headline "Voyager Going To HAL?" compares *Voyager 2* with the evil space-based computer from *2001: A Space Odyssey.*

	USS ENTERPRISE (REFIT)	FIAT PANDA 30
LAUNCHED	JAN 2244	FEB 1980
LENGTH (M)	305.1	3.38
SHAPE	CURVY	BOXY
GROSS WEIGHT (TONS)	235,200	1.05
TOP SPEED (MPH)	522,201,121,422	71
MAX ACCELERATION	45 g	0.08 g
OFFICER COMPLEMENT	76	1
CREW COMPLEMENT	426	0
PASSENGER CAPACITY	150	ONE IN THE FRONT, TWO IN THE BACK
7-POSITION ADJUSTABLE REAR SEAT	NO	YES

Here's that adjustable rear seat in action, converting from fold-up storage to a comfortable bed. Impressive as the *Enterprise* undoubtedly is, the Panda is the clear winner here.

STAR TREK ™

L'avventura dell'uomo sta incominciando.

U.S.S. Enterprise

Fiat Panda. La conquista dello spazio.

MIKE OKUDA

In September 2017, I spoke to Mike Okuda about *Star Trek: The Motion Picture*, futuristic user interface (UI) design, and the Heisenberg uncertainty principle.

Following his graphic-design work on the movie *Star Trek IV: The Voyage Home* (1986), Mike was the scenic-art supervisor for the TV series *Star Trek: The Next Generation* (1987–94), *Star Trek: Deep Space Nine* (1993–99), *Star Trek: Voyager* (1995–2001), and *Star Trek: Enterprise* (2001–5), as well as the associated spin-off movies. If something's on a wall in a modern-day *Enterprise*, it's almost certainly because Mike put it there.

In addition to his scenic-design work, Mike is the coauthor (with Rick Sternbach) of *"Star Trek: The Next Generation" Technical Manual* and (with his wife, Denise Okuda) of *The "Star Trek" Encyclopedia: A Reference Guide to the Future*, now in its fourth edition.

ADDEY: As a long-running franchise, *Star Trek* has to face the challenge of the future constantly catching up with it. What approaches have you taken to keep the things we see on screen one step ahead of the present?

OKUDA: For me, the most important thing is to take a cue from Matt Jefferies, production designer for the original *Star Trek,* which is to do something that has one foot firmly planted in what he called "aircraft logic"—something that seems to be rooted in technical reality—and then to go beyond that and to try to make it look futuristic, imaginative, exciting. Then you inform all of *that* with what you can afford to do: What's the best use of your resources? By starting from those three things, Jefferies was able to do something that was not only cool-looking, not only credible, but also practical to do on a production budget.

If you look back at most other science fiction of the day, they used toggle switches, rheostats, dials, and meters. For better or for worse, Matt couldn't afford to do that back then. Instead, he said, "Here's what I *can* afford to do; I'm going to use a particular style and a particular set of production solutions," which in his case were these backlit panels and little gumdrop buttons. He said, "This, arbitrarily, is my vision of the future. It's not necessarily what I think the twenty-third century's going to be like, but it's my metaphor. I'm going to stick to it, I'm going to believe it." And because he was very good at it, we believed in it, too.

Now, within that context the value of internal consistency is extremely high. If you look through Matt Jefferies's *Enterprise,* there's a sense of consistency to the technology sensors, the art direction, the instrumentation, the architecture. And once you've bought into that, you've bought into the *Enterprise,* even though it was done on an extremely low budget, on an extremely tight schedule.

If it's well done—and I think Matt's world very much did this—you willingly suspend your disbelief. And that's what we all want to do, no matter how much time and money you have. We don't know how to invent warp drive or the transporter; we don't know how to navigate a starship. In order to be successful, we have to persuade the audience to willingly suspend their disbelief.

In addition, there are so many clichés of technology today that it has become much more difficult to come up with something that's as dramatic a departure as the original *Enterprise* was back in 1966. So as a designer in film and television, you try to take a cue from what the screenwriter and director want. In the case of *Star Trek: The Next*

Generation, Gene Roddenberry was very clear that he wanted the *Enterprise-D* to look radically different from the *Enterprise* of *The Motion Picture* and *Original Series*. He wanted it to be obviously user-friendly to a degree that was not common in instrumentation at the time. So that was something that we had the benefit of: "This is what Gene has in mind, let's try to execute that."

The LCARS computer interface you created for *Star Trek: The Next Generation* is a huge part of that unifying visual style for the *Enterprise-D*. It's unusual for a computer interface; it has bold, colorful swooshes and lozenges, which aren't something one typically sees in a present-day computer UI. Was that a deliberate styling, to give it an aesthetic that didn't feel like today?

Very much so. I'd been a fan and a student of graphics and film; I loved the things that were done with the computer screens in *2001: A Space Odyssey;* and I'd seen the remarkable work in films like *Alien.* One thing I brought to the *Next Generation* designs was the understanding that on the one hand you're trying to predict the future, but on a more practical level you need something that looks good in extreme close-up. However, if it's sufficiently intricate to look good in close-up, it's going to turn to mush in a very wide shot—it's going to turn into a pattern of gray. So you want something that, in addition to that fine detail, also has medium detail, and then a much larger-scale detail. With the swooshes—I call them "organization brackets," "L brackets," and "T bars"—I wanted those to convey some kind of organization, flow, and structure that was clear even in a very wide shot, even if the camera is focused on the foreground actor.

But you couldn't *just* have those bold strokes, because when you'd get close it would become uninteresting. So there has to be a second layer of detail on top of that, and then there has to be a third layer of detail on top of *that*.

At the same time, as a fan of science fiction you tell yourself a little story. "OK, here's how you navigate the ship. This must be where you get the coordinates; this must be the power resources; and perhaps this is what you do in an emergency." And as you entertain yourself doing these things, hopefully an interesting organization emerges.

The choice of font [Swiss 911 Ultra Compressed] for LCARS is also unusual for a computer display, in that it's extremely narrow. Is that to balance between small text you don't want people to read versus large text that says, "plot point"?

That's correct. First of all, I wanted to avoid the cliché of what was popular in the seventies and eighties: those OCR [optical character recognition] fonts and fake futuristic fonts. I wanted to do something different from Eurostile and Microgramma—which I love, but which we had done in the *Star Trek* films. I wanted to give the ship its own identity.

That said, yes, I specifically wanted a font that *appeared* to be extremely readable and, if I wanted to label a station, was relatively legible. But below a certain point, I deliberately wanted it to become illegible, or at least something that turned into visual noise. So you could see that it's sufficiently well labeled, and if you were to study it you could see: "Yes, I am scanning the planet, I am analyzing these important sensor readings," but all I really want

Captain Picard uses an LCARS terminal in "Encounter at Farpoint Part 1," the opening episode of *Star Trek: The Next Generation.* In this mid-shot, the random numbers on his terminal screen are readable, with the surrounding colored bars acting primarily as a frame for the data. The use of numbers rather than words removes the danger of the viewer's being distracted, while still suggesting meaningful information.

The same terminal screen is seen from farther away in a later shot. At this size, the text is unreadable, but the curved colored bars still provide a sense of order and organization to the data on screen. An additional benefit of the highly condensed bold font is that at this distance the runs of numbers effectively turn into colored blocks, so that they feel like part of the colored bars rather than becoming a gray mess of blurry text.

you to read is "PLANET ABOUT TO EXPLODE." Because that's the dramatic role of that particular graphic in that particular shot.

It's very easy to draw the viewer's eye, and there are times you don't want to. You want the viewer to believe: "Yes, this is a starship; this is properly labeled for all the things these people need to know," but if I want you to look at the actor's face, the graphic shouldn't distract from that.

***Alien* uses a trick similar to LCARS, often filling screens with numbers that look significant but don't distract from the plot. They would presumably make sense to an operator, but they don't encourage the viewer to read them.**

Absolutely. It's fun to think of things that are technologically plausible and imaginative, but if the viewer stops to read my analysis of how a fusion reactor works, I have taken them out of the

episode, and I've done the filmmakers a disservice. Similarly, it's fun to figure out how the fusion reactor works . . . but if I take half an hour extra to make sense of all the labels, that's half an hour that I could've put into something that actually has value on screen.

How did you approach the design of the LCARS computer system to make sure it could serve stories that hadn't yet been written?

It actually wasn't particularly difficult. As a designer in a more general sense, I want to know what these things do, but as a designer in film and TV, I understand that I can't be the one to tell the director, "You push *this* button to fire the phasers." Because if the director wants the actor to push *that* button for whatever dramatic framing or reason, then that's what they need to do. So I understood the value from the beginning of keeping it relatively generic.

Swiss 911 Ultra Compressed from Bitstream, seen in LCARS interfaces aboard the *Enterprise-D*

ABCDEFGHIJKLMNOPQRSTUVWXYZ

That said, we did have a very specific idea of what station did what on the bridge. In fact, in the very first episode of *Star Trek: The Next Generation* two of the bridge stations were reversed. The actor was sitting at the wrong station. I sent a memo to one of our producers, Rick Berman, noting this and saying, "It's not a big deal; I can change the graphic, and we're fine." And Rick said, "Oh no, no. We can't reshoot the episode, but we're gonna flip the actors. And I want you to come down to the set and explain to the cast how to work the control panels." He took it very seriously.

For *The Motion Picture*, the designers created a guide for cast and crew, indicating which buttons did what. Did you have a similar guide for *The Next Generation*?

That's an amazing book. It was put together by [production illustrators] Mike Minor and Rick Sternbach and [graphic designer] Lee Cole. They did a wonderful job. There's even a couple of pages that Rick put together in response to a request from director Robert Wise, for a scene where he wanted the actor to

push specific buttons. So Rick prepared a memo, saying, "This is how you fire the photon torpedo."

But I also knew that rarely do you have a director who wants that level of detail. I knew which station was wired to do what, but at the same time I was very careful to say, "Look, guys, this is all software-defined. If you want to fire the phasers from this station, you enter the right code, and you can do it."

Marina Sirtis [who played Counselor Deanna Troi] understood that the technology was an important part of the show. She came to me after one of the first days of filming and said, "Mike, I'm kinda concerned about this, because I don't want to mess it up." And I said, "Look, the most important thing isn't the actual button you push—it's the confidence with which you push it. If this is a real starship, I have envisioned that these panels are software-definable. When you sign in to the panel, it's configured to match your training and your personal preferences. These panels have to be so sophisticated that they're simple to use. So the button that you're comfortable pushing to fire the phasers is not necessarily the button that I will push when I'm at that same station." And she said, "OK, that makes sense." And as far I could tell, she was totally fine after that.

In my *2001: A Space Odyssey* research, I discovered that part of the reason the computer displays were created as flat panels was because it wasn't practical to create the display graphics with the computer-graphics systems of the time, so they filmed them and projected them instead. Were there similar practical reasons for the sleek glass surfaces seen for LCARS?

Yes. At the beginning of *Star Trek: The Next Generation,* no one had really put a lot of thought into how the control panels would be executed. This is ordinarily something that the mechanical-effects department does: drilling holes, putting in panel lights and gauges and buttons. I knew that this was not something that was affordable, particularly if you wanted custom-designed switches and buttons. So I went to Herman Zimmerman, our production designer, and said, "Let's look at the choices you can make when you do control panels. What is the fastest, least expensive decision you can make at every step of the way? What gives it the greatest flexibility for the future?" And I said, "This is my opinion as to what the result is—to have photographic, backlit art mounted on acrylic sheeting." It's very inexpensive, very fast to make, and once you have some basic designs, it's relatively easy to repurpose them for other things, which you will need on an episodic basis.

So once those decisions were made, I said, "Well, now—how can I make this look interesting?" And that's when I started the actual graphic-design work.

You mentioned that Gene Roddenberry wanted a very different visual styling for the *Enterprise-D*. What guidance did he give about the aesthetic he was looking for?

I grew up watching the original *Star Trek* and loving the work of Matt Jefferies on *The Original Series.* So I was, frankly, very disappointed when Gene said, "No,

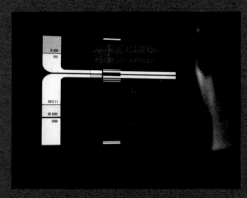

In *The Next Generation*'s season-one episode "The Naked Now," Data and Riker scan the *Enterprise*'s memory banks to find any previous history of someone showering in their clothing. During the scan, they pause briefly on a picture of Gene Roddenberry's head on the body of a parrot wearing a Starfleet uniform. The image is captioned: "The Great Bird of the Galaxy" (a nickname given to Roddenberry by associate producer Robert Justin).

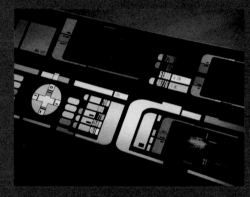

The same interface (along with other images from the sequence) was reused on Data's LCARS terminal a couple of episodes later, in "The Last Outpost," when an unknown being scans the contents of the *Enterprise*'s memory banks, in a similar manner to V'Ger in *The Motion Picture*.

you can't do that." Gene was emphatic that this new *Enterprise* had to be simple to use. These aren't his exact words, but he wanted it to be so advanced that it became simplistic.

In fact, my original concept for the *Enterprise-D* bridge graphics was that most of the lozenge icons would be off most the time and would only come on as needed. And then gradually, I guess, the producers liked the graphics, and they wanted them to stay on all the time. But if you look at "Encounter at Farpoint," the first episode of *Next Generation,*

you'll see that a lot of them are off a lot of the time. That was a conscious decision; that was specifically what Gene wanted.

That "so advanced, it's simple" style evokes a more general design aesthetic for *Star Trek,* which is a distinctly utopian vision of the future. Is that a deliberate philosophical and design choice—to have an aspirational design style?

Very much. I can't speak for other people who have worked on other versions of *Star Trek,* but for me, absolutely yes. And I suspect that's true for Matt as well.

On that utopian theme and making the world—indeed, the galaxy—a better place: The Federation, and Starfleet in particular, seem very reminiscent of the United Nations in terms of their role in the shows and movies.

I think that's a fair statement. I didn't design the version of the Federation emblem that appears in the first three or four movies, but I designed the version that came in *Next Generation,* which we then used in *Star Trek V [The Final Frontier]* and the subsequent spin-offs. In my case, yes, it was very much an homage to the United Nations emblem, with the olive branches on either side and the map of stars.

On that theme: I don't recall the number of nation-states in the UN, but in an episode of *Next Generation* one of the writers called me and asked how many members of the Federation there are, and we settled on a number that was the number of nation-states in the UN at the time.

With so many different series and movies over the years, how have you ensured a consistency in their portrayal of the future?

That's always a difficult balancing act. Because on the one hand, you want to

be consistent. But on the other hand, you need to continuously keep it fresh. If you do exactly the same thing in each subsequent episode and series, it becomes ho-hum, and you don't want to do that.

We had the benefit in *Star Trek: Deep Space Nine* that much of the show was set on an alien space station, so we had the fun of creating this very strange technology that humans didn't necessarily immediately comprehend. And then on *Star Trek: Voyager* and some of the *Next Generation* films, we took what I had done in *Star Trek: The Next Generation* and added a few tweaks on top of it, in the hope of implying that there was some progression of technology.

The biggest departure we made was the last version of *Star Trek* that I worked on, which was *Star Trek: Enterprise,* set some decades before the time of Captain Kirk. What we tried to do there was to say, "Well, the *Enterprise* of Captáin Kirk was relatively streamlined and simplified and highly stylized. Let's make this *Enterprise* clunkier and less user-friendly, with more buttons and more screens and more visual complexity and more mechanical things and gauges." And that was actually a lot of fun to do.

Interestingly, some people didn't understand what we did and felt that

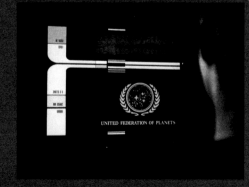

Mike Okuda's redesigned United Federation of Planets logo, seen briefly during a computer scan in *The Next Generation*'s season-one episode "The Naked Now." As with the logo we saw previously in *The Motion Picture,* its olive-branch wrapping and circular map evoke the official United Nations flag.

by adding complexity and computer screens and things we were trying to make the world more advanced. To the extent that they didn't see what we intended, we did not succeed.

When you're putting together a design for a particular piece of scenery, how much do its physical characteristics affect the design choices you make?

They greatly affect the *initial* choices. For example, in the case of *Next Generation* a lot of the physical signage graphics were in the form of preprinted stickers that I would put all over the set. I'd had the benefit of being able to look at not just the *Star Trek* series and movies but a lot of other science fiction, saying, "What do I think would benefit the style, and what is a time- and cost-efficient means of dealing with it?" For example, I think that having signage and labeling throughout a spaceship helps to visually tie it together. And yet signage can be very expensive to do, particularly custom signage for this wall and that door and that console. So for *Next Generation,* I came up with this simplified style of self-adhesive stickers—I called them "capsule labels"—for which I had a number of preprinted things. And again, they had this extremely compact typeface. You could tell it was text, but you didn't necessarily know what it said. So if we rented a console from a prop house or borrowed a wall unit from another set, I could apply these panel labels and visually imply that they were all part of the same ship.

And practically, the use of these preprinted labels meant that I could go in literally minutes before filming and say, "OK, well, let's apply this panel label, which implies that behind this panel are these circuits or in this locker is that equipment." And the intent and hope are that it'll imply there's a great deal of thought and organization behind the system, which we may not have had time

to think on in detail. But hopefully the audience, if they have suspended their disbelief, will accept that this is all part of the same ship.

Have any of the on-screen designs you've created for *Star Trek* over the years gone on to become real-life inventions?

It hasn't become a reality, but in the *Star Trek: The Next Generation* transporter room there is a big backlit graphic behind the transporter operator. This is one of the cases where I put more thought into the labeling because I thought that this might be seen in a fair number of shots. And, in fact, it was. So I invented what I thought was credible technology for various subsystems— molecular imaging scanners, pattern buffers, and things like that.

Now, it's possible to read quantum theory to suggest that you really *can't* digitize all the molecules in a person, for a lot of reasons. One reason is Heisenberg's uncertainty principle, which states that you can't define both the position and the speed of a particle simultaneously. Which could possibly mean that at a fundamental level a transporter simply may not be possible.

So how would one overcome that? Well, because this is Heisenberg's uncertainty principle we're dealing with, I labeled one of the blocks on the schematic as a Heisenberg compensator. How do we deal with the uncertainty principle? Obviously, we use the Heisenberg compensator. Problem solved. And obviously it works—we see it every week.

One of my hopes was that at some point Roddenberry would use it in one of his talks. As far as I know, that never happened. But it has taken on a life of its own. Lawrence Krauss, the physicist, wrote several paragraphs about the Heisenberg compensator, for example.

As someone who is actively involved with the *Star Trek* community, have you met people who've been inspired

Example of a red "capsule label" sticker affixed to a piece of medical equipment in *The Next Generation*'s season-one episode "The Naked Now." The repeated use of these stickers provides a consistent branding, in the manner of the Weylan Yutani logos seen stuck all over the *Nostromo* in *Alien*.

Example of a red "capsule label" sticker affixed to an engineering-room wall behind a sweaty Wil Wheaton in "The Naked Now"

A split-capsule styling was used for the labels on turbolifts and doors all over the *Enterprise,* including this example from *The Next Generation*'s season-five episode "The Next Phase."

The *Enterprise*'s transporter-system graphic, seen behind Chief O'Brien in *The Next Generation*'s season-six fear-of-transporting episode, "Realm of Fear."

Lieutenant Barclay nervously studies the transporter-system schematic in "Realm of Fear." It is fair to say that he is uncertain about the principle.

Lieutenant Barclay and Chief O'Brien scan the Heisenberg compensator for issues in "Realm of Fear."

to follow a career in science after watching the show?

I'm a huge fan of the real-life space program, and one of the coolest things I was ever invited to do was to design the mission patch for space shuttle flight STS-125, which flew in 2009. It was the final servicing mission to the Hubble Space Telescope. I was asked to do this by an astronaut named John Grunsfeld, who at the time was NASA's chief scientist. He was the lead spacewalker on several of the Hubble servicing missions. He told me that one of the reasons he became an astronaut was because he watched *Star Trek* as a child, and he became an astronaut and an astronomer—a professional scientist—because he wanted to be more like Mr. Spock.

Denise and I have been lucky enough to visit several NASA installations, technology companies, and scientific facilities over the years. It's surprising the number of people who say, "I'm here because I was inspired by *Star Trek*." I think this is something Gene Roddenberry was very proud of.

Is this something that science fiction has a duty to do? To inspire people about the future?

Duty is a strong word. Science fiction has a duty to *entertain*. And part of the process of entertaining is telling stories that happen to inspire. In the process of telling a story, you sometimes predict the future, or you warn of dystopia, or you present alternatives. But having that brilliant idea means nothing if you don't tell an entertaining story.

The crew mission patch from NASA flight STS-125, designed by Mike Okuda in 2007. The patch shows the Hubble Space Telescope, together with a representation of its many discoveries, surrounded by the names of the astronauts in Bank Gothic.

BLADE

OFF WORLD

Blade Runner's vision of 2019 LA introduced the now common sci-fi trope of an advertising-laden multicultural cityscape. According to FX supervisor David Dryer, the movie's iconic geisha ad is actually for a birth control pill—a product Dryer imagined would be heavily advertised in 2019's overpopulated future.

R
UN
NE
R

THE FINAL CUT

After studying *Alien* in intimate detail, it's time to look at the typography and design of Ridley Scott's other classic sci-fi movie, *Blade Runner.* The movie, based on Philip K. Dick's novel *Do Androids Dream of Electric Sheep?* cements Scott's reputation for beautiful, gritty science fiction.

Blade Runner's opening crawl is decidedly *un*-futuristic in its choice of font, using the decidedly old-school Goudy Old Style, designed by Frederic W. Goudy way back in 1915.

Goudy Old Style, by Frederic W. Goudy, 1915

ABCDEFGHIJKLMNOPQRSTUVWXYZ

This somewhat traditional choice fits well with *Blade Runner*'s film noir aesthetic, in which moody detective tropes from 1940s and 1950s movies are restyled for a futuristic setting. Indeed, *Blade Runner* pretty much invented a new genre with this crossover, latterly known as "tech noir," after the name of a nightclub in 1984's *The Terminator*. A similar noir/sci-fi crossover can be seen in movies such as *Brazil, Twelve Monkeys, Ghost in the Shell,* and *Minority Report.*

Early in the 21st Century, THE TYRELL CORPORATION advanced Robot evolution into the NEXUS phase — a being virtually identical to a human — known as a Replicant.

The NEXUS 6 *Replicants* were superior in strength and agility, and at least equal in intelligence, to the genetic engineers who created them.

Replicants were used Off-world as slave labor, in the hazardous exploration and colonization of other planets.

After a bloody mutiny by a NEXUS 6 combat team in an Off-world colony, *Replicants* were declared illegal on earth — under penalty of death.

Special police squads — BLADE RUNNER UNITS — had orders to shoot to kill, upon detection, any trespassing *Replicant.*

This was not called execution.
It was called retirement.

ABOVE: A page from *Mary Poppins* by P. L. Travers, showing several examples of Mid-Sentence Capitalized Words

LEFT: *Blade Runner*'s opening title crawl, set in Goudy Old Style

The opening crawl uses Goudy Old Style for a veritable typographic cornucopia. Within five and a bit paragraphs, we are treated to several inconsistently spaced examples of SMALL CAPS (all of which make me think of Terry Pratchett's anthropomorphic personification of Death TALKING INSIDE MY HEAD) and five—count them!—examples of particularly chunky em dashes. (Thankfully, they do not follow the strange American style of removing—for no reason at all—their surrounding spaces, as I myself am being forced to do at this very moment by my American publisher.)

My favorite aspects of this opening crawl, however, are the arbitrary examples of Mid-Sentence Capitalized Words, as popularized by A. A. Milne (*Winnie-the-Pooh*) and P. L. Travers (*Mary Poppins*). There's no real Reason for "Robot," "Replicant," or "Off-world" to be Capitalized, but it certainly does Make an Impact when you Read the Words in your Head.

With the opening crawl's typographic anomalies fresh in our minds, it's time to meet our first suspected replicant. Leon, a potential NEXUS 6, is being tested with a Voight-Kampff machine in the offices of the Tyrell Corporation. We know we're in the offices of the Tyrell Corporation because the chairs have "TYRELL CORP." stenciled on their backs in what might be Akzidenz-Grotesk Extended, though it's impossible to be sure. As we saw in *Alien,* omnipresent corporate branding is the single most important sign of a successful international conglomerate.

Akzidenz-Grotesk Extended, by
H. Berthold, 1898

ABCDEFGHIJKLMNOPQRSTUVWXYZ

The Voight-Kampff machine measures contractions of the iris muscle to gauge the subject's empathetic response to a range of questions. We see a close-up of one of Leon's green eyes as the test is administered:

This is odd, given that Leon's eyes are blue:

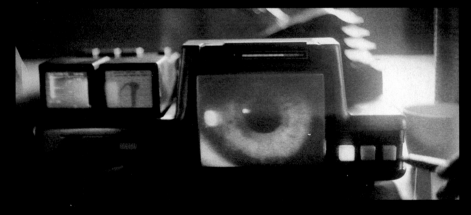
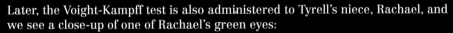

Later, the Voight-Kampff test is also administered to Tyrell's niece, Rachael, and we see a close-up of one of Rachael's green eyes:

This is odd, given that Rachael's eyes are brown:

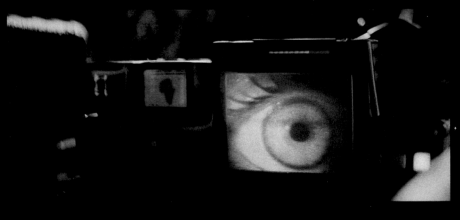

Thankfully, this mystery is easy to explain: The eyes we see on these Voight-Kampff screens are taken from stock footage by Oxford Scientific Films, not from actual replicants. This is almost certainly because the eyes of a *real* replicant are notoriously hard to film without a bad case of red-eye effect.

We see an example of this phenomenon the very first time we meet Leon:

The same is true when we meet Rachael (purportedly Tyrell's niece, but later exposed as an unsuspecting replicant):

The trademark tinge is also there when Pris is reunited with Roy Batty in J. F. Sebastian's apartment:

And even a top-of-the-range NEXUS 6 like Roy Batty suffers from a bad case of the red eye:

The red-eye effect is *so* common, in fact, that it seems a bit unnecessary to use a Voight-Kampff machine to identify potential replicants. *Blade Runner*'s blade runners could have saved themselves a lot of time and inconvenience if they'd just checked for glowy eyes instead.

Perhaps the most inexplicable example of the red-eye phenomenon is a blurry background shot late in the movie, featuring central protagonist (and definitely *not* a replicant) Rick Deckard, played by Harrison Ford:

How strange! I'm sure it won't turn out to be significant.

Deckard reads a copy of the *Independent Sentinel* in the Los Angeles rain.

The first time we meet Deckard, he's sitting in the Los Angeles rain, idly reading a copy of the *Independent Sentinel.* (You'll see this newspaper prop several times later in the movie—it's also at the Snake Pit Bar and inside a drawer in Leon's apartment.)

The newspaper's headline reads, "FARMING THE OCEANS, THE MOON AND ANTARCTICA" in Futura Demi, with the subtitle "WORLD WIDE COMPUTER LINKUP PLANNED" in Optima Bold. While the idea of a WORLD WIDE COMPUTER LINKUP might seem passé for 2019, the year in which *Blade Runner* is set, it was still very unusual in 1982, when the film was released. Indeed, it wasn't until March 1982 that the US Department of Defense, creators of pre-Internet network ARPANET, declared TCP/IP as the standard for all military computer networking, kick-starting the Internet we know and love today.

Futura Demi

ABCDEFGHIJKLMNOPQRSTUVWXYZ

Optima Bold

ABCDEFGHIJKLMNOPQRSTUVWXYZ

LEFT: *Blade Runner*'s sole use of Eurostile Bold Extended

BELOW: LP cover for *An Evening with Groucho* (A&M Records, 1972

But we're getting ahead of ourselves. Back at the beginning of the movie, Deckard folds up his newspaper and buys some tasty noodles from a street restaurant. As he noms the noodles, he's approached by Gaff, a shady agent of the Los Angeles Police Department. Gaff takes Deckard back to his flying car, which is a Spinner, as indicated by a beautiful insignia on the door. The Spinner also features *Blade Runner*'s sole instance of Eurostile Bold Extended, via a "CAUTION" sticker and the number 44 on the vehicle's side.

With this one exception, it's notable that Ridley Scott skipped the de facto typeface of the future in both *Alien* and *Blade Runner*. Neither movie presents a future that could be considered utopian; foregoing Eurostile avoids an association with the aspirational, sixties-influenced future seen in *2001: A Space Odyssey* (1968) and *Star Trek: The Motion Picture* (1979). Sometimes, avoiding a particular typographic choice is just as important as making one.

Before we move on, there is one more typographic curiosity to be noted on the side of the Spinner. See that "POLICE 995" logo in wonky, pixelated type? You're probably thinking that it looks suspiciously like the cover of Groucho Marx's 1972 album, *An Evening with Groucho*, right? Well, you are correct. Production illustrator Tom Southwell took inspiration from the album's cover, creating his own hand-lettered version for the Spinner.

AN EVENING WITH
GROUCHO

2 RECORD SET

A&M

As the Spinner takes off into the rain, its dashboard TV displays a couple of screens that might seem familiar to the more observant among you. Its "ENVIRON CTR PURGE" display looks remarkably like a screen seen in Ridley Scott's *Alien* just before the *Nostromo* explodes, and its yellow-and-blue symmetrical pattern looks uncannily like the *Nostromo*'s disconnect sequence. The reason these images were recycled is unclear; nonetheless, both work well in either context.

Gaff's Spinner displays an "ENVIRON CTR PURGE" message in *Blade Runner*.

The *Nostromo*'s computer displays an "ENVIRON CTR PURGE" message in *Alien*.

Gaff's Spinner displays a pretty yellow-and-blue graphic as it ascends into the LA sky.

The *Nostromo*'s computer displays a clamp release graphic as the command craft disconnects itself from its floating refinery.

That "ENVIRON CTR PURGE" display was almost certainly created with an Aston 1 Character Generator, a device used to add captions and overlays to live TV events such as sports and election coverage in the 1970s and 1980s. Happily for us, TV character-generator buff Dave Jeffery has re-created the Aston's typeface in digital form, thereby enabling me to provide a specimen for your delight and delectation.

The Aston 1 Character Generator's typeface

ABCDEFGHIJKLMNOPQRSTUVWXYZ
0123456789

As Deckard and Gaff continue their flight through the Los Angeles skyscape, a technical-looking message tappity-taps itself onto a screen in Gaff's Spinner. (Confusingly, this is a *portrait* CRT display—the landscape display we saw earlier is notably absent.) This being *Typeset in the Future*, we are, of course, duty-bound to take a closer look at the on-screen text. It's a sign of my misspent youth that "ALT / VEL / PTCH" at the top of the screen immediately makes me think, 1UP / HIGH SCORE / 2UP. However, the fuzzy text on the main body of the screen is even more interesting, because it seems to be adapted from a 1980s ad for the Matrix Color Graphic Camera System by Matrix Instruments.

The text seen in the movie is a chopped-up amalgam of several parts of this ad:

MICROPROCESSOR BASED ELECTRONICS PROVI

OUR SYSTEM DOES WHAT NO OTHER INS

TRUMENT CAN DO- IT PRODUCES INSTANT, ON

THE SPOT RESULTS WITH XXXXX 8X10 FILM,

8X10 COLOR TRANSPARENCIES FOR BACKLITE

DISPLAYS AND OVER HEAD PROJECTION, 35MM

COLOR SLIDES, 60 IMAGE XXXXX MICRO

RELATED AND SEQUENTIAL IMAGES CAN BE RE

CORDED IN ORDERLY ARRAYS, ON A SINGLE

SHEET OF 8X10 INSTANT PRINT FILM. THE

The two "xxxxx" words don't look to match the advert, so I'm not taking a chance on guessing them. (I am, however, entirely unsurprised by the font that Matrix Instruments chose for their company logo.)

Gaff's Spinner journey also introduces us to a recurring piece of typography from the movie's backdrop. The *Blade Runner* production team reused city background scenery in different configurations throughout the movie, which is why the glowing "NUYOK" sign seen here is remarkably similar to the glowing sign for the "YUKON" hotel seen thirteen minutes later (also known as the temporary home of replicants Leon and Zhora).

Shortly after this revelation, the Spinner lands at an LAPD station. This station turns out to be a smoke-filled version of LA's real-world Union Station (for trains, not policemen). The stunning art deco room seen here is the station's original ticket concourse, and the beautiful wooden structure along its left-hand side is a 110-foot ticket counter (sadly, no longer in use).

The original ticket concourse at
Union Station, Los Angeles, in 2017

Deckard is briefed by Harry Bryant, captain of the LAPD's Rep-Detect department, about the replicants he is meant to retire. We're presented with the serial numbers and details of all four replicants, starting with Leon, who we learn is a combat replicant and nuclear fission loader. (We discover this fascinating fact via some decidedly non-futuristic on-screen Cheltenham Bold.)

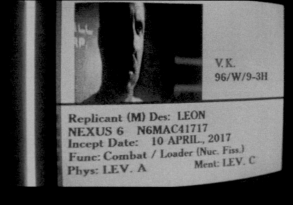

Cheltenham Bold

ABCDEFGHIJKLMNOPQRSTUVWXYZ

Next up, we meet Roy Batty, lead replicant in *Blade Runner*. We learn that Roy is trained in combat for the colonization defense program and is a general all-around badass.

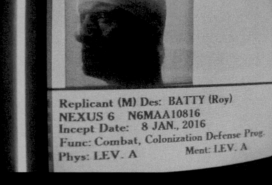

Roy is followed by Zhora, who someone at the Tyrell Corporation decided it would be a great idea to retrain in political homicide.

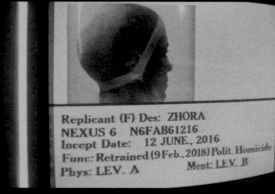

Finally, we meet Pris, who unifies the sadly-not-as-disparate-as-one-might-hope disciplines of military and leisure.

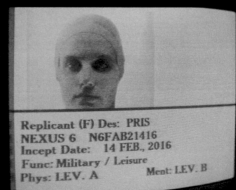

On the surface of it, the serial numbers of these replicants look easy to decode. The format seems to be:

[N6 FOR NEXUS 6][GENDER][PHYSICAL][MENTAL][MONTH][DAY][YEAR]

For example, Pris's serial of N6FAB21416 corresponds to:

[N6][Female][LEV. A][LEV. B][FEB][14][2016]

On closer inspection, however, these serial numbers contain several typographic oddities. The first is the use of an American *month-day-year* format in the serial number but a British *day-month-year* format for the incept date. Surely a serial number, of all things, would benefit from placing year *before* month, for chronological sorting of SKUs? Even if not, the inconsistency between the two is disappointing, especially for a movie so clearly set in America.

Secondly, why use a single digit for the month? We know that the day is zero-padded, at least going by Roy's serial number. The lack of comparative zero padding for the month means that any replicant incepted in October through December will have an eleven-character serial, and not a ten-character serial like their colleagues.

Thirdly, and most importantly, the date section of Leon's serial number is just plain wrong. He's listed with a serial number date section of 41717, and yet he was incepted on 41017. Sadly, even though 2007's *Blade Runner: The Final Cut* re-release rectified many on-screen glitches, these typographic errors are still awaiting correction.

FOLLOWING HIS BRIEFING on the target replicants, Deckard drives back to his apartment through the crappy LA weather. Indeed, it's hard to recognize the Los Angeles of November 2019 through *Blade Runner*'s incessant rain (especially given that it didn't rain there at all during November 2015). Nonetheless, the city's residents have found a way to work around the combined smog and rain with ingenious umbrellas, whose handles are fluorescent tubes.

The design of Deckard's apartment is both classic and oppressive, with its instantly recognizable concrete-tiled walling and an impressive balcony overlooking the city's streets. Like so many of the movie's locations, Deckard's apartment is based on a real-world LA landmark—in this case, the Ennis House, built in 1924 and designed by famous American architect Frank Lloyd Wright.

LEFT: Interior shot of Deckard's apartment, showing its repeated wall-block pattern

RIGHT: Exterior of the Ennis House, at 2607 Glendower Avenue, Los Angeles

The Ennis House hasn't appeared just in *Blade Runner*. You may also recognize it as:

The exterior location for 1959's Vincent Price low-budget horror classic *House on Haunted Hill*

The abanoned mansion where Angel, Spike, and Drusilla hang out in "I Only Have Eyes for You" (season two, episode nine of *Buffy the Vampire Slayer*)

A villain's hideout in *The Karate Kid, Part III*

"The Towers" in *Invitation to Love*, a bad soap opera watched by the residents of Twin Peaks in *Twin Peaks*

. . . and, according to Wikipedia, a variety of locations in *Black Rain*, *The Glimmer Man*, *The Replacement Killers*, *Rush Hour*, *The Thirteenth Floor*, *The Rocketeer*, and *Mulholland Drive*.

Perhaps most famously, of course, the Ennis House is the music-video setting for Ricky Martin's classic 1998 single "Vuelve." Let's take a tour of the house, with Ricky as our guide.

The interior design of the Ennis House mirrors its exterior, just like Deckard's apartment in *Blade Runner*. To break the monotony, a variant of the geometric pattern appears on narrower corner stones, which are handy for leaning against while singing.

This particular corner abuts a corridor along the building's west elevation, which is flooded with light from nine floor-to-ceiling windows. The presence of so much natural light is a major difference between Ricky's domestic arrangements and those endured by Deckard in *Blade Runner*.

Architectural students may be interested to know that the corridor is roughly as wide as a man's outstretched arms.

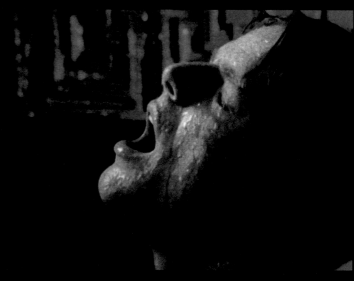

According to "Vuelve" and *Blade Runner*, it rains at the Ennis House every time someone turns up with a video camera. Meteorological records suggest that this strange phenomenon is atypical for the area's climate.

Thank you, Ricky, for that beautifully melodic introduction to Mayan Revival architecture.

The repeating interior design of Deckard's apartment is lifted directly from the Ennis House and is based on the twenty-seven thousand concrete blocks that make up the house's interior and exterior. These concrete blocks have weathered somewhat over the years, and many have been patched up or restored to reinstate the original geometric pattern.

Close-up of a renovated Ennis House exterior block

FEET 0 10 20 30
METERS 0 5 10

Schematic of the Ennis House's west elevation. Historic American Buildings Survey, 1969

There's surprisingly little of the actual Ennis House in *Blade Runner,* however. The only two shots of the house's exterior that I've identified are the Spinner's on-road approach to Deckard's apartment complex:

. . . which looks like a matte painting superimposed over the top of the house's front wall:

. . . and the Spinner's arrival through the apartment gates:

. . . which looks mighty familiar from *House on Haunted Hill:*

The rest of Deckard's apartment was created from scratch on a sound stage, using replicas of those Mayan concrete bricks with substantially lower and more oppressive ceilings than the original.

After a brief encounter with Rachael, Deckard is left studying one of her childhood photos. The photo shows a young Rachael sitting on the porch of a stereotypical American house:

This is eerily reminiscent of a porch-based photo from Deckard's own collection, seen later in the movie:

How strange! I'm sure it won't turn out to be significant.

During a close-up, we see Rachael's photo briefly come to life—an effect replicated in the movie's sequel, *Blade Runner 2049,* for a photograph of a dead tree. To make sense of these animated memories, I checked in with *Blade Runner*'s literary origin, *Do Androids Dream of Electric Sheep?* It turns out Philip K. Dick decided that photographs in the future will be holographic, thereby explaining *Blade Runner*'s brief animated-GIF interlude. Dick wasn't far off the money, either—animated photography became commonplace in 2015, when Apple launched Live Photos as a feature on its iPhone 6S and 6S Plus devices. Live Photos record 1.5 seconds of video and audio before and after a photo is taken, producing an effect spookily similar to the one seen in *Blade Runner.* (At the time of writing, Apple had not yet developed a way to print animated Live Photos on photographic paper.)

LEFT: Rachael's holographic childhood photograph shows animated shadow and lighting movement when viewed in close-up by Deckard.

RIGHT: *Blade Runner 2049* reaffirms the holographic nature of printed photographs as K views his own animated capture of a plot-significant tree.

Having studied Rachael's photo in detail, Deckard next leafs through the photographs he collected from Leon's hotel room, which are printed on Polaroid paper. We know this because of their "POLAROID" label, and some technical-sounding terms on their right-hand edges, in red Helvetica Medium:

When *Blade Runner* was made, there was an obvious and popular way to add arbitrary text to everyday objects such as the photos above. Regardless of whether you were an amateur or a professional designer, your solution of choice would have been a dry transfer sheet of Letraset Instant Lettering. This fantastic rub-on lettering gave a simple (if slightly imprecise) way to add text to pretty much any surface, and it's the option that *Blade Runner*'s design team chose for Leon's photographs.

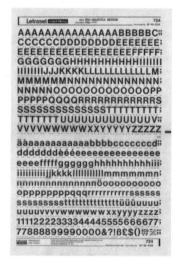

However, there's something odd about those technical-sounding codes on the edges of Leon's photos. Let's take a closer look at their wording.

Hmm. "HELCLN/IUM." "VETICA MED/CLN." That sounds . . . familiar, somehow.

Let's look again at our sample Letraset sheet from before, but rather than studying the body of the sheet, we'll focus on the header and footer instead.

I *thought* that text sounded familiar. Leon's photographic labels are constructed entirely from the sheet's throwaway content. If I didn't know better, I'd suggest that someone in the *Blade Runner* production department had a used sheet of Letraset hanging around and didn't want the leftovers going to waste.

In the time that we've been distracted by dry transfer lettering, replicant Pris has arrived at a building called "the Bradbury," intending to woo Tyrell Corporation genetic designer J. F. Sebastian. This is in fact the real-life Bradbury Building, built in 1893 and located at the corner of South Broadway and West Third Street in downtown LA.

The Bradbury Building, as it looked in 2005

ABOVE: The Bradbury's actual main entrance, shown here as it looked in 1960

RIGHT: The Bradbury's main entrance, seen when Pris arrives to visit J. F. Sebastian

The highly decorative future noir frontage seen in *Blade Runner* is, sadly, not the building's real entrance—though it does feature some very lovely Block Heavy for its signage. (The *real* entrance to the Bradbury has more of an art nouveau style and was designed so long ago that its type is probably custom.)

RIGHT: The Bradbury's logotype, re-created in Block Heavy

BELOW: Block Heavy, from Berthold. Block's initial release in 1908 contained a bold weight only; other weights followed, with Block Heavy released in 1920.

The BRADBURY

ABCDEFGHIJKLMNOPQRSTUVWXYZ

The Bradbury's interior is a beautiful, wrought-iron representation of abandoned industrial chic. In addition to *Blade Runner,* you might recognize it from the similarly apocalyptic *(500) Days of Summer,* in which Joseph Gordon-Levitt fawns incessantly over Zooey Deschanel's manic pixie dream girl. It's also in Oscar-winning 1920s throwback *The Artist* and in plenty more movies and TV shows besides.

ABOVE: The Bradbury's twin-elevator ironwork, as seen when Deckard arrives for his boss-battle show-down with Roy Batty

LEFT: The Bradbury's twin-elevator ironwork, as seen in *(500) Days of Summer* when Tom arrives for a job interview

The Bradbury Building is now a mix of governmental and commercial offices. The lobby seen in *Blade Runner* is open to LA tourists, who can explore as far as the second-floor landing. I myself have visited said lobby, which is how I know that when J. F. inserts his key to call one of the building's elevators, he's actually sticking his hand into a letter box at the bottom of the Bradbury's mail chute.

BELOW LEFT: J. F. Sebastian inserts his key into the Bradbury's letter box to summon one of its elevators.

BELOW: The Bradbury's letter box, situated at the base of a mail chute that runs the entire height of the building

Directly opposite the Bradbury Building is the Million Dollar Theatre, which exists in real life as a theater located directly across from the Bradbury Building. Built in 1918, it did indeed cost well over one million dollars to construct, as one of America's first great movie palaces.

We see an illuminated sign for the theater's upcoming events a couple of times in the movie, as characters arrive at the Bradbury's dramatic main entrance.

ABOVE: The Million Dollar Theatre, as it looked in 2005

TOP RIGHT: A view of the Million Dollar Theatre from the Bradbury's main entrance, just before J. F. Sebastian encounters Pris in the building's lobby

ABOVE RIGHT: Alternate image of the Million Dollar Theatre's marquee, listing an upcoming gig by Gilberto Valenzuela

RIGHT: *El asesino,* by Gilberto Valenzuela

I have not been able to confirm if *Blade Runner* intentionally promoted a 1980s gig by Peruvian indie-alternative band Los Mimilocos Mazacote y Orquesta, though I sincerely hope it did. However, we can be pretty confident that this scene was filmed just before an upcoming gig by famous Mexican crooner Gilberto Valenzuela, whose name can be seen along the far right of the marquee.

In fact, Gilberto released cover art for his 1980 album, *El asesino* (The assassin), that featured a photograph of the Million Dollar Theatre's marquee announcing him as its headliner.

Back in the Bradbury, we glimpse a blimp through the building's roof, with yet more Coca-Cola promotion on its underside. The blimp's giant screens are showing an ad for the multinational Shimata-Dominguez Corporation, which (like *Alien*'s Weyland Yutani) assumes a future in which international business conglomerations are commonplace.

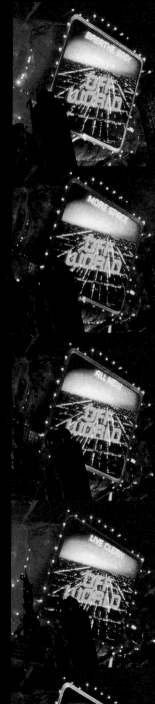

The blimp's ad audio has different voice-overs in different cuts of *Blade Runner*, but if you mix them all together, this is the message you get:

> *A new life awaits you in the off-world colonies. The chance to begin again in a golden land of opportunity and adventure. New climate, recreational facilities, easy advancement, great pay. Plus, a loyal trouble-free companion, given to you on arrival, absolutely free. Use your new friend as a personal body servant or a tireless field hand. The custom-tailored genetically engineered humanoid replicant, designed especially for your needs.*

I don't know about you, but using a replicant as a "personal body servant" or a "tireless field hand" sounds a lot like out-and-out slavery to me. (It also makes it hard to blame Roy and company for rebelling.)

This ad is similar to *WALL·E*'s Buy n Large infomercials, which we'll hear more about later in this book:

> *Too much garbage in your face? There's plenty of space, out in space! [. . .] Spend your five-year cruise in style, waited on twenty-four hours a day by our fully automated crew, while your captain and autopilot chart a course for nonstop entertainment.*

In addition to promoting slavery and advertising Coca-Cola, the *Blade Runner* blimp preempts both *Total Recall* and *WALL·E* with soothing platitudes encouraging off-world colonization. Residents are encouraged to leave Earth so that they can "BREATHE EASY" and have "MORE SPACE," because off-world colonies are "ALL NEW" and enable you to "LIVE CLEAN."

Just visible at the end of this montage is a fifth colonial selling point. If you look very closely before we cut back to Pris, you'll spot a mention of a "PAN AM SHUTTLE" on the blimp's side screen. (There's some *2001: A Space Odyssey* influence here after all.)

Deckard decides that it's time to study Leon's photographs in more detail. In his doing so, *Blade Runner* gives us perhaps the definitive example of the "enhance button" trope, via the suspiciously amazing ESPER machine.

This chunky-looking gadget is a voice-controlled photographic enhancer with an almost supernatural ability to follow its controller's verbal instructions.

Deckard's ESPER machine

When Deckard inserts Leon's photo into the ESPER and asks it to "enhance 224 to 176," it diligently enhances 197 to 334 as requested.

Deckard continues to direct the ESPER to navigate around his blurry, out-of-focus photo. He asks it to "enhance 34 to 36," and it obediently enhances 197 to 334 as instructed.

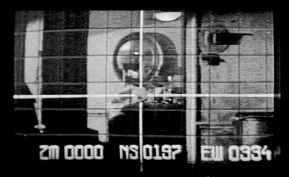

The ESPER zooms in further still, focusing on the mirror on the far wall of the next room. As image quality becomes more and more challenging, the ESPER's enhancement algorithm automatically switches from "blurry VHS" to "high-quality film stock."

Deckard asks the ESPER to "enhance 34 to 46." It follows his instructions to the letter, enhancing 197 to 334 as before.

At this point, things get kind of ridiculous. The ESPER machine zooms so far into the mirror that we can see individual snakeskin sequins on an item of clothing hanging on a wardrobe on the other side of a room, *behind the wall we're looking at:*

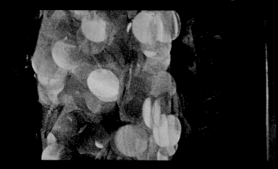

After moving left a bit and right a bit and left a bit and right a bit, Deckard asks the ESPER machine to "enhance 15 to 23." True to its roots, it enhances 197 to 334.

The end result is a close-up photo of replicant Zhora, who is conveniently recognizable owing to the large snake tattoo on her face.

I'm not going to lie: This whole scene is spectacularly geographically confusing. By my reckoning, the final photo above is a reflection in a mirror of a reflection in a mirror, though even then I'm not entirely sure.

Indeed, things got *so* confusing at this point in the movie that I painstakingly re-created the entire ESPER sequence,* *just* to work out how far we crop, zoom, and enhance at each stage of the machine's photoprocessing. By my calculation, that final photo of Zhora is a *667.9-times zoom* in on the original photograph. It's no wonder, then, that the image Deckard prints from the ESPER machine is a little bit grainy. (It's also a completely different angle from the final frame of the ESPER we saw above.)

---

* https://typesetinthefuture.com/esper

Deckard's Polaroid printout of Zhora, showing an angle different from the ESPER's on-screen image

On his way to track down Zhora, Deckard makes a video call to Rachael in a handy "VID-PHŌN" booth at the bar. (In case you're wondering, that line above the O is a macron, which draws out the vowel sound to make the word sound like "phone" rather than "phon.")

In a special guest appearance by optical character recognition font OCR-A, we discover that the fictitious 555 exchange code is still going strong in 2019. This code is reserved for use by services such as directory assistance and operator service in all US area codes. Due to its resultant low fill rate—there aren't many such services—it is also recommended for use by Hollywood movies that want to ensure the phone numbers they show on screen don't lead to accidental nuisance calls for real-world telephone users. Strictly speaking, only the numbers 555-0100 through 555-0199 are reserved for fictitious use, but *Blade Runner,* like many other movies, merrily strays outside that range.

OCR-A

ABCDEFGHIJKLMNOPQRSTUVWXYZ

You might have noticed that the VID-PHŌN service is run by the Bell System group of companies, who were behind the Picturephone video-calling service we saw in *2001: A Space Odyssey.* The cost of video calling has definitely gone up in the intervening eighteen years—Dr. Floyd's call in *2001* cost just $1.70 for ninety seconds. (This is substantially cheaper than the $9-a-minute that Picturephone actually cost when the system first launched.) By comparison, Deckard's thirty-second call to Rachael costs a whopping $1.25.

Let's do the realism math here, to check that this holds up. The events of *Blade Runner* are set in 2019. Deckard's thirty-second, $1.25 call to Rachael works out at $2.50 a minute. This is substantially more expensive than the $1.33 per minute that Bell Systems charged Dr. Floyd in *2001*. However, it's only a 3.5 percent call-cost increase year over year, so it is roughly in line with inflation. (Never let it be said that Ridley Scott doesn't sweat the details.) The irony for both of these scenes? In the real November 2019, a thirty-second video call will cost zero dollars and zero cents per minute. Some things about the future really are hard to predict.

Back in the Bradbury, we discover that J. F. Sebastian is in the middle of a chess game with Dr. Eldon Tyrell, head of the replicant-creating Tyrell Corporation. Roy Batty recognizes the chess game as an opportunity to meet his maker and gives J. F. some top chess tips to advance his cause.

As he does so, we see that J. F.'s chess pieces are elaborately carved animals, perhaps representing the fact that real animals were all but extinct in *Do Androids Dream of Electronic Sheep?* (as its name implies). By comparison, Tyrell's board features equally intricate carvings of people—entirely appropriate for the creator of superhuman replicants, who are nearly indistinguishable from the real thing.

Urban myth tells us that this game is based on the topically named Immortal Game, won by Adolf Anderssen against Lionel Kieseritzky in 1851. After a careful study of J. F.'s and Tyrell's boards and dialogue, I can confirm that this is indeed the case.

The Immortal Game is notable in that Anderssen defeated Kieseritzky despite sacrificing a bishop, both rooks, and his queen. By the time Batty meets Tyrell, he has already sacrificed Leon, Zhora, and two other replicants in his quest to meet his maker.

Something something *significant*.

Batty finishes off J. F. and Tyrell, and heads toward the Bradbury for an inevitable show-down with Deckard. As the movie draws to its climax, Batty delivers his famous "tears in rain" monologue on a bleak, rain-soaked rooftop. This speech, improvised by Rutger Hauer during the scene's filming, is universally acclaimed as one of the most moving death soliloquies in movie history. However, as a thing constructed solely from words coming out of a mouth, it is typographically insignificant and is therefore of zero interest to *Typeset in the Future*. This is in stark contrast to the multistriped neon TDK logo just over Rutger's shoulder, which I think we can all admit is a pretty spectacular rendition of a classic company logo.

FROM ITS IMPRESSIVE neon to its crowded, living streets, *Blade Runner* both earned and deserves its position as a sci-fi noir classic. *Blade Runner* demonstrates that deep, detailed production design has a profound effect on the believability and consistency of the world we see on screen. In *Blade Runner*'s case, concepts were created for everything from newsstand magazines to parking meters, none of which ended up in the movie. Nonetheless, the time and thought that went into their conception makes the city we *do* see all the more believable as a fully thought-through reality. It's a testament to the success of this deep preparation that flying cars feel like a natural extension of a living city, not an anachronistic nod to sci-fi expectation. As with *2001* before it, *Blade Runner*'s attention to detail means its aesthetic has stood the test of time—and its futuristic LA will be just as believable in 2019 as it was in 1982.

ANTONIO CAVEDONI

In August 2017, I spoke to Italian type designer Antonio Cavedoni about superellipses, microscopic fonts, and the creator of Eurostile, Aldo Novarese.

ADDEY: Novarese is known for designing Eurostile and Stop, two of the all-time classic sci-fi typefaces. What led to his creating such futuristic designs?

CAVEDONI: Aldo was born in 1920 and studied design at the Scuola Vigliani-Paravia in Turin. The school was directed by Giulio da Milano, who designed Neon, published by [Milan type foundry] Nebiolo. Neon already has the square curves that Microgramma and Eurostile would have later on. It's an unusual typeface—it starts very small and is vaguely reminiscent of Microgramma, especially in the numbers, but as it gets bigger, the letters only grow vertically, so they become very skinny and narrow.

Another of Aldo's teachers was Nebiolo's art director, Alessandro Butti. He recognized Aldo as a promising student and called him into Nebiolo when he was sixteen.

Now, whether Aldo was always taught to draw these kinds of angular shapes, I don't know. Butti himself, I think, is the originator of that style. Butti was a very experimental designer—pos-

Neon Bold, by Giulio da Milano, 1935. Specimen from *Caratteri Nebiolo*, a Nebiolo catalog

sibly the craziest typeface he designed is Fluidum, which has squarish shapes somewhat similar to the ones in Eurostile, but it's a script, like an English round hand. It's crazy.

There's another one, called Quirinus, which is an upright, Bodoni-like version of the same concept. It has a vertical axis, but you can see—if you look at the O, for instance—the same rounded rectangles are still there. And it wasn't just Butti doing it; Imre Reiner had also done it with his Corvinus type from 1934. So Aldo came into a world of design where these squared-off shapes were already normal.

When Microgramma and Eurostile were released, how were they marketed? Were they positioned as futuristic? Or was it their usage, such as in *2001: A Space Odyssey*, that led to their being perceived that way?

I think the latter. These typefaces, when they were first introduced, were actually positioned as something for *today*. Butti and Novarese were saying, "The typefaces that we use no longer represent us. We need something of *our* time, something that looks like now."

That squared-off-rectangle shape was very much in the air at the time, particularly in architecture and industrial design. If you look at television sets in the fifties, they literally look like squared-off rectangles. Likewise train windows from the fifties and sixties, where they use this rectangular shape with rounded-off corners, at least here in Europe.

Aldo wrote an article about this, in which he shows a Roman arch and a Roman letter; a Gothic cathedral and then a Gothic letter; and then a modern building and a Eurostile letter. He was saying, "Look—this is the shape of our time, we see it everywhere."

Indeed, Butti even went as far as to propose [the square form] as a whole new genre of typeface. There's a

Fluidum Bold, by Alessandro Butti, 1951

Quirinus Bold, by Alessandro Butti, 1939

Corvinus Skyline, a 1991 digital revival of the 1934 original by Imre Reiner

classification system for fonts, invented by Maximilien Vox, that divides them into several different categories. And Butti came up with a new one, which he called Quarres. He said, "Look, there're all these classes of typefaces, but there's one that's missing, which is one from our time." Essentially, that rounded-rectangle, squared-off type. He put forward this new category and showed Microgramma, which he'd just designed, as an example.

So if Microgramma and Eurostile were the shape and form of their time, what led to their becoming associated with the future?

That's a question I really don't have an answer for. Perhaps it was *such* a strong shape, it became a little bit too . . . flavorful, if you will. Other typefaces quickly migrated away from it, because it was such a strong flavor. And so because it

was so closely associated with that one era–which had sci-fi movies like *2001* and other things about the future–I think the association stuck.

The shapes themselves also look very technical–almost machined, if you will. They're very industrial-looking shapes. And if you want to make a design look technical and engineered, these shapes give you something that almost feels like a knob or button, like something you can push and interact with.

Another part of it is that the square-circle shape is completely synthetic. In nature, you don't find a plant that looks like a square circle; you don't find an animal that looks like a square circle. It's a very man-made thing. The circle you can find; the square, possibly; but the square circle? It's a purely synthetic kind of shape.

It also ties in with the concept of superellipses, which are that round-rectangle shape expressed in mathematical form. Someone came up for a new word for these shapes, which I find dreadful: They call it a "squircle," a squared circle. But anyhow, this kind of shape has been used a lot in the 1960s and 1970s in industrial design, architecture, and even in typeface design. Besides Microgramma and Eurostile, Melior, designed by Hermann Zapf in 1952, has a structure based on squared-off circles.

Did these shapes also have practical benefits, in addition to their aesthetic relevance?

Oh, definitely. Butti believed that these squared-off shapes were good for small

sizes; indeed, that's why Microgramma is called "*Micro*-gramma." To prove the point, in the late forties/early fifties, Nebiolo engraved the entire Hail Mary prayer onto a single sort [a piece of metal type] to show how well they could do small type.

Think of it this way: If you have a circle, it can only hold so much air. But if you make it slightly squarer, the edges of the square make the central shape bigger. We know that counter shapes [the spaces inside letters] are critical to making letters legible, so if you increase their volume, you have a chance to make them work even better when they're small. And Butti exploited this fact to make Microgramma as a typeface for really tiny sizes.

ABCDEFGHIJKLMNOPQRSTUVWXYZ

ABCDEFGHIJKLMNOPQRSTUVWXYZ

The Ave Maria (Hail Mary), engraved on a single sort in Microgramma. Fountain pen shown for scale

A superellipse (blue) with an overlaid circle (red) of the same diameter. A superellipse with a diameter of 1m has an area of ~0.86m², whereas a circle with the same diameter has an area of only ~0.79m².

Of course, when you have something that small, lowercase is just useless because you have two counters on a lowercase *e*, and we're talking about type that is a fraction of a millimeter high. So they didn't even think of doing lowercase, which may be why Microgramma was only released as an uppercase design.

That "micro" aspect is particularly interesting in light of my conversation with Stephen Coles. He noticed that Bank Gothic, the other bold extended font used in sci-fi movies, was also designed for use at very small sizes. And yet it's now used at the other extreme. What is it about Microgramma and Bank Gothic that makes them work so well large, even though they were designed to be small?

Small sizes are a continuous fascination for type designers. They present the most radical problems, and because they are so small they are full of opportunities—you can get away with a lot.

In 1905, a French ophthalmologist by the name of Émile Javal wrote a treatise titled *Physiologie de la lecture et de l'écriture* in which, amongst other things, he published some experiments on letter shapes suitable for typesetting at really tiny sizes. His collaborator, Charles Dreyfuss, drew a set of letters based on Javal's ideas, in variants for progressively smaller sizes, down to two points. At that size, the lowercase *o* is just a little square—it doesn't even have a counter anymore.

These extremely small typefaces are kind of like Formula One cars, in that you can make unusual choices and experiment with the craziest components and materials. And then you bring some of these into the larger text faces. But occasionally, there are some ideas that work so well that you just want to use them at every size.

One example of this is Freight Micro by Joshua Darden. It's an optical size of an existing classic-looking serif design. Josh made the micro version, which was crazy, with very squared shapes, and, of course, what happens? Everyone starts using it for titles.

What happens is: The solutions you find for small sizes, they have a flavor to them, a voice to them. And if you have a graphic designer working on a piece that needs a strong voice, one way they can easily achieve that is by taking a typeface designed for small sizes and using it big. I think that's what happened with Microgramma. Because it worked so well small, and it had such flavorful shapes, when you blew it up it was unusual and novel.

What was the relationship between Microgramma and Eurostile? How did the former lead to the latter?

We don't know exactly, but I think it was simply commercial success. When Aldo became art director at Nebiolo in 1952, he started making his own designs. But he also revisited older designs, and if they were successful he expanded on them to make them bigger. Microgramma was missing a few weights and didn't have a lowercase. They wanted to make it bigger and better, and that's how Eurostile was born. I don't know that there are any significant differences between the two—they were meant to be the same family, in a way.

Minuscule Deux, designed by Thomas Huot-Marchand and published by 205TF in 2007. Minuscule is a revival created to test the "theory of compact printings" set out by Louis Émile Javal. The font is available in five sizes, each intended for use at a decreasingly small point size: Minuscule Six (6pt), Cinq (5pt), Quatre (4pt), Trois (3pt) and, the most extreme, Minuscule Deux, shown here (intended for use at 2pt).

ABCDEFGHIJKLMNOPQRSTUVWXYZ

Minuscule Deux's lowercase characters. The lowercase o and g use a small square without a counter.

abcdefghijklmn▪pqrstuvwxyz

Lowercase characters from Freight Micro Pro Bold, by Joshua Darden, 2009

abcdefghijklmnopqrstuvwxyz

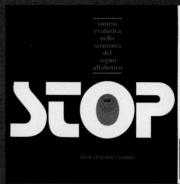

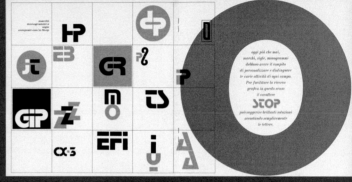

Nebiolo marketing specimen for Stop

Novarese's other famous sci-fi typeface is Stop, which is notable for removing elements and slicing aspects out of its glyphs. What inspired that design, and was Stop the first time someone had formalized it into a reproducible face?

I think Stop is one of a kind because of the way it does what it does in such a successful way. There are precedents, however—most notably Bifur, designed in 1929 by Cassandre. Instead of the letters being sliced like Stop, Bifur is designed as a chromatic face, which means that it's meant to be printed in two different colors. All the thick strokes are in black—the *F* has two thick black strokes, for example—and then it has a shaded second version that you put underneath in a different color.

So the thing about Bifur is it doesn't actually work if you remove the chromatic aspect. The black parts of some of the letters are just not self-sufficient. The *E* works, but if you remove the chromatic aspect the *N* doesn't look like an *N*. Stop has similar shapes for the *P* and *R*, but without the chromatic layer in Bifur it's really hard to read the *G* as a *G*. And if you look at the shapes on their own, like the *S* next to the *P*, they really don't feel like they belong in the same visual vocabulary. Whereas Stop is much more cohesive and does it in a way where the letters work on their own in isolation.

Stop's device of using three vertical sections, slicing them horizontally, is what really brings it together. That, and the use of lowercase shapes in place of some uppercase ones, I think, is the genius of Stop. It's what makes it work

in just black and white when compared to Bifur. The three horizontal lines give it consistency, even though the glyphs are quite abstract in some cases.

Is there a practical aspect to these geometric typefaces, in addition to their flavorful design?

Definitely. Aldo had a preoccupation throughout his career with helping graphic designers, with creating shapes that would make it easy to construct logotypes and lockups. In the marketing material for Eurostile, he says, "These letters, because they are made out of squared-off rectangles, they have a graphic aspect to them. Each letter looks like a little decorative widget." And then he puts them together in logotypes, with an *R* upside down next to another one, and you can make a logotype with this typeface really easily. The typeface is meant to help designers do these kinds of things—treating shapes not just as words but as actual shapes.

Stop, to my understanding, is the final point in his research on that. It's an extreme because the letters become almost abstract shapes: they no longer look like letters. It's the reductionist approach to letter design: How much can I take away from letters before they stop being legible? How much can I remove and still get away with it?

About ten years ago, I start noticing this trend of people taking Stop and modifying it, extending it, changing it. At the time, I was living in a part of Italy that was very busy with factories and trucks, and the trucks would always have Stop on them. I noticed it in the truck liveries first, and then I started noticing it *everywhere.* You'd find it in any environment where people didn't have a lot of money for graphic design, where Stop became the company's identity instead. They'd have a name, they'd use Stop, and that was it.

And the thing I noticed is that most of the time people would go in and change things. Because Stop really is kind of strange. It has some choices that are extreme, like the *H* only having one vertical bar. It's a bit extreme, especially if your name has an *H* in it.

So I set up a group on Flickr called Custom Stop, and I started getting tons of pictures from everywhere, of people customizing Stop. I would only collect items if they were customized. I got things from Mexico, Hawaii, Japan . . . anywhere in the world that Stop was used. It was kind of incredible.

What is it about Stop that makes it so inherently customizable?

I think there are two aspects to it. Firstly, Stop has the right weight and spacing to make logotypes. That's by design; Aldo nailed that one.

Secondly, that vertically divided three-part system, where essentially everything fits into the same module, makes it very easy to extend parts of each letter. For instance, if you have an *E* next to a *T,* it's very easy to take the crossbar from the top of the *E* and drag it over—you don't even have to join them in Photoshop or Illustrator. They make a chain, and now you have a ligature.

Now, whether people think that that's in poor taste or not, I don't know. In Italy, Stop is considered by some

ABCDEFGHIJKLMNOPQRSTUVWXYZ

ABCDEFGHIJKLMNOPQRSTUVWXYZ

Custom Stop on a motorbike handle, spotted in Reading, UK

Custom (and hand-painted) Stop for a barber's window sign in Viareggio, Italy

Stop in use in signage for the Palazzo di Giustizia, Naples, Italy

Custom Stop for Baraldini Trasporti Industriali, spotted in Mirandola, Italy

Custom Stop for Baroni Legno, spotted in Modena, Italy

Custom Stop spotted in Fiorano, Italy

Stop in use on a tombstone in the Cimitero Monumentale, Milan, Italy. Here, the name "SACCHI" illustrates why "HI" is a problematic pairing of glyphs in Stop.

graphic designers to be a bit of a taboo. If you start using Stop, it's like giving up your credibility as a graphic designer because it's so easy to make a logotype. And you end up with a logotype that looks like the future of the past, which is not always appropriate. For example,

we've seen Stop on the Palazzo di Giustizia in Naples, which is the courthouse. Having that name in this futuristic face is not necessarily what you would want to do. We've even seen it on a tombstone.

How much did the emergence of Letraset help with this use for logotypes?

Stop was an early Letraset design, and I think it was huge. Because with Letraset it was even easier to do the customization that we talked about before. It was absolutely critical for the success of the design. But the success of the design, to me, is the design itself. It was a happy coincidence that it became ubiquitous in a transitioning format.

What more recent typefaces have become the modern-day equivalent of what Novarese set out to achieve?

I don't think there's anything quite like these two designs, especially Stop. There is one design that tries to capture

the rounded-rectangle aesthetic, which is Biome by Carl Crossgrove. It's definitely a descendent of Eurostile—it's in the wide category of typefaces that I think are the most successful styles of Eurostile and Microgramma. This one adds aspects to it like rounded corners, and it has a successful lowercase as well.

Biome, voice-wise, goes a little bit more in the alien world—it has an organic quality to it, which Eurostile doesn't. You could consider it an organic Eurostile. But look at those shapes—that's prime sci-fi material right there.

So if you were making a sci-fi movie, what kind of design would you choose?

For my own movie, I'd probably design something custom-based on the principles of Stop and carry it even further. I like the "kit of parts" thing, and I also like stencil typefaces, because they are inherently mechanical. They have an engineered look right away because of the way they have to be reproduced.

Combining Stop's *E* and *T* (LEFT) into a ligature (RIGHT) is as simple as dragging the corner points of either top bar to overlap with the other (MIDDLE).

Biome Pro Wide Bold, designed by Carl Crossgrove in 2012 and published by Monotype

ABCDEFGHIJKLMNOPQRSTUVWXYZ

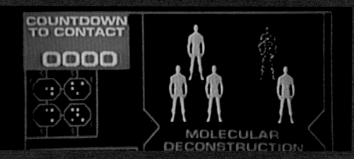

Stargate's primary on-screen "text" is formed of hieroglyphs and pictograms, such as this diorama of slaves being transferred through a star gate.

Thankfully, *Stargate* still finds a place for Eurostile Bold Extended at the American end of the connection.

And Stop, by the way, is almost completely a stencil typeface—it has virtually no counters. It's even used by Banksy as his logo, spray-painted onto walls.

If you stick with semisquare shapes, that's also going to help. The alphabet has three kinds of shapes: triangles like *A* and *V*; round shapes like *O*; and straight shapes like *I*. The problem is always how to make something work with the round shapes and the straights. In Futura, for instance, they solve it by having a "ball and stick" texture. So you have always the circle. Whereas if you stick with squared-off shapes, you're

more free, because you don't have to solve that problem—it's inherently solved for you.

It also depends on what kind of sci-fi movie it would be. As we've seen with Biome and Eurostile, you can have genres of "future" in typography. You can have the future that's more classic or more organic or more technical. You could also have a future where everything went backward, like *Stargate* [1994], where everything goes back to Egyptian times, and what looks futuristic there is more rune-like or hieroglyphic.

Are there any other typefaces you'd recommend for people who want to make their designs feel futuristic?

There are some recent typefaces by Hoefler & Co.—Forza, Vitesse, and Tungsten—that have the squared-off shapes and the Eurostile feel to them. Two relatively obscure typefaces that should be mentioned here are recent releases by young designers, both of which explore the angular side of futuristic typefaces. The first is Bismuth (and Bismuth Stencil) by Ondrej Jób, which has a wide stance and inventive

Forza, from Hoefler & Co., 2010

ABCDEFGHIJKLMNOPQRSTUVWXYZ

Vitesse, from Hoefler & Co., 2000

ABCDEFGHIJKLMNOPQRSTUVWXYZ

Tungsten, from Hoefler & Co., 2009

ABCDEFGHIJKLMNOPQRSTUVWXYZ

Bismuth, by Ondrej Jób, 201

ABCDEFGHIJKLMNOPQRSTUVWXYZ

Bismuth Stencil Black, by Ondrej Jób, 2012

ABCDEFGHIJKLMNOPQRSTUVWXYZ

Pilot Black, by Aleksandra Samuļenkova, 2017

ABCDEFGHIJKLMNOPQRSTUVWXYZ

glyph constructions. The second is Pilot by Aleksandra Samuļenkova, which is narrower and a little retro-looking.

From Aldo himself I'd recommend Metropol, which was conceived as an extension of the Eurostile family but released with a different name because it was a little bit different. It's basically "Eurostile Tilting." Another is Geometry, also by Aldo. Yet another is Avenir, which he designed for a French company called Tygra. He calls it "the square shape of the twentieth century." And there's one more of his that I have to share because of its name—Spazio. It literally means "space."

At the other extreme is Aldo's Stadio, which is kind of a reverse-contrast Eurostile. Although that one works better if you want to make a futuristic western movie. And of course, Aldo designed Estro, which is the iconic Italian spaghetti-western-movie typeface. If you've ever seen a spaghetti western with a Morricone soundtrack, you'll find this typeface in it. It's one of his masterpieces.

A selection of Novarese's typefaces, from the back cover of *Il segno alfabetico*. Spazio (*spazio* is the Italian word for "space") is near the bottom of the first column.

Metropol, by Aldo Novarese, 1967

ABCDEFGHIJKLMNOPQRSTUVWXYZ

Geometry, by Aldo Novarese

ABCDEFGHIJKLMNOPQRSTUVWXYZ

Avenir, by Aldo Novarese

ABCDEFGHIJKLMNOPQRSTUVWXYZ

Stadio, by Aldo Novarese

ABCDEFGHIJKLMNOPQRSTUVWXYZ

Estro, by Aldo Novarese, 1961

ABCDEFGHIJKLMNOPQRSTUVWXYZ

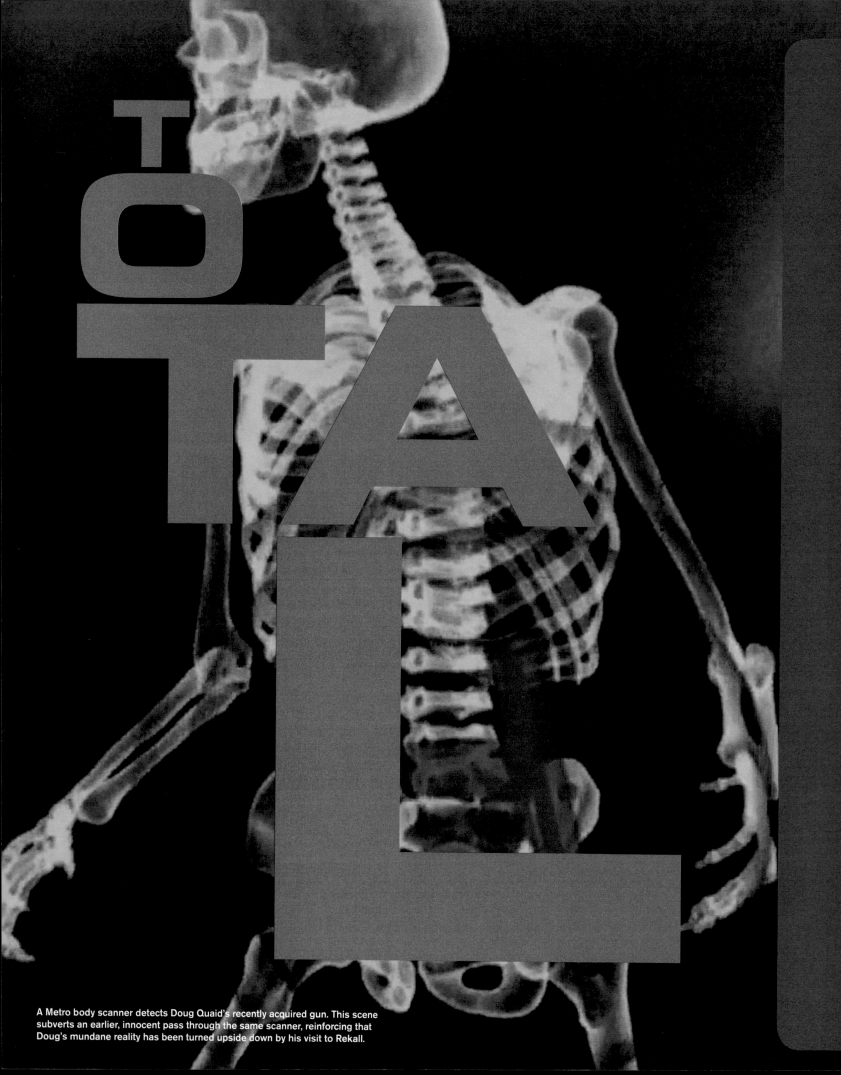

A Metro body scanner detects Doug Quaid's recently acquired gun. This scene subverts an earlier, innocent pass through the same scanner, reinforcing that Doug's mundane reality has been turned upside down by his visit to Rekall.

RECALL

Our next movie will bring back memories. It's our second movie penned by *Alien*'s Ronald Shusett and Dan O'Bannon, and our second Philip K. Dick adaptation, this time based on his 1966 short story "We Can Remember It for You Wholesale."

SCHWARZENEGGER

Get ready for the ride of your life.

TOTAL RECALL

There are a few differences, however, between the book and the film. For a start, the movie's mind-bending company is called Rekall, not REKAL. Its protagonist's surname is Quaid, not Quail—a change supposedly made to avoid any negative connection with Dan Quayle, US vice president at the time of the movie's release. And most importantly, the movie actually has a second and third act, in which Quaid gets his ass to Mars (at least if *Total Recall*'s reality is to be believed).

There is one final way in which the movie might feel familiar to sci-fi fans: *Total Recall* features an evil corporate overlord played by Ronny Cox, who is in no way reminiscent of *RoboCop*'s evil corporate overlord played by Ronny Cox.

LEFT: Evil corporate overlord Dick Jones, from *RoboCop* (1987)

RIGHT: Evil corporate overlord Vilos Cohaagen, from *Total Recall* (1990)

Total Recall is set in 2084, but its opening titles are pretty old-school, at least going by their usage of Imre Reiner's tall, condensed 1934 typeface, Corvinus. I haven't been able to track down a version of Corvinus that contains a capital letter *A* as rectangular as the one seen in *Total Recall*'s opening, leading me to assume that the title's designers adapted the font's capital *H* to suit their descending glowy effect instead. The remainder of the titles are set in Information Extra Bold Wide to impressively chunky effect, albeit with a misspelling of "Philip K. Dick."

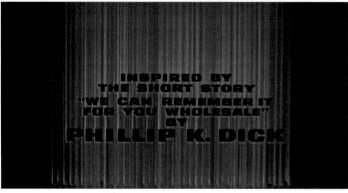
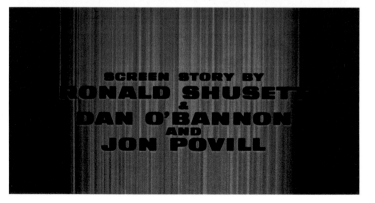

As we discovered earlier, in this book's interview with Antonio Cavedoni, Corvinus is based on the same rounded-rectangle principles as Eurostile, despite its serif style. The same is true for Information, whose rounded letters are based on a predictable geometric shape. *Total Recall*'s title designers may not have gone for the sci-fi typography classics, but they were certainly inspired by their aesthetic.

Corvinus Skyline, a modern digitization of Corvinus, showing its far less rectangular *A*

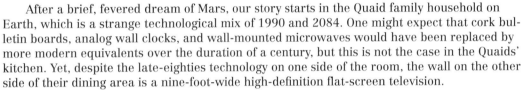

ABCDEFGHIJKLMNOPQRSTUVWXYZ

Information Extra Bold Wide, by Friedrich Karl Sallwey, 1956

ABCDEFGHIJKLMNOPQRSTUVWXYZ

Silhouettes of (FROM TOP TO BOTTOM) the capital letter *O* from Eurostile Bold, Corvinus Skyline, and Information Extra Bold Wide, showing their common synthetic rounded-rectangle shape

After a brief, fevered dream of Mars, our story starts in the Quaid family household on Earth, which is a strange technological mix of 1990 and 2084. One might expect that cork bulletin boards, analog wall clocks, and wall-mounted microwaves would have been replaced by more modern equivalents over the duration of a century, but this is not the case in the Quaids' kitchen. Yet, despite the late-eighties technology on one side of the room, the wall on the other side of their dining area is a nine-foot-wide high-definition flat-screen television.

Despite its capacity for wide-screen, when the Quaids watch network TV they use only the middle square of their high-definition video wall. At the time *Total Recall* was made, broadcast TV had a standard definition aspect ratio of 4:3, not the HD ratio of 16:9 we're accustomed to today. It would have felt odd to 1990s viewers if the Quaids' TV picture had appeared any wider, and so the full capacity of the TV wall was saved for landscape video, such as the *actual* landscape they switch to when the news broadcast ends.

RIGHT: Doug and Lori's 2084 kitchen has a cork bulletin board, an analog wall clock, and a microwave with an LCD timer.

BOTTOM LEFT: The aspect ratio of broadcast TV in 2084 is closer to that of 1984 than that of today.

BOTTOM RIGHT: Doug and Lori enjoy the tranquil beauty of a video nature scene on their wide-screen wall-size TV.

In switching to this beautiful lake scene, the Quaids are following a long-standing sci-fi tradition of using a wall-size TV as a replacement for an actual outdoors. Fake outdoors scenes show up in *Soylent Green, Outland, Aliens* (at least in its special-edition form), *Prometheus, The Hunger Games,* and *Passengers,* to name but a few. The underlying reason for the scenery's fakeness is usually the same—to emphasize that the alternate, real-world location for which the protagonist yearns is currently unattainable.

TOP: Ellen Ripley in *Aliens (Special Edition)* enjoys the tranquil beauty of a video nature scene from Earth, shortly before learning that her daughter back on Earth died while Ripley was in hypersleep.

In a nod to the future decor of *Aliens,* Meredith Vickers's grudging presence aboard *Prometheus* is reinforced by an entire wall showing the tranquil beauty of a video nature scene.

MIDDLE: In 2012's *The Hunger Games,* Katniss Everdeen is taken to a Capitol bedroom with a window

. . . whose view switches among a number of natural environments, including a tranquil video nature scene that is eerily reminiscent of the District 12 forests she can no longer visit.

BOTTOM: Aging detective Sol Roth chooses assisted suicide as an escape from an overpopulated New York City in 1973's *Soylent Green,* a process he describes as "going home." As a lethal anesthetic ends his life, he basks in a panoramic view of Earth as he remembers it from his childhood.

Jim Preston upgrades to a fancy cabin with an outdoors video wall in 2016's *Passengers.*

In fact, the TV-as-outdoors trope is so deeply connected to futurism in film that in *Back to the Future Part II,* the very presence of a SceneScreen video window makes Jennifer realize she is no longer in 1985. As a smooth TV voice-over croons that the window is "broadcasting beautiful views twenty-four hours a day. . . . You're tuned to the Scenery Channel," Jennifer looks distraught and cries, "I'm in the *future!*"

After distressing 1980s Jennifer in *Back to the Future Part II,* a malfunctioning SceneScreen causes Lorraine Baines-McFly to give up on its aspirational projection . . .

. . . and reveal the uninspiring suburban scene behind it.

According to director Paul Verhoeven, the inclusion of this idealistic reality wall, which contrasts sharply with the mundanity of Doug's life, is one of several opening-act cues that allude to an alternative story line for Doug's lowly construction worker. Perhaps the subtlest subliminal prompt can be spotted on the Quaid family bookcase during this scene: an upside-down copy of *The Widow's Handbook,* a 1988 guide to coping with the death of a husband. This seems an odd book for Lori to own, given that nobody is currently trying to kill Doug.

A copy of *The Widow's Handbook* is visible behind Doug as he gazes wistfully at the outdoors video wall.

The Widow's Handbook, by Charlotte Foehner and Carol Cozart (Fulcrum, 1988)

Also visible on Doug's big TV is some blatant product placement for ESPN, whose logo looks exactly the same as it does today. That's because it is *already* the most futuristic company logo in the world, scoring a solid five out of ten according to our rules for future-positioned text, with particular credit for slicing. (I'm sure it's entirely coincidental that this logo was launched in 1985, just a few years after the release of *Blade Runner.* In either case, both logos clearly owe a debt to Aldo Novarese's Stop.)

ESPN's product placement is an ad for an upcoming baseball game: "Tonight on ESPN, the fifth game of the World Series, live from Tokyo. Be there as the Tokyo Samurais go for a fourth and decisive victory over the Toronto Bluejays."

Today, Major League Baseball's amusingly titled World Series is composed entirely of teams from the United States of America, with the notable exception of one Canadian team, the Toronto Blue Jays. In an example of *Total Recall*'s prescience, the Blue Jays became the first non-US team to compete in (and win) the World Series just two years after the movie was released. Sadly, unlike the Blue Jays, the Tokyo Samurais are not yet a real-life team. Nonetheless, based on *Total Recall*'s predictive track record, we can assume that the MLB will have expanded the World Series to other baseball-loving markets by 2084, making it entirely reasonable for a Japanese team to challenge a Canadian team for the title.

ESPN's 1985 logo, which looks a lot like *Blade Runner*'s 1982 logo

● SLANT	● SLICE
● CURVE	● METAL
● STRAIGHT	○ BEVEL
○ SHARP	○ EXTRUDE
● KERN	○ STARS

If only they'd made the *E* a bit pointier.

Done with breakfast, Quaid takes the metro to work, passing behind a futuristic X-ray metal detector device on the way. The complete absence of incident during this scene is, of course, subverted later, when he returns through the same device with a gun in his pocket, causing a disturbance.

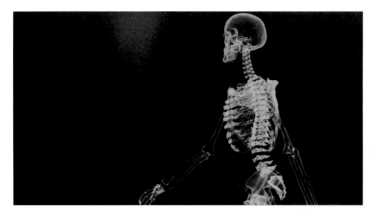

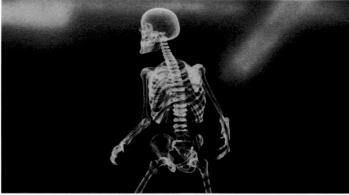

Here, *Total Recall* is partially on the money. Full-body scanners are a commonplace experience at airports today, even if they don't have real-time skeletons. The initial wave of backscatter X-ray scanners, introduced in 2007, were highly controversial, producing images of passengers that directly showed their skin layer, making them appear naked on screen. *Total Recall* solves the problem by going one step further and simply removing their skin altogether.

LEFT: Early in the movie, Quaid strides behind an X-ray detector.

RIGHT: Quaid later returns to the X-ray scanner, this time with a gun in his pocket. The security guards are not pleased to see him.

ADVERTISING IS EVERYWHERE in *Total Recall*, just as it was in *Blade Runner*. Here, a metro train is packed with CRT (cathode-ray tube) TVs, streaming nonstop ads on bulky displays whose boxiness is hidden by a shrewd choice of camera angle. One such ad introduces Quaid to Rekall, a company that sells virtual Mars memories as "cheaper, safer, and better than the real thing." Despite warnings about the memories' safety from a construction worker buddy, the advertising works its magic and Quaid decides to pay Rekall a visit.

One botched memory implant later, Arnie returns to the metro, where the same TV screen shows a counter-ad for good old-fashioned space shuttles. "Don't settle for pale memories, don't go for fake implants. Experience space travel the old-fashioned way on a real live holiday you can afford," says the Northwest Airlines sales rep, with perfect plot-advancement timing. (Indeed, the timing of this ad is so perfect, one could almost believe it was part of a scripted memory intended to get Quaid's ass to Mars.)

LEFT: Rekall's Dr. Edgemar pitches fake memories of Mars.

RIGHT: Quaid contemplates a Northwest Airlines shuttle to Mars.

Sadly, the real-life Quaid won't be able to take a Northwest Airlines shuttle to Mars when 2084 comes around. That's because Northwest, like *2001: A Space Odyssey*'s Pan Am, is no longer in existence. The company merged with Delta in 2008 and stopped using the Northwest name in 2010. (In a double kicker, the Northwest logo seen later on Mars was replaced in 1989, one year before the movie's release.)

One final advertising detail: Just before the Northwest promo, we see the end of an ad for Botco, offering "Tomorrow's Fuels" at "Tomorrow's Prices," which doesn't sound like a good deal at all. This ad wasn't created for *Total Recall*, however. It's a snippet from *Botco*, a 1985 animated short by pioneering computer-graphics company Pacific Data Images, which went on to create *Antz* and *Shrek*.

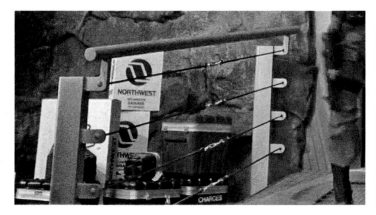

LEFT: **The pre-1989 Northwest logo, seen in 1990's *Total Recall***

RIGHT: **"Botco. Tomorrow's Fuels, Tomorrow's Prices"**

But back to Quaid's Rekall visit. As Quaid arrives at Rekall to meet sales rep Bob McClane, we see Bob's secretary, Tiffany, use a futuristic nail varnish pen to change the color of her nails from blue to red, simply by tapping each of them in turn—another piece of foreshadowing for the indeterminate, changeable nature of Doug's reality.

Tiffany taps each nail with a stylus, turning it from blue to red.

"Check out those statistics."

Lost luggage . . .

. . . lousy weather . . .

. . . crooked taxi drivers.

Bob pitches Quaid on a Rekall trip to Mars. Doubting the reality of Rekall's dreams, Quaid quizzes Bob about the company's reputation for lobotomizing its customers. Ever the salesman, Bob isn't fazed and notes that traveling with Rekall is safer than getting on a rocket. He invites Quaid to "check out those statistics," while showing a graph of "FATALITIES" plotted against "YEARS," with "SHUTTLE" clearly looking a lot worse than "REKALL."

There are four big problems with Bob's graph, each of which undermines his claim. Let's take a look at them in more detail.

First, a lobotomy is not a fatality. It is a very bad thing to have happen to you, but it is not actually being dead.

Second, neither axis of the graph has numbers on it, making it very hard to know how much worse "SHUTTLE" really is.

Third, the "SHUTTLE" curve does not indicate its defining data points, suggesting (for example) that two and a half people died from "SHUTTLE" in year six. (It is not technically possible for half a person to die from "SHUTTLE," or for one person to have half died.)

Finally, we don't know where the zero y-axis lies. If it's the thick black line across the bottom of the graph, we could assume that one person has died from "REKALL," reliably and consistently, in each of the years shown on the graph. (Quaid might be wise to ask if this year's fatality has already happened.)

Having failed to provide convincing statistics to back up his safety claim, Bob continues his sales pitch regardless: "Besides, a real holiday is a pain in the butt! You got lost luggage, lousy weather, crooked taxi drivers; when you travel with Rekall, everything is perfect." Intriguingly, all three of these butt pains show up in Quaid's post-Rekall adventures. First, he nearly loses a suitcase left by his agency buddy and ends up fighting a passing woman to retrieve it. Second, the weather on Mars is so lousy that it causes your eyes to pop out and your neck to swell up something horrible. And third, there is no taxi driver more crooked than Benny, who sells the entire Mars resistance out to Cohaagen and his goons in order to feed four (or five) fake hungry kids.

This is not Bob's only prediction of the future, either. His description of Rekall's Secret Agent package makes a strong argument for the majority of the movie's taking place in Quaid's imagination, given that he neatly sums up the entire second and third acts:

> *You are a top operative, back under deep cover on your most important mission. People are trying to kill you left and right. You meet this beautiful exotic woman. . . . I don't want to spoil it for you, Doug, but you rest assured, by the time the trip is over you get the girl, kill the bad guys, and save the entire planet.*

Yup. Pretty much.

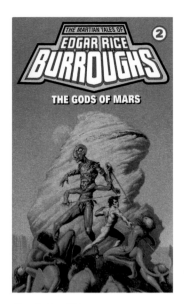

The Gods of Mars, by Edgar Rice Burroughs (Del Rey Books, 1979). Cover illustration by Michael Whelan

Sold by Bob's suggestion of the Secret Agent package, Quaid decides to take a fake trip to Mars. As Rekall's Dr. Lull prepares him for his memory injection, she notes that the company is offering alien artifacts as an optional add-on package. A number of fantastic-looking alien images flash up on the Proton CRT behind her, including one particularly intriguing image of a multiarmed chap in a loincloth, brandishing swords in two of his four hands.

This image is unmistakably adapted from a book cover illustration by Michael Whelan for a 1979 paperback edition of Edgar Rice Burroughs's *The Gods of Mars.* In fact, the befanged green gentleman seen in the picture is none other than Tars Tarkas, the primary Thark befriended by John Carter during his time on Barsoom, Burroughs's fictionalized version of Mars. Why he crops up as an alien artifact in *Total Recall* is a mystery, as is the fact that the original cover image has been adapted to show a red (rather than white) background and blue tentacles wrapped around Tars's legs.

Dr. Lull introduces Rekall's range of alien artifacts.

Tars Tarkas is not the only significant artifact on the list. Dr. Lull continues Bob's foreshadowing by showing a pretty massive spoiler for the movie's closing act. Artifact F45.55 from her catalog looks suspiciously like concept art for the huge alien reactor seen inside the Pyramid Mines at the end of the movie.

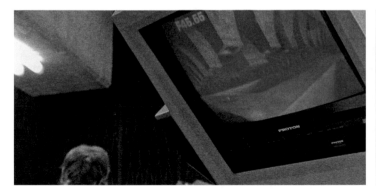

Dr. Lull shows Quaid an image of a million-year-old alien artifact, with lots of rectangular shapes jutting out of the ceiling.

Quaid and Melina look at a million-year-old alien reactor, with lots of rectangular shapes jutting out of the ceiling.

Rekall employees *still* aren't done with their foreshadowing. After pitching the alien artifacts, Dr. Lull throws a data disk to her assistant, Ernie, who looks at it and says, "That's a new one: blue sky on Mars!"—clearly a reference to the movie's terraforming ending. This is immediately followed by Dr. Lull asking Quaid if he's "been married long"—a nod to his eight-year marriage to Lori, which he later discovers began just six weeks earlier.

After establishing that Quaid has an interest in fake memory infidelity, Dr. Lull presents him with a selection of disembodied rotating lady heads, asking: "How do you like your women? Blonde? Brunette? Redhead?" She tactfully skips the second line of captions, which read "Negro," "Oriental," and "Creole." Clearly, white women are distinguished by hair color, and everyone else by ethnicity, even in 2084. (If you're wondering why these spinning mannequins look familiar: Cast your mind back to the rotating replicant profiles in *Blade Runner*. To make pseudo-humans look like property, simply stick 'em on a turntable.)

Racial stereotyping is sadly still a reality in 2084, with accompanying clichéd makeup and hairstyles.

HAVING MADE HIS SELECTION, Quaid undergoes the Rekall procedure. Everything goes horribly wrong, and there is an altercation. Quaid wakes up to find he has been unceremoniously dumped in a cab—specifically, a Johnnycab, a fully autonomous taxi of the future. In this regard, *Total Recall* is bang on the futuristic money. As we approach 2019, several of the world's biggest technology companies, including Google, Tesla, and Uber, are on their way to making autonomous taxis a reality. (Indeed, with its combination of autonomous vehicles, Mars colonization, and underground tunneling, *Total Recall* is pretty much Tesla CEO Elon Musk's idealized dream of the future.)

To make passengers slightly less uncomfortable about the lack of human control, each Johnnycab has a humanoid robot in the front, voiced by (and modeled after) Robert Picardo, better known as the Doctor from *Star Trek: Voyager*. In Quaid's case, his robot is whistling the Norwegian national anthem as he awakes. (The reason for this is unclear.)

According to director Paul Verhoeven, Johnnycab's use of a humanoid driver was less a futuristic prediction and more a moviemaking convenience for storytelling interaction. (It would be weird to enter a car that was itself whistling the Norwegian national anthem.) Thankfully, despite Johnnycab's lack of realism, its futurism is saved by the fact that "JOHNNYCAB" is written down the side in Eurostile Bold Extended.

Quaid's Johnnycab is—of course—decorated with Eurostile Bold Extended.

After leaving his Johnnycab, Quaid kills his work buddy, Harry, plus three other random men. He begins to wonder if all is not what it seems. Back at the Quaid apartment, Lori is learning tennis from a HOLD-TENNIS holographic instructor. Like all good movie holograms, the tennis instructor's projection glitches occasionally, just to make it clear it is a hologram. (It is less clear, however, why the HOLD-TENNIS base unit is an oscilloscope with "HOLD-TENNIS" written on it.)

Lori practices her swing with a virtual holographic instructor.

The holographic instructor glitches each time the swing cycle repeats, to remind us that this is a hologram.

This simple, everyday use of 3-D holographic technology is a neat setup for Quaid's later holographic wristband, normalizing our expectation of 2084 technology so that it doesn't seem too far-fetched when called upon to advance the plot. Indeed, this is a common theme throughout the movie's opening sequences: Quaid's initial uneventful jaunt through the metro X-ray screen, and his innocent Johnnycab journey, also preempts later action sequences when there isn't enough time for viewers to grasp each new technology.

Quaid arrives home, hoping for sympathy and understanding from his wife, Lori. Instead, she goes all *Widow's Handbook* on him, attacking him in an action-packed fight sequence and nearly killing him in the process. Richter, the movie's central bad guy, arrives just after Quaid escapes. (I will henceforth refer to Richter as "Bad Guy" for convenience.) He is in every way exactly like Clarence Boddicker, the central bad guy in *RoboCop*. (Indeed, Kurtwood Smith—who played bad guy Boddicker in *RoboCop*—declined the role of Richter because he felt they were too similar.)

Bad Guy's primary henchman (whom I will henceforth refer to as "Primary Henchman") uses a handheld motion detector to follow Quaid's escape. This device is very similar to the handheld motion detector seen in Shusett and O'Bannon's earlier *Alien,* except that this one shows 3-D maps of the surrounding architecture and appears to be made by Casio. That's almost certainly because Casio was one of the main manufacturers of portable LCD televisions in the late 1980s, and the industrial-looking device seen in *Total Recall* almost certainly has an off-the-shelf Casio TV inside it.

Primary Henchman's motion detector, which takes the *Blade Runner* ESPER-machine approach to arbitrary coordinate systems

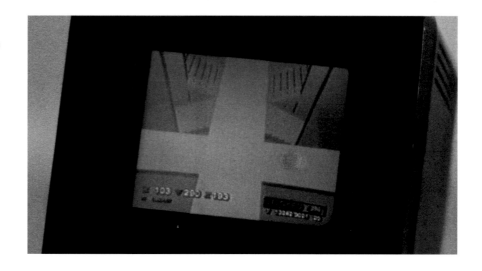

Despite the motion detector, Bad Guy and Primary Henchman fail to track down their quarry. As Quaid escapes on the metro, Bad Guy receives a "live transmission from Mr. Cohaagen." This is impressive, given that Bad Guy is on Earth and Cohaagen is on Mars. Live transmissions between the two planets are physically impossible because of the distances involved and because radio signals are constrained by the speed of light. Indeed, when the two planets are at their closest, it takes around four minutes for a radio signal to travel between them; when they are farthest apart, it takes a whopping twenty-four minutes. And that's just in one direction. You can double those times if you're hoping for a two-way conversation.

All of which makes real-time communication entirely impossible, unless by 2084 humans have managed to break the speed of light (in which case it's highly unlikely they'll be making their video calls on CRT displays). The other possibility is that *Total Recall*'s video calls are transmitted via the mechanics of bad news. As Douglas Adams noted in 1992's *Mostly Harmless,* "Nothing travels faster than the speed of light with the possible exception of bad news, which obeys its own special laws."

So why does video calling show up time and time again in science-fiction movies, despite its inherent real-world limitations? The failure of Picturephone some twenty years before *Total Recall* proved that video-based communication is not necessarily a future that human beings feel comfortable with. Nonetheless, it still appears in the majority of sci-fi movies studied in this book. Given its social challenges, I am convinced that it recurs solely for the purposes of convenient visual storytelling. Video calling is an excellent way for two characters to advance the plot in an inherently visual medium, without the need for such boring details as traveling or actually being in the same location. (Pesky details such as human psychology or the fundamental laws of physics should never get in the way of good storytelling.)

QUAID SURFACES from the metro in a busy shopping complex, only to find near–*Blade Runner* levels of product placement, including an inevitable Coca-Cola billboard. Sadly for *Total Recall*'s futurism, Quaid also sees plenty of ads for 35mm camera film, both on Earth and later on Mars. Unless film cameras are having a vinyl-like resurgence in the late twenty-first century, it seems unlikely that either Fujifilm or Kodak will be advertising in 2084 the products and services seen here.

An Earth billboard advertising "FUJI FILM: FILM OF THE CENTURY XXI"

LEFT: A twenty-four-hour Kodak photo service on Earth

RIGHT: The Fox Photo store on Mars, with a neon sign saying, "FOX PHOTO: We sell Kodak film"

Also visible after Quaid's metro escape is a neon ad for Peñafiel, a brand of mineral water in Mexico. The reason for its presence is surprising but simple: Most of the movie's Earth-based locations were filmed in Mexico City, whose new brutalism architecture was chosen by Paul Verhoeven as a convincing vision of a concrete-first near future.

TOP LEFT: A neon ad for Mexican mineral water brand Peñafiel

TOP RIGHT: Quaid walks past the all-concrete entrance to the Metro Insurgentes station in Mexico City.

BOTTOM LEFT: Quaid's Johnnycab drives him into the all-concrete Heroico Colegio Militar complex in Mexico City.

BOTTOM RIGHT: Quaid walks into the all-concrete offices of Rekall—also known as Infonavit, the Mexican federal institute for workers' housing.

LCD, by Alan Birch, 1981

ABCDEFGHIJKLMNOPQRSTUVWXYZ

This sequence also introduces us to a rare appearance by popular eighties font LCD, on the license plate of Bad Guy's futuristic car. LCD, named after the liquid crystal displays popularized by eighties pocket calculators and digital watches, is a classic example of a font that was futuristic for the briefest of moments. Sadly, it now looks as anachronistic as *Alien*'s Pump Demi, especially when positioned a century after its heyday.

"PASSENGER JRP 601 DRIVE SAFELY"

Quaid takes a second and slightly more destructive Johnnycab journey, ending in a fireball at an abandoned industrial complex. Here, he investigates the contents of his mysterious case.

In addition to a painful-looking location tracker–removal gadget, the case also contains a holographic wristband and a portable TV screen that plays a video of Quaid, who tells Quaid he is actually Hauser and should get his ass to Mars. After removing a painful location tracker, he dutifully obliges.

We know from earlier Rekall scenes that Quaid's secret-agent ego trip included first-class travel on a shuttle to Mars. Based on today's spaceflight technology, this flight to Mars would take between six to eight months, depending on timing and fuel cargo. Even then, this is assuming that the orbits of Earth and Mars are in their optimal alignment, which happens only every twenty-six months. Even if Hauser's video message was perfectly timed for this biennial event, his half-year Martian flight would still make for a very boring movie. Thankfully, the filmmakers choose to skip the details of this flight and cut straight to the red planet instead.

After some Mars positioning shots (think "red, dusty, bonus moon"), we find ourselves in Mars Immigration, where space passports are stamped "MARS IMMIGRATION ADMITTED," just in case there was any doubt. These stamps also give a precise date reference of June 19, 2084, for this scene.

An administrative check when visiting another celestial body is not without real-world precedent. After returning to Earth, *Apollo 11*'s three-man crew completed a standard US customs and immigration form, showing a departure place and country of "MOON." More ominously, the form's declaration of onboard conditions that could lead to the spread of disease read "TO BE DETERMINED." That's because the crew was quarantined for *three weeks* after returning to Earth—first in a Mobile Quarantine Facility (a converted Airstream trailer) and then at the Lunar Receiving Laboratory—under NASA's Extra-Terrestrial Exposure Law, to be sure that nothing dangerous returned with them from the moon. (After our previous study of *Alien,* you can't blame NASA for playing it safe.)

TOP RIGHT: A Federal Colonies logo seen as part of a Mars Immigration passport stamp. "FEDERAL COLONIES" is, of course, set in Eurostile Bold Extended. The logo is missing the foreground moons seen in other instances of this logo.

BOTTOM RIGHT: Neil Armstrong, Michael Collins, and Buzz Aldrin in the Mobile Quarantine Facility aboard the USS *Hornet* recovery ship. On the right is President Richard Nixon, being careful not to catch moon cooties.

FAR LEFT: The Agriculture, Customs, Immigration, and Public Health form completed by the *Apollo 11* crew after their return to Earth. According to NASA historians, the form was not signed by Neil, Buzz, and Mike immediately after splashdown; rather, it was created by the Customs Service in Hawaii, with the astronauts' signatures auto-penned into place later in 1969.

Back on Mars, a perfectly normal-looking lady in a plain yellow jacket is smiling her way through immigration. Unfortunately, this innocent setup is totally spoiled by the presence of a plain yellow jacket and perfectly-normal-looking-lady mask in Hauser's bag of technical goodies a few moments earlier, proving what you've no doubt been suspecting: It's not a lady but Arnold Schwarzenegger, wearing *Total Recall*'s most memorable special effect.

You wouldn't have guessed it was Arnie from looking at the lady's passport, where the signature reads "Priscilla Allen." (This is because the lady is played by actress Priscilla Allen, who simply signed the passport herself.)

Ironically, Arnie missed out on the role of RoboCop in *RoboCop* because his overly muscular frame wouldn't fit inside the movie's robo-suit. He probably wouldn't fit inside a Priscilla Allen suit, either, but a clever use of camera angle means the characters' mismatched statures are not noticed.

A perfectly normal-looking lady makes her way through Mars Immigration.

Moments earlier, a perfectly-normal-looking-lady costume can be seen hidden inside Hauser's bag.

OMG! It's a lifelike model of Arnold Schwarzenegger's head, hiding inside the costume!

"THIS PASSPORT IS NOT VALID UNTIL SIGNED BY THE BEARER." Priscilla should be fine, then.

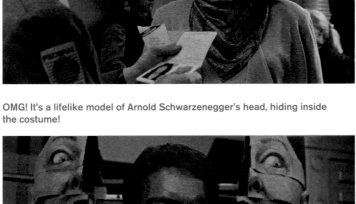

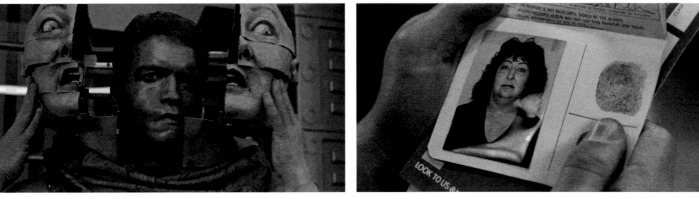

ABCDEFGHIJKLMNOPQRSTUVWXYZ

Eurostile Extended

As Quaid's true identity is revealed, a group of heavily armored Mars guards prepare to attack. Surprisingly, some of the guards have 1989 Casio fx-250c scientific calculators strapped to their wrists. It's an appropriately on-brand choice, given that the device makes extensive use of Eurostile Extended.

These guards work for Federal Colonies, *Total Recall*'s inevitable intergalactic megacorp. We see the Federal Colonies logo several times in the movie, often (but not always) with its associated text in Eurostile Bold Extended.

It's not entirely clear what the Federal Colonies logo represents, but one might assume that it pictures Mars and its two moons, Phobos and Deimos. If this assumption is correct, then the scale is spectacularly wrong—Phobos and Deimos are tiny rocks, with diameters of just 13.8 and 7.8 miles, respectively. Mars, on the other hand, is over half the diameter of Earth, at 4,220 miles.

ABOVE LEFT: Federal Colonies guards look on in shock as Arnie's identity is revealed. Note that the guards on the left and right have interesting-looking devices strapped to their left wrists.

ABOVE RIGHT: A subsequent close-up of one of the guards shows that the device strapped to his wrist is in fact a Casio scientific calculator.

LEFT: A 1989 Casio fx-250c scientific calculator, liberally labeled with Eurostile Extended

FAR LEFT: A stitched Federal Colonies badge on the shoulder of a Mars Immigration official, in Eurostile Bold Extended

BELOW LEFT: A blue-and-orange Federal Colonies logo on the helmet of a guard, in Eurostile Bold Extended

It turns out that Bad Guy and Primary Henchman are also in the Mars Immigration hall, apparently having made the six-month trip to Mars without bumping into Quaid. Because he is an idiot, Bad Guy shoots his gun several times at Quaid, hitting and rupturing a glass window in the arrivals area. This turns very bad indeed, with everyone and everything pulled out into the low-pressure Martian atmosphere.

Quaid escapes on a train with a poster featuring more Eurostile Extended. He overhears a conversation about how annoying Cohaagen is, having apparently raised the price of air again.

As he leaves his train, we also discover that Mars doesn't yet have Johnnycabs, instead relying on good old-fashioned humans to drive people around. (Given that Earth's taxi infrastructure seems to be entirely formed by Johnnycabs, it's not clear why Mars has a human-powered fleet, especially given that the cost of living is probably astronomical, in every sense of the word.) Quaid brushes off the advances of Benny, an innocent-looking cabdriver, and heads to a nearby hotel. It is, of course, a Hilton hotel, suggesting that the chain's moon outpost eighty-three years earlier (in *2001: A Space Odyssey*) was a resounding success. (Sadly, Hilton stopped using this logo in 1998.)

The man in reception inserts Quaid's identity card into the authorization-card slot of a Sargent System 45 device. This is a real-world 1980s hotel device from Sargent Locks, which the Hilton receptionist is using entirely incorrectly. This device is actually for coding hotel room keys; the receptionist's *own* identity card should be inserted into the authorization-card slot, followed by a room key in the upper slot, to encode it for room access. (After using the System 45 erroneously, the hotel receptionist says, "I'll go and code your room key," and leaves the front desk to do so on an alternate device.)

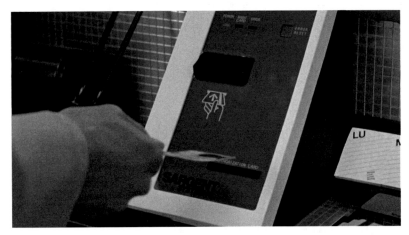

As he leaves his Hilton hotel to visit Melina, Quaid is once more accosted by Benny and finally accepts his offer of a taxi. There are explosions, and shooting breaks out between rebels and guards as the duo set off in the direction of Venusville.

As the shooting continues, our gaze rests briefly on an ad for *Mars Today,* the "newspaper of the universe" and "no. 1 in the galaxy." This is a clear riff on *USA Today,* one of the largest-circulation newspapers in the United States. The logo seen in *Total Recall* is an adaptation of *USA Today*'s Futura Bold logo, with "MARS" instead of "USA," red instead of blue, and an understandable lack of continents on its globe. (The other main difference is that the *M* in "MARS" doesn't look anything like Futura Bold, for which I have no explanation.)

A newspaper stand for *Mars Today,* "the newspaper of the universe"

Futura Bold

ABCDEFGHIJKLMNOPQRSTUVWXYZ

Sadly for 2084, *USA Today* stopped using its original masthead logo in 2012, replacing it with a simpler design that employs a circle instead of an explicit globe. The newspaper also switched to its own custom form of Futura, known as Futura Today, during the same rebranding.

Futura Today Bold, from *USA Today*'s custom variant of Futura

ABCDEFGHIJKLMNOPQRSTUVWXYZ

Total Recall is not the only time *USA Today* has been envisaged as the newspaper of tomorrow. *Back to the Future Part II* (1989) also shows an issue of *USA Today,* this time with a futuristic curved-and-sliced logo proclaiming news that befits the movie's October 2015 setting.

Let's put this newspaper through its paces. First, it claims to have three billion daily readers, which is at least 1,000 percent higher than *USA Today*'s actual 2015 daily readership. Second, it predicts that the country's female president will be tired of being asked the same questions by reporters, which was almost (but not quite) a reality in November 2016, if not October 2015. Furthest from the mark, tragically, is the suggestion that Queen Diana would visit Washington, D.C., in the fall of 2015.

A reimagined *USA Today* also appears in 2002's *Minority Report,* during a scene in which John Anderton is on the run from his Precrime colleagues. As Anderton escapes on the subway, a businessman across from him sees the front page of his E Ink–like newspaper update with "Breaking News," finally displaying an image of Anderton alongside the headline "Precrime Hunts its Own!"

TOP: The *USA Today* logo, rendered in Futura Bold, 1982–2012

ABOVE: The *USA Today* logo, since 2012

LEFT: *USA Today* in 1989's *Back to the Future Part II,* as published via compu-fax satellite

There's plenty more product placement to be seen when Quaid and Benny arrive at Venus-ville. Pepsi seems to be the sugar-water choice of a new colonization, while fast-food chain Jack in the Box and electronics outlets Sharper Image and Curtis Mathes all make an appearance.

TOP LEFT: A Mars-based Sharper Image store, seen when Quaid checks in to the Hilton hotel

TOP RIGHT: A Mars-based Curtis Mathes store, seen during Quaid's visit to Venusville

BOTTOM LEFT: A Mars-based Jack in the Box restaurant, and a second Sharper Image, seen behind Benny and Quaid during their visit to Venusville

BOTTOM RIGHT: An ad for the Ricoh MIRAI camera, the logo looking just as fresh as it did ninety-six years earlier

Also advertised is the Ricoh MIRAI, a futuristic-looking 1988 SLR camera whose name is literally the Japanese word for "future." (This might explain why its slanted/curved/sliced *Blade Runner*–style logo looks just as futuristic as ESPN's.)

Several more outlets have taken the *Mars Today* approach of colony-specific branding, including the imaginatively named Mars Burger and the inevitably colored Coors Martian Red, which takes pride of place behind the bar at the Last Resort.

LEFT: Mmmm. Mars Burger.

RIGHT: A neon sign for Coors Martian Red, in the Last Resort bar. (Killian's Red, seen on the right, is also a Coors brand but was red before it got to Mars.)

The Last Resort is notable for two more typographic curiosities: It features the only neon Eurostile Extended I've seen in a movie, and it features a wrestling poster for "ERIC STEEL vs RORY THE DOG-FACED BOY," which is a glorious name for a wrestling matchup on any planet in the solar system.

LEFT: "LAST RESORT," in neon Eurostile Extended

RIGHT: "WRESTLING: ERIC STEEL vs RORY THE DOG-FACED BOY"

At the Last Resort bar, Quaid finally meets Melina. They have a fight, and he returns to his hotel. Here, he is unexpectedly visited by Rekall employee Dr. Edgemar, who adds further credence to the theory that *Total Recall* is all a dream:

> *Your dreams started in the middle of the implant procedure. Everything after that—the chases, the trip to Mars, the suite at the Hilton—are all elements of your Rekall holiday and ego trip. You paid to be a secret agent.*
>
> *And what about the girl? Brunette, athletic, sleazy, and demure, just as you specified. Is that coincidence?*

You have to admit, he's got a point.

Dr. Edgemar asks Quaid if it's possible that he's "really an invincible secret agent from Mars, who's the victim of an interplanetary conspiracy to make him think he's a lowly construction worker." Yup. Sounds about right.

Dr. Edgemar offers Quaid a chance to return to normality, noting that if he doesn't:

> *. . . the walls of reality will come crashing down. One minute you'll be the savior of the rebel cause, and the next thing you'll know, you'll be Cohaagen's bosom buddy. You'll even have fantasies about alien civilizations.*

He's pretty much summed up the remainder of the movie right there.

In a neat twist, when Doug shoots Dr. Edgemar square in the forehead, the wall behind him immediately comes crashing down, and people try to kill him left and right. (You can't say they didn't warn him.)

The walls of reality come crashing down, and by "reality" I mean a Hilton hotel suite on Mars.

During his prescient monologue, Dr. Edgemar notes that if Doug wants to awake from his dream, he must swallow a red pill as a symbol of his desire to return to reality. This is in itself prescient of 1999's *The Matrix,* in which Neo is offered a remarkably similar option by Morpheus. *Total Recall* definitely got there first, however, in both the real and fictive worlds: It's set in 2084, whereas *The Matrix* doesn't take place until 2199.

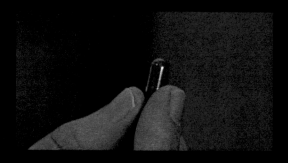

LEFT: In *Total Recall,* Quaid refuses to take the red pill, perpetuating his illusion of reality.

RIGHT: In *The Matrix,* Neo chooses to take the red pill, rejecting his illusion of reality.

Quaid is captured but escapes when Melina arrives and shoots his guards. She has a boss fight with Lori, and they are both totally badass. There is an extended chase sequence, containing nothing of typographic significance, and the good guys inevitably escape. Cohaagen seals up Venusville, cutting off its air supply, because he is evil. Quaid ends up at the Resistance underground headquarters, where a man called George promises to introduce him to Kuato, leader of the Resistance.

George speaks to Quaid from behind a laptop that has a cable plugged into it from one camera angle only. Worryingly, his laptop seems unable to boot beyond its BIOS (Basic Input/Output System), at least going by the following text on his screen:

```
CMOS system options not set
CMOS checksum failure
CMOS ??????? configuration mismatch
*** RUN SETUP UTILITY ***
Press <F1> key to RESUME
American Megatrends Inc
```

All 1980s PCs were reliant on their BIOS for access to their keyboard, disk, and text display systems. American Megatrends, established in 1985, grew to become the world's largest PC BIOS firmware vendor, so it's not surprising to see its name on screen if something is fundamentally wrong with George's laptop. Nonetheless, given that the Resistance is using one-hundred-year-old computer hardware in their fight against Cohaagen, it's worrying that their leader can't even get his PC to boot.

LEFT: Crop. Zoom.

RIGHT: Enhance.

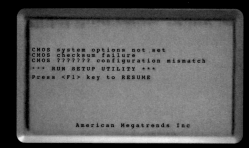

George and Quaid are betrayed by Benny. There are explosions and expositions, all of which we will skip. Quaid and Melina are strapped into yet more Rekall machinery, but they escape because Arnie is strong. Cohaagen, having made the classic Bond-villain mistake of not waiting to see his evil plan succeed, is livid to hear of the pair's escape.

To make his anger clear to the audience, Cohaagen kicks over a nearby tank of goldfish, who flap about desperately on the floor. This whole scene reinforces that Cohaagen is an important man who controls the ability to breathe, though there's good news, too. Larger gold-fish like these can survive for several hours out of water, so there's plenty of time for Cohaagen to have a change of heart, so long as he doesn't asphyxiate himself in the meantime.

 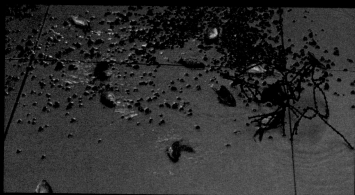

Just in case we haven't gotten the point, we then cut to Venusville, where the air is still turned off and everyone is gasping. No one will shed a tear, then, when Cohaagen's payoff boss death involves his being exposed to the harsh Mars atmosphere and dying from a lack of oxygen. He won't shed a tear himself, either, because his eyes are out on their stalks, and any liquid that came out of his tear glands would evaporate on contact with the thin Martian atmosphere.

Quaid and Melina encounter Benny again, this time in a drill tank that features an excellent example of surplus Letraset being put to good use. If you look closely, you can just make out a spurious "4 CLN" beneath the "MANIFOLD PRESSURE" dial inside the tank:

As we saw previously with Leon's photos in *Blade Runner*, this "CLN" comes from the header or footer of a sheet of Letraset that would otherwise have gone to waste.

ABOVE: The header and footer of a sheet of 42pt Letraset red Helvetica Medium type

RIGHT: The handheld motion detector from *Alien*. The "47-30-CLN" text seen beneath the detector's screen almost certainly comes from the header or footer of a sheet of 30pt Letraset red Helvetica Medium type.

Blade Runner is not the earliest example of surplus Letraset that I've spotted, however. That credit goes to 1979's *Alien*, which features the same telltale "CLN" text on its handheld motion detector.

Benny gets a deserved Bad Guy Death, as Quaid drills through his tank just beneath some Univers 67 Bold Condensed. This being an eighties/nineties Arnie movie, Benny's drill-based death is accompanied by an obligatory Arnie Death Line—in this case, a determined cry of "SCREW YOUUUUUU!"

"SCREW YOUUUUUU!"

Univers 67 Bold Condensed

ABCDEFGHIJKLMNOPQRSTUVWXYZ

Benny's drill tank opens a pathway to Cohaagen's alien reactor, which looks remarkably like alien artifact F45.55 from page 161. Arnie notes that the whole core of Mars is ice, which the alien reactor can melt to create an atmosphere. He's wrong, of course—Mars's core is made of liquid iron, not water—but he's right in that there is *some* ice on Mars. Both poles of the planet have permanent ice caps, believed to contain water ice alongside frozen carbon dioxide. Large sheets of ice have also been discovered underneath the planet's surface, closer to its equator. Indeed, in August 2017 researchers discovered that it even snows on Mars, though only at night. Sadly the snow rarely reaches the ground, making Martian snowmen impractical.

Bad Guy and his goons turn up to ambush Quaid and Melina. Arnie dons his holographic wristband (remember that?) and walks straight into their ambush. The goons gun him down but fail to kill him because he is a hologram. We can be confident that he is a hologram because his image blips in exactly the same way as the tennis training hologram we saw early in the movie. (Turns out Paul Verhoeven was training us how to spot holograms, not how to play tennis.)

Given Arnie's holographic nature, it is unclear how the goons fail to kill one another in a horrific self-inflicted massacre during this scene. Their ambush clearly targets Quaid's noncorporeal image from both sides, and so one would expect their many bullets and grenades to hit their colleagues opposite. Thankfully, their cheating of physics turns out not to be crucial, as the real Quaid and Melina turn up and shoot them afterward anyway.

ABOVE LEFT: As Arnie laughs at the goons' inability to shoot him . . .

ABOVE RIGHT: . . . his image blips to indicate that he is, in fact, a hologram.

Whatever's going on with the wristband, it seems likely that it's more for plot convenience than realistic futurism. Indeed, it seems the band even works when you're not wearing it, as Melina demonstrates during her own moment of goon deception. (This time, the goons successfully kill one another as her hologram disappears.)

ABOVE LEFT: Bad Guy's goons somehow manage not to shoot one another through a holographic Quaid.

ABOVE RIGHT: Melina demonstrates that you don't need to wear the chunky holographic wristband in order to be duplicated.

Arnie and Bad Guy have a boss battle, which ends with Bad Guy getting his arms ripped off. The movie's writers miss a great opportunity for an Arnie Death Line, opting for "See you at the party" rather than the infinitely more punny "Now you are 'armless."

Quaid reaches the alien reactor's trigger room and has a standoff with Cohaagen, resulting in an explosion. Everyone is sucked toward the outside, but Arnie manages to enable the alien reactor anyway, because he is strong. As the reactor activates, Cohaagen, Quaid, and Melina are all sucked out onto the Martian surface, where they argle in pain owing to the lack of atmosphere.

Cohaagen dies a grisly death due to being out there a little bit longer than the other two. Mercifully, the alien reactor generates a perfect working Martian atmosphere just before Quaid and Melina go the same way, and they do not end up dead. In a neat throwback to the movie's opening, Quaid and Melina gaze at the beauty of a blue sky on Mars, without the need for the protective suits they wore in Quaid's opening dream.

AS THE SUN COMES OUT from behind some instant clouds, Melina says, "I can't believe it—it's like a dream." In doing so, she neatly summarizes the philosophical question that has perplexed watchers of *Total Recall* since 1990. *Is* Quaid truly a spy, or is he lying lobotomized in a Rekall lab, drooling and dreaming of Mars? There's only one man who can answer that question definitively—and there's an interview with him on the next page.

PAUL VERHOEVEN

In September 2017, I spoke to Paul Verhoeven, director of *RoboCop* (1987), *Total Recall* (1990), and *Starship Troopers* (1997), about futurism, violence, fascism, and philosophy in science fiction.

ADDEY: Let's start by looking at some of the futurism in your science-fiction movies. *Total Recall* has Johnnycab, a self-driving taxi, which is pretty close to becoming a reality today.

VERHOEVEN: That's true. In general, what you're doing with this kind of futuristic thinking is not a prophecy—certain elements are already there in society, and you extrapolate them and use them in perhaps a hyperbolic way. And then you shouldn't be too amazed when some of these things become a reality.

Other people might see it in a different way, but I don't think that these movies have anything to do with the real future. I don't think the brain can invent something completely out of nowhere—it's always based on details of the now, which become more mainstream twenty to thirty years later.

Starship Troopers, for example, has a lot to do with what's happening now, you know. But *Starship Troopers* was taking political situations that were already visible at the end of the nineties and extrapolating them. And it was only half a year ago that some of these things became much closer and much more realistic than we thought when we originally wrote it.

There's a line in *Starship Troopers,* in the schoolroom, where Rasczak says, "We explored the failure of democracy, how the social scientists brought our world to the brink of chaos."

Total Recall's autonomous Johnnycab, complete with smart-ass robotic driver

Yeah. You could say it's prophetic, but I really feel that it is based on events we saw already in American society, that were already there. Notably, we took some stuff from Texas, where [George W.] Bush was at that time the governor. When Ed Neumeier and I wrote it, it's not that we really thought this *would* happen; it was more that this *could* happen. I was amazed this year that it seems to be happening much more precisely than I had anticipated. You take elements out of the now and extrapolate them in a hyperbolic, over-the-top way, and then you find out that these tendencies that you noticed after a certain amount of time became a reality.

The interpretation of Johnnycab is interesting for having a robotic human as a person in the car, rather than an entirely autonomous vehicle.

That, I think, was already in the script, as an attempt to visualize this kind of automatic driving, this driving without touching the wheel. And we visualized it in a movie that has a certain kind of exaggeration; it's an action movie, but it's also lighthearted.

It plays to the medium of the movie to have a physical character you can interact with, rather than a faceless voice.

Yes. And especially in this kind of movie, where everything is hyperbolically treated. I mean, it's not *Blade Runner.* And that's because of Arnold [Schwarzenegger].

The original story of *Total Recall,* if you read the Philip Dick story, is about this guy who is like a secretary, an accountant. And absolutely not Arnold Schwarzenegger. When I got the script of *Total Recall,* I realized I got the last version, and there turned out to be thirty-nine other versions before. And they were all using the character from the Philip Dick story: this accountant who was not a hero, was not strong, who then turns out to be a secret agent.

Ultimately, this movie was made purely because Arnold Schwarzenegger wanted to do it. All other attempts to do it had failed. It was in the hands of Dino De Laurentiis, and Arnold had worked with Dino before. And he wanted to play the part, but Dino felt that he was not the accountant described in the short story and in the previous scripts.

So he refused Arnold to participate. Dino was looking at Richard Dreyfuss and others. And it was only because Dino's company bankrupted that Arnold could convince [*Total Recall* executive producer] Mario Kassar to buy the script out of the bankruptcy.

Arnold must have felt that this was really an interesting philosophical story. You don't think about Arnold so much as a philosopher, but I think he had a very good intuition that this was something very special, and he finally secured the rights through Mario. So Arnold was fundamental to the making of the movie.

When I got to the project, it was already known that Arnold would be the main actor, the protagonist. But the script didn't fit Arnold at all. So Gary Goldman, a new writer I brought in, and I decided that the script had to be adapted to Arnold. To this kind of superman, this supermuscular man. But still to make that possible with a script that from a philosophical point of view was very interesting. And we realized that with Arnold, we had to do it in a different way than the scripts before; we needed to do it in a lighter style. And so that's what we did.

In all three of your science-fiction movies, a lot of that lighthearted feel comes from the use of advertising—and in the case of *Starship Troopers*, propaganda—as a storytelling medium. Why did you opt for advertising as such a prominent storytelling tool?

The idea of integrating newsreels and commercials into the narrative came from the writers of *RoboCop,* Ed Neumeier and Michael Miner. When I came to *RoboCop,* I accentuated it because I felt that it was interesting to have a really disruptive metanarrative. You would have the main narrative, but that there would be a secondary narrative that would put heart into the main narrative. It's not like the police are looking at the television and saying, "Let's see what's on the

television." Rather, the main narrative, about RoboCop, is interrupted in a very harsh way by this secondary narrative in the newsreels and the commercials.

What I had in mind was the paintings of [abstract Dutch painter] Mondrian, with these blocks of color, these squares of red and blue. In some of his paintings, these are interrupted by very harsh vertical and horizontal black lines. This harshness between the color and the black lines, that was my inspiration for how to do *RoboCop*—that the television would not be connected into the scenes; it would just be cut in.

Composition with Red, Blue, and Yellow, by Piet Mondrian. Oil on canvas, 1930

Then when we were doing *Total Recall,* and notably when we were doing *Starship Troopers*—which had the same writer as *RoboCop*—we accentuated that. Working with the same writer, we came to the same conclusion, or at least the same pleasure, in doing that again, but in a more political way. That trick, or that kind of structure, was given to me by the writers of *RoboCop,* and then I used it whenever possible. I think it's still a lot of fun to do it.

***Starship Troopers* takes it a step further, into something that's actively propaganda. How did your experience as a documentary maker, particularly**

A laughing family plays a happy game of *NUKEM,* "another quality home game from Butler Brothers," in an ad from 1987's *RoboCop.* The ad is not only a funny pastiche of TV board game marketing; it also reinforces a more serious message: Militarized violence is *everywhere* in future Detroit.

working with the Dutch military, lead into that kind of propaganda filmmaking for *Starship Troopers*?

Certainly that did. When I was young and drafted in the Navy, which was obligatory at that time, I made propaganda: a very tough, almost James Bond–like documentary [*Het Korps Mariniers*] about the Dutch Marines. And I think that experience, from before I made narrative movies, is certainly visible in some scenes in *Starship Troopers.* So yes, that contributed to my style, to have made documentaries that were already propaganda in the first place.

In *Starship Troopers,* I also used a lot of elements and even images from Leni Riefenstahl's *Triumph of the Will* [1935]. That was made in 1934, in the party congress of the Nazis. Hitler had come into power in 1933, and Leni

Title card from *Het Korps Mariniers* (The Royal Dutch Marine Corps), directed by Paul Verhoeven in 1965

During a propaganda reel, members of *Starship Troopers'* mobile infantry are shown beneath slow dissolves of the organization's flag.

The same propaganda reel zooms in on infantrymen and infantrywomen within a huge crowd, each of whom states, "I'm doing my part!"

The Citizens Federation in *Starship Troopers* has a striking hooked-beak-eagle emblem on its official flag.

Though dead
In spirit march on with us yet

Verhoeven's shots are a clear adaptation of slow dissolves through the Nazi flag in *Triumph of the Will*.

We dam the North Sea!   We plant trees.
We build roads   We provide new soil for the farmer

In *Triumph of the Will*, at a rally for the German Reichsarbeitsdienst (Labor Service), the camera focuses in on individual laborers within a huge crowd, each of whom announces the effort he is making toward the rebuilding of Germany.

The Federation logo evokes the official emblem of the Nazi Party, the Parteiadler (Party eagle), which is seen multiple times in *Triumph of the Will*.

made *Triumph of the Will* in 1934, about the rallies in Nuremberg. Hitler appears out of the sky; it's very symbolic. Many images, many shots that you see in Leni's work, I used in the propaganda reels and newsreels in *Starship Troopers.*

I was trying to tell the audience—but it didn't work so well—that these people were living in a fascist utopia. And then, of course, the movie *itself* was accused of being fascist. But what I tried to do, which at the time was not very well understood, was to say, "These people—[actors] Casper Van Dien, Denise Richards, Dina Meyer—these heroes and heroines are basically, by the way, also fascist. They live in a fascist utopia."

And are seemingly unaware that they live in that kind of culture.

Sure, that was the fun. I hoped that the audience would be aware, but the actors and actresses . . . like happens

in a lot of fascist countries, the people go with it—certainly the German people went with it. And so these people that are the main characters in the movie are not aware of their position in a fascist utopia. They think this is the norm. As I said, I had the feeling that it was not very well understood at the time. Even the *Wall Street Journal* or *Washington Post* accused Ed Neumeier, the writer, and me of being neo-Nazis.

When the intent was to satirize that, rather than represent it?

And nobody saw that. They saw it later; they saw it maybe more after 9/11 than before.

The main difference with *Starship Troopers*, in terms of how it tells the story, is that both *RoboCop* and *Total Recall* have a protagonist who

is actively fighting against the evil federation or corporation.

Yes. And in *Starship Troopers* that's not the case. In *Starship Troopers,* we went more the other way—we were saying, "People who are sympathetic to you could be fascist." I don't have to compare it to what happened with the neo-Nazis a couple of weeks ago [in Charlottesville, Virginia, in August 2017], after which the president said, "Both sides were not nice guys," but it's a little bit in that direction, isn't it?

There's some pretty extreme violence in the news stories and footage in these movies. However, it doesn't seem to shock the characters; they seem to have become desensitized to that level of violence.

Sure, but that is also my vision of the world. I think we're living in a very cruel and violent world. We have the situation with North Korea right now, but the potential for violence has always existed; it was there in medieval times, and it was there in the time of Jesus. I think we are really a very violent species.

Sometimes you can call us humane, and there is certainly an aspect of humanity and generosity and compassion in the world. But there is also the other thing: The violence, and the destruction, and aggression is also dominantly there. So if I show violence, I always try to show it as it is, because I think that's the reality. These three movies, and perhaps even *Hollow Man* [2000], are, let's say, highly influenced by my . . . not-so-positive view on this universe.

I mean, the whole universe is violent. If you look at the sky, and you know that galaxies far away are being pulled together because of gravity, and what that would mean for life in these galaxies—I mean, that is a destruction on a degree that we have no idea of. It's like being in the middle of the sun.

So that is our universe. The creation of new planets and stars is certainly there, and human beings are probably one of the more interesting aspects of life, but life is all over the place. It's not like we are the grand exception. Neither does the sun go around the earth—it's the other way around. So I think we are just a very insignificant planet around a very insignificant sun. And I think that the universe is violent. And we are built into that, and we cannot escape.

Whenever there's a vision of a utopian future in these movies—from the proposed Delta City in *RoboCop* to the off-world colonies in *Total Recall*—the reality always seems to be just as corrupt as the world they are proposing an escape from.

Sure. And certainly what happened under the philosophical thinking of communism has been extremely violent.

Even the United States has often been extremely violent. As I said, there is no escape. The violence and aggression is so much a part of this universe that we are all participating in it and are all basically violent, you know. And are willing to be violent, and sometimes happy to be violent.

I mean, I made other movies, too. But by coincidence, perhaps, the movies that I made in the United States are more violent than the ones I made in Europe.

In *Total Recall*, and also in *RoboCop*, there seems to be a blurring of lines between corporations and governments, with OCP contracted to run the police force, and Federal Colonies running Mars.

And privatized presidents and all that stuff. Yes. A lot of that thinking came from the original writers; it was already in the script. When I came to *RoboCop*, coming from Europe and not knowing much about American politics, I'm certainly not the one that invented that. Although I understood it when I read it.

I think I was much more informed about the United States when I was doing *Starship Troopers* than when I was doing *RoboCop*. In *RoboCop*, I think all these political things were based on Reagan's development of Reaganomics, which I had only read about, living in Holland. And if you see the connections between government and politics, with Jones saying, "We *are* the military," it's the military-industrial complex that Eisenhower talked about at the end of his presidency. This connection of interwoven goals of government and military . . . that was not something that I brought to the movie; that was already there.

You mentioned earlier that the philosophical aspects of *Total Recall* were a big part of what appealed to both yourself and Arnold. The movie is unusual for keeping two opposing

RoboCop has a clear protagonist and antagonist . . .

. . . as does *Total Recall*. (Their antagonists are even played by the same actor.)

The good versus evil dynamic in *Starship Troopers* is far more ambiguous, with human characters universally positioned as "good guys," and the arachnid "other" as bad. When a news reporter observes that "some say the bugs were provoked by the intrusion of humans into their natural habitat," lead human Rico ignores the suggestion, refers to a recent attack against Earth, and cries, "I say, kill 'em all!"

yet believable interpretations alive throughout the entire story. How did you approach that story to keep the audience guessing?

What we tried, and I think to a large extent we succeeded, is to tell the audience that there is *no* position, that we don't take a position. We tell them two narratives. One narrative is that he's dreaming, and at the end his brains are basically blown away—he's brain-dead. Or he's the hero. Either he dreams that he's the savior of Mars or he's really the savior of Mars. And more so than the other thirty-nine drafts, we tried to push it as much as possible to the fact that there are *two* narratives, and we don't decide—we will not decide, we will not give information to the audience as to which is the right one. You could see it as a postmodern movie in that regard.

Rashomon, the Kurosawa movie from the fifties, has done this already, of course. It has four narratives, and they're all true. You don't know, at the end, which one is the right one because they all make sense. What we did in *Total Recall* was certainly inspired by that—I'm a big fan of Kurosawa, from when I was young, and *Rashomon* is a really great movie.

For me, the best and most interesting scene in the movie is when Arnold arrives at Mars, and he's there in the hotel, and Dr. Edgemar comes in and tells him, "Well, sorry—you think you are a secret agent, but you are still in the chair at Rekall and you are dreaming." Then he tells him the rest of the movie's plot, tells him what's going to happen in the next fifty, sixty minutes. Then Arnold kills Edgemar, and then it all really happens. But the audience seems to have forgotten that they knew the plot already.

Indeed, between the first visit to Rekall and the Dr. Edgemar scene, the movie's entire story is laid out by Rekall employees.

Yes, it's all laid out. And the audience doesn't remember. It's interesting, because they could say, "OK, now everything we heard is happening," but no, you forget it. Even if you are reminded halfway through the movie by Dr. Edgemar that what you're seeing could well be a dream, you don't believe it.

I think we pushed that very hard, although that scene with Edgemar was already in the original scripts from Ron Shusett and Dan O'Bannon. But we pushed that even further, into this ambiguity about what is true and what is

In a Martian hotel room, Dr. Edgemar spoils the plot of *Total Recall*'s closing act for both Arnie and the audience.

not, and not telling the audience what is true.

One thing that has not been observed by critics is that we tried very hard from the beginning of the movie to prepare the audience for this duplicity of reality. There are many aspects, many small visual things that we pointed out. I mean, the walls of the kitchen turning out to be artificial—it's the walls, and it's a television screen, or it's all just a beautiful landscape. Even just changing the color of your nails in a split second by touching them was a little instrument. We were continuously trying to tell the audience: "What you see might not be true. Or *both* things might be true."

I think we were very aware, Gary [Goldman] and I, that we should bring the audience, especially in the first fifteen to twenty minutes, into believing that things could be different than what they thought. Even Johnnycab can be put under this umbrella. We tried to find elements that would continuously say to the audience, "Well, you thought it was *this,* but it's *that.*" There are four, five, six, seven times that this happens in the first twenty to thirty minutes, all trying to have the audience prepare for the big ambiguity: Is it a dream or not?

There are several cases—the subway X-ray scanner, Johnnycab—where we see things once in their everyday

form and then we see them again in their alternate form. That was a very deliberate choice, to repeat them?

That was a deliberate . . . I wouldn't say "trick," but that was a deliberate decision to prepare the audience for the scene in the middle where Dr. Edgemar says, "Well, by the way, everything you have seen . . ."—and also to the audience— ". . . everything you have seen is not true." And then overruling that again by saying, "Well, it was true anyhow," or "perhaps not." I always felt that critics had not really seen these things that we brought in from the beginning to unbalance the audience and prepare them to accept the ambiguity of the narrative.

And to make it possible for both narratives to coexist—neither one is true; both are equally valid.

Or both are true *at the same time.* That's a very interesting thought, isn't it? That there are multiple realities. And it's not a new thought, but I think it was well done.

I've actually tried, several times, to work on a script where you would even have the two realities next to each other and that you would go from one to the other. Attempts have been made by others to do that, too, but I think we never found a good enough story to tell that.

It's interesting that people want to associate with the "hero" version of *Total Recall*, because they've gone along with it, they've suspended their disbelief in it—

And then they lose it, and then they get it again, and at the end they just don't know anymore.

The last line of the film is Rachel Ticotin saying, "Kiss me quick, before you wake up." Edgemar promises Arnold that at the end of the story he will lose his brain; he will be lobotomized. That's why the last shot of the movie, when they're standing there, Rachel and Arnold, we fade to white—not to black; we fade to white. At that time, his brain is taken away from him, he's lobotomized at that point. And [composer] Jerry Goldsmith uses this special theme that he has for "what's true and what's not true."

Or they kiss each other, and it's great, and he saved Mars, and they fall in love and have many beautiful children. Or he's lobotomized. That was the idea. I mean, it's not expressed very precisely, but it was certainly how we wanted to end it.

Have you ever been tempted to return to science fiction as a storytelling medium?

I would love to do that, but I have not been able to find a script or book or short story that is as interesting as the three movies that we just discussed. For me to do it again, it has to be something new, something that I have not done. Something that has not been done by anybody. So how to find that . . . It might be that our idea of science fiction, that the ideas of the last twenty, thirty years are not so interesting to me. I would love to do something that is really different, in a philosophical way—like *Total Recall* is interesting because of the philosophy. And even *Starship Troopers*, because of the politics.

My doing science fiction in the United States has always been like a shield of protection, because I grew up in

As *Total Recall* ends, Quaid and Melina kiss . . .

. . . as the movie fades to white . . .

. . . leaving the viewer uncertain about how Quaid's story really ends. The reality, according to Verhoeven, is that both versions of Quaid's story are true simultaneously.

Europe. And Europeans are different from Americans, but in science fiction nobody can check me out, you know. They cannot see really that I am not American, that I cannot feel completely American, that I feel a bit more European. In science fiction, that's allowed. So I think me doing science fiction was the way to go for a European director that in general didn't know anything about science fiction. It was my way, I think, to survive here.

AUTO's view of EVE combines a Terminator red-hued HUD with a HAL 9000
fish-eye lens, informing well-versed sci-fi fans that this robot is not to be trusted.

WALL·E is something of a departure from our previous five films. Every single frame of this computer-animated movie, made by the best in the business, has been painstakingly constructed by hand entirely from zeroes and ones. Nothing is accidentally visible in the back of the shot here, unless someone at Pixar *deliberately* left it in the shot as a sneaky visual gag.

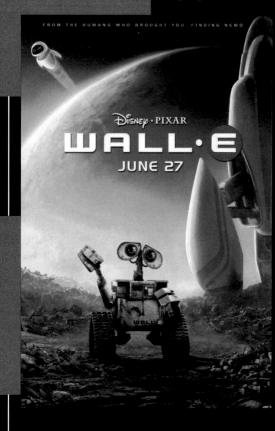

From its opening study of a trash-filled Earth to the futuristic *Axiom* and back again, *WALL·E* is a finely crafted balance between consumerist dystopia and space-race optimism. Our study therefore must go deeper than before—into the uniquely robotic future of a remarkably human film, as seen through the eyes of its eponymous hero, WALL·E.

WALL·E's front plate, clearly showing his interpunct

BEFORE WE GET STARTED, however, there is an important detail we must clear up. Our hero's name is not, as you might think, WALL-E. Moreover, it *definitely* isn't WALL•E. His name is WALL·E, and that dot is an *interpunct,* not a hyphen or a bullet.

An interpunct is, of course, a vertically centered dot originally used to separate words in Latin and ancient Greek. (Spaces weren't invented until several centuries later.) The interpunct is still in use today—it's the official decimal point in British currency (£9·99) and is used to represent the dot product of two vectors in mathematics (x · y). Most relevantly, it's used in Japanese to separate titles, names, and positions, as in "課長補佐 · 鈴木" (Assistant Section Head · Suzuki). It is therefore entirely appropriate as the separator in WALL·E, which is short for Waste Allocation Load Lifter · Earth Class.

[handwritten margin note: also used in some N Am First Nations' languages, like]

The bold extended typeface seen on WALL·E's front plate is Gunship, designed by Dan Zadorozny, one of the unsung heroes of modern sci-fi type design. Dan is an amateur type designer from Texas whose Iconian Fonts website (iconian.com) features more than six hundred free hand-crafted typefaces, many of which have been used by sci-fi movies, TV shows, and book designers.

In addition to WALL·E's front plate, Gunship is seen on Earth and aboard the *Axiom,* the flagship spacecraft of megacorporation Buy n Large (BnL, for short), most notably for robot-facing wall and door typography. Its upper- and lowercase variants include different combinations of cutouts and curve orientations, giving designers flexibility when crafting robot signage. (Strictly speaking, this means that our hero's name, correctly capitalized, is "waLL·e," with the interpunct as a further customization—Gunship's own interpunct is rectangular.)

Gunship (uppercase characters)

ABCDEFGHIJKLMNOPQRSTUVWXYZ

Gunship (lowercase characters)

ABCDEFGHIJKLMNOPQRSTUVWXYZ

The movie begins with an insight into WALL·E's typical workday, which is spent building gigantic piles of trash by compacting waste into neat, stackable cubes. After his hard day's crushing, we follow him on his journey home, learning some useful exposition along the way. This includes a bank of electronic ads for BnL, promoting everything from liquid air to quadruple-patty burgers. Common throughout these ads is an insistence on immediate consumption—"DRINK NOW," "HUNGRY NOW," "RUN NOW," "CONSUME." And if consuming a product once isn't enough, you can repeat the experience a second time—the signage includes ads for "100% Reused Food" and "Regurgi-Shake: Twice the Flavor."

We've seen how corporate mergers, such as *Alien*'s Weylan Yutani and *Blade Runner*'s Shimata-Dominguez, are an inevitability in sci-fi futures. *WALL·E*'s Buy n Large is similar, except that this company was formed by a merger between a frozen yogurt manufacturer (Buy Yogurt) and a maker of suits for the larger gentleman (Large Industries). Clearly a marriage made in heaven, this corporate combination led to a rapid expansion, culminating with Buy n Large owning every company and government in the world.

The Buy n Large logo is an over-italicized customization of Futura Extra Bold Oblique. (This theory is borne out by a superdistinctive capital *G* in the BUY N LARGE BANK logotype that WALL·E passes early in the movie.) If the red-and-blue logo feels familiar, it shouldn't be a surprise—it's because BnL uses the exact same typeface and color scheme as real-world retail giant Costco Wholesale Corporation.

Futura Pro Extra Bold Oblique, released by Berthold. Original Futura design by Paul Renner

ABCDEFGHIJKLMNOPQRSTUVWXYZ

BELOW: The Costco Wholesale Corporation logo, in Futura Extra Bold Oblique

RIGHT: "BUY N LARGE BANK" signage, set in Futura Extra Bold Oblique, showing its distinctive capital *G*

There's another curious BnL subsidiary to be found among the city's electronic ads, on a beaten-up billboard advertising "Eggman Movers (Creating More Space)." This company is an Easter-egg reference to *WALL·E* production designer Ralph "Eggman" Eggleston, and it shares the name of the moving company from 1995's *Toy Story,* for which Ralph was art director.

LEFT: Eggman Movers, from 2008's *WALL·E*

RIGHT: Eggman Movers, from 1995's *Toy Story*

THE PRESENCE of a Buy n Large–branded bank means Buy n Large–branded banknotes, which are unusual for being strewn across the floor of the deserted city. If you look closely at the notes, you'll see that some of them have "10^6" in the corner and are marked "ten million dollars." Others look to be marked "99^6," suggesting that Buy n Large stores continued the classic $9.99 pricing trick even after adding six zeroes to the end of everything. (Indeed, it says much about the Buy n Large approach to consumerism that it prints notes with the 99s already included, to avoid customers having to receive any change.)

$10 million and $99 million bills lie abandoned on the ground near a Buy n Large Bank.

We discover later in the movie that the *Axiom* left Earth in the year 2105. This suggests that in the preceding years of overconsumption there was a period of severe hyperinflation, making a $10 million note a necessity. This is not without historical precedent—Earth's most extreme example of hyperinflation occurred in Zimbabwe in November 2008, just a few months after *WALL·E*'s release, when the inflation rate for the Zimbabwe dollar reached a staggering 79,600,000,000 percent per month. At this point, a single US dollar was equivalent to 2,621,984,228 Zimbabwe dollars. The largest-denomination note printed during this time was the $100 trillion note, which makes Buy n Large's $10 million bill seem like small change by comparison.

A $100 trillion bill from the Reserve Bank of Zimbabwe, showing some impressively pointy Futura

WALL·E leaves the bank behind and continues his journey via the disused tracks of the BnL Transit monorail system. In the absence of working trains, these concrete tracks provide a convenient route through the middle of the deserted city.

Despite their association with aspirational futures, monorails have been failing to become a global mass-transit system for almost two hundred years. The first passenger monorail opened in 1825 in Cheshunt, England, primarily to transport bricks, though it was also utilized for transporting people, mostly for novelty purposes. Unlike the top-of-rail system seen in *WALL·E*, Cheshunt's monorail consisted of carriages suspended beneath an overhead track and was powered by a single horse.

The Cheshunt style of monorail—with suspended carriages hanging beneath a single rail— was also adopted by the Wuppertal Schwebebahn, which began operation along the Wupper River in Cologne, Germany, in 1901. The Wuppertal's suspended system is still in operation today, carrying more than sixty-five thousand passengers on an average weekday.

LEFT: A Wuppertal Schwebebahn monorail train arrives at the Werther Brücke station in Cologne, 1913.

RIGHT: WALL·E climbs an escalator to a BnL Transit monorail station.

The monorail seen in *WALL·E* is of the style popularized by Swedish entrepreneur Axel Wenner-Gren, whose prototype ALWEG (Axel Lennart Wenner-Gren) monorail system came to the attention of Walt Disney after a family visit to Wuppertal gave him monorail fever. Disney saw the potential for a monorail attraction at his Disneyland theme park in California, and the Disneyland-ALWEG Monorail System opened in June 1959. The system remains in operation today (under the name Disneyland Monorail), and there are similar attractions at Disneyland Tokyo and Walt Disney World in Florida. In total, Disney monorails have transported more than one billion passengers into an aspirational transportational future.

It's not entirely clear what US city WALL·E lives in, but the presence of a monorail network certainly positions it as a location that was once optimistic about the future. This mid-century futurism is borne out by other architectural features of the city, most notably a curved building seen among the billboards encountered earlier. This building is strongly reminiscent of the Space Needle observation tower in Seattle, Washington, which was built for the city's 1962 World's Fair, together with an ALWEG monorail system that is still in operation today.

MIDDLE: Seattle's ALWEG monorail passing in front of the city's Space Needle, 2008. Both were built for Seattle's 1962 World's Fair.

RIGHT: The Disneyland-ALWEG Monorail System at Tomorrowland station, 1963

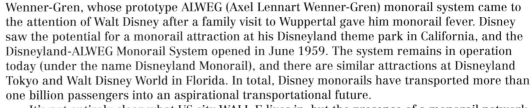

Near the monorail, WALL·E passes a promotional poster for himself, with the caption "Working to dig you out!" This poster has definite communist propaganda undertones, showing a stylized army of WALL·Es working together to build a brighter future. The implication of this design choice—that communist values are the solution to decades of rampant consumerism—is a pretty bold political statement for what is only the fourth minute of the movie.

Buy n Large poster for WALL·E robots, with the caption "Working to dig you out!"

The future to which these WALL·Es aspire is apparently just above and behind the viewer— a common trope for communist propaganda, where the aspirational group gaze is almost always in this direction. Indeed, it's *such* a common trope that it became the primary styling of the promotional poster for 2014's banned comedy movie *The Interview*, in which two Americans travel to North Korea to interview the country's leader, Kim Jong-un. (The WALL·E poster's bottom-edge caption, punctuated by an exclamation mark, is a common trope in North Korean propaganda posters.)

This aspirational style is an example of socialist realist design, the officially sanctioned visual aesthetic of the Soviet Union, which positioned broad-shouldered, purposeful workers as the true heroes of the age. As a robot who is literally a rectangle, there is surely no worker more broad-shouldered and purposeful than our movie's eponymous hero, WALL·E.

TOP LEFT: Chinese communist propaganda poster with the caption "To go on a thousand 'li' march to temper a red heart." A "li" is about 500 meters, so a thousand-li march is about 310 miles.

TOP RIGHT: Soviet communist propaganda poster, with the caption "Let's raise a generation utterly devoted to the cause of communism!" Designed by Victor Ivanov, 1947

BOTTOM LEFT: North Korean propaganda poster, with the caption "The party calls! To important construction!"

BOTTOM RIGHT: Chinese communist propaganda poster, with the caption "Turn philosophy into a sharp weapon in the hands of the masses."

BELOW: Promotional poster for *The Interview*, with the Korean-language caption "Don't believe these American bastards!"

WALL·E's self-promotional poster is also a fine example of Handel Gothic, one of the movie's supporting typefaces. Originally designed in 1965 by Donald J. Handel, the font has become a mainstay of design futurism. (Indeed, it is quite possibly the originator of our rule 2 for futuristic type: Make straight things curved.) My favorite use of the typeface in WALL·E occurs later in the movie, when we see the distinctly curved *E* of some Handel Gothic . . . on a handle. (I refuse to believe this is anything but a deliberate typographic joke.)

Handel Gothic Com Bold, from Linotype. Handel Gothic was originally designed in 1965 by Donald J. Handel for FotoStar.

ABCDEFGHIJKLMNOPQRSTUVWXYZ

"Handle" Gothic

Original logo for the EPCOT Center theme park at Walt Disney World, Florida

Handel Gothic enjoyed a particular resurgence when the type family was expanded in the 1980s, and will be immediately familiar to anyone who visited EPCOT Center at Walt Disney World in Florida, which opened in 1982. (Later in this chapter, we'll look in detail at the theme park, which is now named simply Epcot.) The original EPCOT Center logo was Handel Gothic all the way, making particularly good use of a lowercase *n* in "Center" to bring some extra curviness and choosing a font variant with a curved leg in its *R* for consistency. (It also added letter joining and slicing for good futuristic measure.) Handel Gothic will also be familiar to *Star Trek* fans, from its appearance in the credits for both *Star Trek: Deep Space Nine* (1993–99) and *Star Trek: Voyager* (1995–2001).

LEFT: Opening credits from the *Star Trek: Deep Space Nine* episode "Emissary," showing some shiny metallic Handel Gothic (in this case, with a straight-legged *R*)

RIGHT: Opening credits from the *Star Trek: Voyager* episode "Unimatrix Zero: Part II," showing Handel Gothic with a similarly straight-legged *R*

BELOW: Opening credits to 1977's *Close Encounters of the Third Kind*

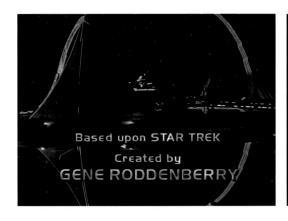

The movie that made Handel Gothic synonymous with sci-fi, however, was almost certainly Steven Spielberg's *Close Encounters of the Third Kind,* released in 1977. *Close Encounters* used the typeface for its theatrical poster and for its opening credits, with the very words "Close Encounters" offering not one but three opportunities to recognize Handel Gothic's trademark *E*.

But back to WALL·E's journey. Toward the end of his trek home, he passes many more WALL·E units, all of them rusted and dead. The sole remaining WALL·E happily cannibalizes a Caterpillar track from a nearby broken unit to replace his own damaged part and motors onward with the new track in place.

It's an easy detail to miss, but WALL·E's home is a broken-down "BnL WALL·E Transport" vehicle, which may once have housed all the dead units he just passed. When he reverses himself into a WALL·E-size bin in a rotatable storage rack a few minutes later and rocks himself to sleep, his loneliness as the last robot on Earth is made all the more acute by the uninhabited bins around him, now filled with ordered trash.

Before he climbs into bed, WALL·E retrieves his favorite VHS cassette from a nearby toaster and pops it into a VCR. It turns out this is a beaten-up copy of *Hello, Dolly!*—1969's awkwardly punctuated Jerry Herman musical. Delightfully, the typography of this cassette is taken directly from the movie's 1991 VHS release, though the identity of its non-futuristic title font—half Century Schoolbook, half Benguiat Caslon—has, sadly, eluded my detective skills.

WALL·E watches his *Hello, Dolly!* cassette via a small, portable device that looks almost exactly like an Apple iPod Video. I say "almost," because the real-world iPod Video had a smaller click wheel than the one seen in *WALL·E,* had white labels on its buttons, and did not support external playback from a VHS cassette player. Nonetheless, this iPod is just one example of many in WALL·E's home that evoke nostalgia for gadgets past, reinforcing that WALL·E himself is the discarded, unwanted technology that humanity left behind.

Barbra Streisand • Walter Matthau
Michael Crawford

TOP: WALL·E's much-watched copy of *Hello, Dolly!*

ABOVE: The front cover of 1991's US VHS release of *Hello, Dolly!*

LEFT: WALL·E watches a movie on his iPod's small screen through a rectangular Fresnel lens.

BELOW LEFT: In 1985's *Brazil,* Ministry of Information employees watch movies on a small CRT screen through a rectangular Fresnel lens.

BELOW: WALL·E's iPod, showing *Hello, Dolly!* on its LCD color screen

To work around the tiny scale of his iPod's screen, WALL·E uses a plastic Fresnel lens as a magnifying device to enlarge the image to several times its original size. In doing so, he follows a trend started in Terry Gilliam's similarly dystopian *Brazil,* in which employees at the Ministry of Information Retrieval huddle around tiny CRT screens to watch westerns through Fresnel lenses when their boss isn't looking.

WALL·E awakes from robotic sleep on day two of the movie, low on power and dynamism. The fact that his head is a big pair of binoculars gives a great opportunity for a visual gag, as we see him literally bleary-eyed before activating the zoom lock on first his left eye, then his right, to reveal an eye-test chart in the opposing rack.

WALL·E's binocular form is mimicked in the shape of his heads-up display (or HUD), which has the classic "two circles" shape used in many movies to indicate that we are looking from a character's viewpoint through a pair of binoculars. This HUD raises an interesting question, however. *Why* does WALL·E have a heads-up display, with information overlaid on a video stream? A heads-up display really makes sense only if you are a human who has eyes; for a robot, any video input is combined with additional metadata from environmental sensors (such as direction, zoom, and power) and fed directly into the robot's processor. Overlaying environmental information on a video stream implies that the robot has cameras that look at the world, and then *more* cameras that look at the augmented output of those cameras, which doesn't make sense at all.

The answer, of course, is that WALL·E has a HUD because movie robots have HUDs, and movie robots have HUDs because they enable the viewer to visualize what the robots are thinking, even if it makes zero sense in technical reality. This trope began in 1973's *Westworld,* whose final act shows us the world from the vantage point of Yul Brynner's gun-slinging robot. Although Brynner's HUD is not augmented with data, it is nonetheless the first use of computer-generated imagery in a feature film. Director Michael Crichton cuts several times from a real-world scene to the robot's pixelated version of the same, including a thermal image when Brynner chases his prey in the movie's final act.

There is one further question raised by WALL·E's binocular HUD. How does his directional compass—seen at the top center of his HUD—continue to work when he is aboard the *Axiom*? Lots of planets may have a north, but the same is not true of spacecraft—north, south, east, and west make sense only when you're on the surface of a sphere.

From his bleary beginnings . . .

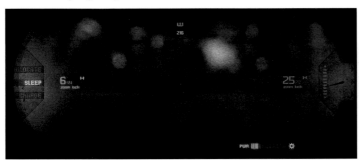

A canyon in *Westworld* . . .

. . . WALL·E focuses his binoculars on an eye chart in the distance.

. . . and Yul Brynner's pixelated view of the same

Westworld's "robot viewpoint" trope was codified by 1984's *The Terminator* and 1987's *RoboCop,* both of which augmented their HUDs with additional data and text. Following these two movies, a heads-up display pretty much became the de facto expectation for any on-screen robot whose motives need to be understood.

A HUD screen from the T-800 Terminator, in 1984's *The Terminator.* Here, the T-800 is determining an appropriate auditory response to a question from its apartment's superintendent.

A HUD screen from the OCP Crime Prevention Unit 001, in 1987's *RoboCop.* Here, RoboCop's visual tracking system is being put through its paces by detecting the location of a pen. (Note that RoboCop's HUD has highly visible scan lines, to make sure we know we are watching a live video stream in a movie.)

Pixar's robot HUDs tend to include the shape of the robot's eye(s) within the heads-up display, to help us associate the HUD with the character it represents. *The Incredibles'* Omni-droid predates WALL·E's binoculars in this regard. Other *WALL·E* robots—M-O, SECUR-T, and EVE—also follow suit.

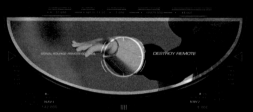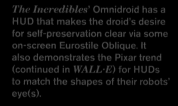

The Incredibles' Omnidroid has a HUD that makes the droid's desire for self-preservation clear via some on-screen Eurostile Oblique. It also demonstrates the Pixar trend (continued in *WALL·E*) for HUDs to match the shapes of their robots' eye(s).

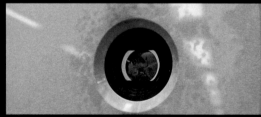

The SECUR-T sentry robot's eye in *WALL·E* is explicitly a camera, as reinforced by a SLR (single-lens reflex)-camera-like HUD when taking a CAUTION photo of WALL·E's rogue robots.

EVE's curved, lined HUD mirrors the curved, lined styling of her eyes and face.

M-O's wide, flat eye-panel shape is mirrored in his wide, flat on-screen HUD display. This shape, of course, requires his HUD to use a certain wide, flat typeface for its informative text.

Pixar's neatest variation on the robot HUD trope, however, occurs all the way back in 1999's *Toy Story 2*, where a plastic toy's marketing gimmick (plus some clever camera framing) enables us to literally see through the eyes of the movie's robotic bad guy.

As Buzz Lightyear runs away from his archenemy, Zurg, in 1999's *Toy Story 2*, a camera movie brilliantly subverts the robot HUD trope . . .

. . . turning a plastic toy's "LOOK HERE" scope . . .

. . . into the bad guy's evil robot HUD . . .

. . . complete with ZURG VISION logo in Eurostile Bold Oblique.

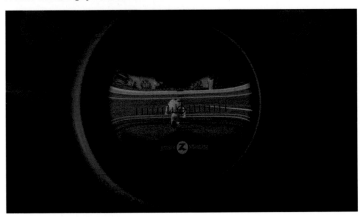

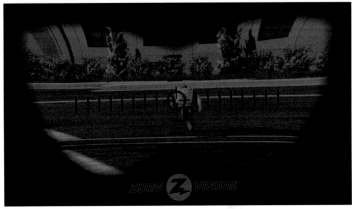

BELOW: Side view of an iMac G4, released in 2002, with an EVE-head-like base

BELOW RIGHT: An Apple Macintosh 128k, released in 1984, with a WALL·E-like beige body

DAY TWO (and act two) of *WALL·E* see a Buy n Large scout ship arrive on Earth, disrupting WALL·E's routine. Most importantly, it introduces us to EVE, who is everything WALL·E is not. EVE's shiny white design is technologically advanced; she's the curvy iMac G4 to WALL·E's boxy Mac 128K. Her design evokes sleek Apple products of the 2000s, with her head, in particular, highly reminiscent of a 2002 iMac G4's base. Even her reboot sound is a futuristic take on Apple's famous startup chime, whereas WALL·E's post-charge chime is the version Apple introduced in 1998 and removed altogether in 2016.

EVE's evocation of Apple product design is not entirely coincidental. In a 2008 interview with *Fortune* magazine, director Andrew Stanton stated: "I wanted EVE to be high-end technology—no expense spared—and I wanted it to be seamless and for the technology to be sort of hidden and subcutaneous. The more I started describing it, the more I realized I was pretty much describing the Apple playbook for design." This led to a 2005 call to Steve Jobs—at that time, both owner of Pixar and CEO of Apple—which in turn led to Apple design head Jony Ive spending a day at the Pixar headquarters in Emeryville, consulting on the EVE prototype. (It is surely entirely coincidental that EVE's wireless arms and hands are reminiscent of Apple's wireless Magic Mouse, released the year after *WALL·E*.)

DURING A DUST STORM, WALL·E takes EVE back to the safety of his home, where he presents her with a small multicolored cube. In the three seconds the camera pans away for WALL·E to retrieve *Hello, Dolly!,* EVE solves the Rubik's Cube and returns it to her astonished host. EVE's cube-solving time would be impressive for a human; the current world record is 4.69 seconds, set by fifteen-year-old Patrick Ponce in Middletown, Virginia, in September 2017. Sadly, because of the camera pan, we'll never know if EVE broke the world record for a robot, which currently stands at a mind-boggling 0.637 seconds. This record was set in November 2016 by Sub1 Reloaded, a cube-solving robot built by German engineer Albert Beer. Six high-performance stepper motors turned the cube twenty-one times to complete the task, averaging just 0.03 seconds per rotation.

Spare a thought, then, for poor WALL·E. His surprise at EVE's accomplishment is understandable—he lacks color vision and has only three digits on each hand, which means that Rubik's Cubes are really not his specialty. (There's a reason *Guinness* doesn't have a "fastest dog" Rubik's Cube category.)

One other point of note: This scene is the only time the color green appears in *WALL·E* in a scene unrelated to the plant. While this breaks the movie's careful color scripting, it's worth it for a good gag.

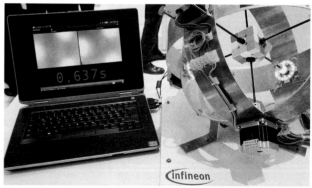

ALL SEEMS TO BE going well with WALL·E and EVE's introductions, until they are rudely interrupted by EVE's spotting a plant that WALL·E has excavated from the trash. She subsumes the plant, as per her "directive," and enters hibernation mode. WALL·E's attempts to wake her invariably end in comedic pain, though one of them does reveal EVE's serial number, 051682, set in Handel Gothic. (I can't help but wonder whether someone in Pixar's art department was born on May 16, 1982.)

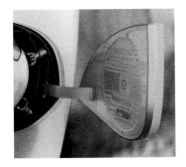

EVE's serial number, seen on the inside of the door above, is 051682.

WALL·E gives up on reviving EVE and disconsolately returns to his trash-crushing routine. Shortly afterward, the *Axiom*'s scout ship returns to Earth and collects EVE to take her home. Desperate not to lose his new friend, WALL·E hitches a ride on the outside of the scout, causing him grief when the ship blasts through Earth's surrounding satellite trash. As the satellites fall away, we see that WALL·E has a Soviet-era *Sputnik 1* satellite on his head. This is impressive, especially given that *Sputnik 1*—the first man-made object to orbit Earth—burned up on reentry to Earth's atmosphere in 1958.

We see *Sputnik 1* again later in the movie, as a model in Captain McCrea's display cabinet. This model is accompanied by a NASA space shuttle launch/entry helmet, as worn by space shuttle astronauts between 1982 and 1986 during launch and return from space.

This "retro space tech" theme can also be seen on Earth during EVE's scan for plant life. After scanning a *Toy Story* Pizza Planet truck and a portable lavatory, EVE checks a rusting *Apollo* command module before slamming the door shut in disgust at its absence of plant-based life.

Showing recent space technology as trash or as museum pieces positions our personal experiences of space as archaic and quaint in comparison to the *Axiom*'s futuristic styling. This further reinforces WALL·E's own obsolescence as a discarded piece of technology and sets us up neatly for a transition to the shiny futurism of the *Axiom*.

TOP LEFT: A replica of the *Sputnik 1* satellite, showing its 58cm-diameter aluminum sphere and four spindly antennas

TOP RIGHT: As the *Axiom* scout ship breaks through Earth's satellites WALL·E is briefly left with *Sputnik 1* on his head.

MIDDLE LEFT: Payload specialist Sharon Christa McAuliffe is briefed on the space shuttle's launch/entry helmet during training for the January 1986 launch of flight STS-51L.

MIDDLE RIGHT: A space shuttle launch/entry helmet and a Sputnik model in Captain McCrea's display case

BOTTOM LEFT: The *Apollo 14* command module, nicknamed "Kitty Hawk," at the Kennedy Space Center in Florida

BOTTOM RIGHT: A BnL-branded *Apollo*-style command module in a pile of trash on Earth

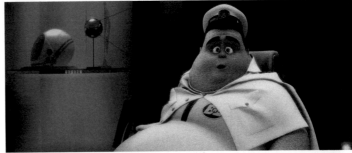

The *Axiom* paints a vision of the future where every menial task, no matter how small, has a dedicated robot created expressly for the purpose. Like *2001: A Space Odyssey*'s HAL and *Alien*'s MU/TH/UR, all these robots have cute acronyms to make them human-friendly.

SAUT-A (chefbot)

BUF-4 (bufferbot) and SPR-A (spraybot) in action cleaning EVE

HAN-S (massagebot) and PR-T (beauticianbot)

SR-V (tennisbot)

BIRD-E (golfbot)

SECUR-T (stewardbot)

BURN-E (maintenancebot)

GO-4 (gopherbot)

VN-GO (painterbot)

NAN-E (nannybot)

Of particular note is VN-GO, the painterbot, whose acronym perpetuates a common yet incorrect pronunciation of Dutch painter Vincent van Gogh's surname. (According to the BBC Pronunciation Unit, it is "van Gokh," with the *kh* pronounced like the *ch* in the Scottish word *loch*.)

EVE's acronym, sadly, is even worse. Her denomination as Extraterrestrial Vegetation Evaluator could not be more inaccurate, given that her entire reason for existing is to evaluate vegetation *on* the planet Terra (as Earth is known in Latin). Presumably, her moniker was chosen for cuteness rather than linguistic accuracy—after all, this movie is about WALL·E and EVE, not WALL·E and TVE.

Also of note is TYP-E, a typingbot who is designed solely to press keys when someone approaches the elevator shaft to the captain's quarters. TYP-E provides an excuse for one of the movie's best visual gags—as a robot, he has a keyboard made entirely, of course, from ones and zeroes.

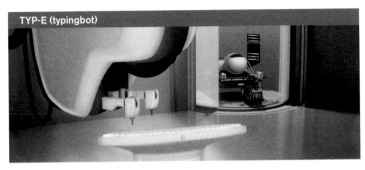

TYP-E (typingbot)

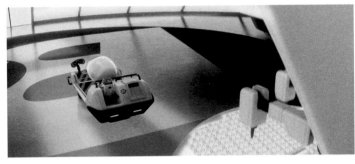

In a brief over-the-shoulder shot, we see that TYP-E's keyboard is made entirely from keys labeled *1* and *0*.

M-O's cleaning colleagues (VAQ-M, SPR-A, and BUF-4) may bring back memories for fans of 1997's *The Fifth Element*. In Luc Besson's over-the-top vision of the future, evil industrialist Zorg demonstrates his own array of task-specific robots by dropping a glass tumbler on the floor to trigger their "lovely ballet." As two sentrybots stand guard, a sweeperbot, a spraybot, and a bufferbot clean up his mess before returning to a nearby storage station.

The Fifth Element preempts WALL·E's cleaning robots with its own sweeperbot . . .

. . . and spraybot . . .

. . . and bufferbot.

The *Axiom*'s robots travel around the ship via their own dedicated corridors, separate from the craft's passenger areas. These passenger areas are split into three classes—economy, coach, and elite—each of which has a distinct architectural style. The classes themselves do not play a functional role in the movie's plot, but one has to wonder what they mean for the *Axiom*'s society. Are children born into the classes their ancestors originally purchased, as if into some kind of futuristic caste system? Would the *Axiom* have its own *Titanic* moment if a passenger from economy bumped hover chairs with someone from elite? One thing's certain: The styling of each class is extremely useful for helping viewers orient themselves within the ship's overall structure as the action moves back and forth along its length.

Our introduction to the passenger area starts with the economy deck (below), which is compact, angular, and concrete in texture and color. Its palette is deliberately sparse, rarely moving outside the Buy n Large blue, red, and white, and making extensive use of the corporation's Futura Extra Bold Oblique. The deck's design is highly reminiscent of the interior of the Contemporary Tower at Walt Disney World Contemporary Resort, whose A-frame concrete-and-steel structure was so futuristic when it opened in 1971 that it even had a monorail running through the middle. (As anyone who has stayed at the Contemporary can attest, however, its rates can hardly be considered "economy.")

The coach deck (below right), unlike the economy deck, is curved, eclectic, and spacious, with brightly colored holo-ads scattered everywhere. It mimics Las Vegas's Strip in gaudiness and style, with artificial neon colors used extensively and every sign encouraging *Axiom* passengers to spend more money. (How the ship's financial economy continues to function after a seven-hundred-year flight continues to remain a mystery.)

The ceiling of the coach deck is a gigantic animated screen that can switch between day and night, complete with a BnL-branded sun or moon. The ceiling's relationship to *actual* time is somewhat tenuous, as we see when Captain McCrea winds the sky back from 12:30 P.M. to 9:30 A.M. in order to make his morning announcements. In this regard, the ceiling is essentially an amalgam of two Las Vegas landmarks: the painted cloud ceilings of the Forum indoor arcade at Caesar's Palace, whose lighting ebbs and changes without ever making it nighttime enough for you to want to stop buying things, and the four-block-long overhead screen of the Fremont Street Experience—the world's largest video screen—whose 12.5 million LEDs illuminate Vegas partygoers every night. The result is an entirely fake sky for the *Axiom*'s population, allowing finely tuned control over their artificial environment, and our most extreme example yet of the "virtual outdoors" trope previously seen in *Total Recall*.

BELOW: Interior of the Contemporary Tower at Walt Disney World Contemporary Resort, as it looked in 2011. The blue raised platform on the right is a monorail station, with a green-line monorail currently boarding.

BOTTOM AND OPPOSITE BOTTOM: The economy deck, as seen by WALL·E shortly after his arrival on the *Axiom*. Apart from a few hints of yellow, it follows the BnL corporate color scheme exclusively, with plenty of Futura Extra Bold Oblique.

TOP RIGHT: The painted, vaulted ceiling of the Forum Shops arcade at Caesar's Palace, Las Vegas

CENTER RIGHT: The coach deck's sky dome ceiling, transitioning from midday to early morning

BELOW LEFT: The four-block-long LED ceiling of the Fremont Street Experience, Las Vegas

BELOW RIGHT: A section of the Las Vegas Strip at night, showing a similar palette of oversaturated cyan, purple, pink, and yellow hues, combined with omnipresent ads encouraging consumption

The coach deck leads to the elite deck, whose styling resembles that of a high-class lido or spa. Despite their very different palettes, the coach and elite decks share a curved, futuristic environmental styling that unifies their overall architecture. According to production designer Ralph Eggleston, the architecture of this shared area is inspired by the work of architect Santiago Calatrava, whose signature curved supports and arches can be seen throughout both decks' central concourse.

TOP: The coach deck's central plaza, with arched supports for its passenger shades

MIDDLE: Close-up of the arched supports in the central coach-deck plaza

BOTTOM: An arched glass half-dome in the coach deck's food court

LEFT: Transitional area between the coach and elite decks, showing arched supports around the central transportation line

TOP RIGHT: The elite deck, with its clean, spa-like lido styling

BOTTOM RIGHT: Close-up of the base of the captain's control tower, showing its arched, glass-fronted entrance

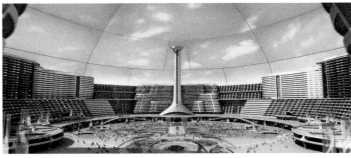

LEFT: Café Calatrava, Milwaukee Art Museum, Wisconsin. Designed by Santiago Calatrava, completed in 2001

RIGHT: Concourse and roof supports, Lyon–Saint-Exupéry Airport Railway Station, Colombier-Saugnieu, France. Designed by Santiago Calatrava, completed in 1994

BOTTOM LEFT: Arched wall supports, Palau de les Arts Reina Sofia, Valencia, Spain. Designed by Santiago Calatrava, completed in 2006

MIDDLE RIGHT: Exterior detail, Milwaukee Art Museum, Wisconsin. Designed by Santiago Calatrava, completed in 2001

BOTTOM RIGHT: Arched exterior of the Adán Martín Auditorio de Tenerife, Santa Cruz de Tenerife. Designed by Santiago Calatrava, completed in 2003

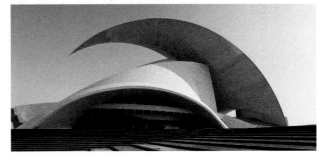

The other main influence for the *Axiom*'s architecture is the design of the Tomorrowland area of Disneyland, in California. According to production designer Ralph Eggleston, during the movie's production *WALL·E*'s design team visited an exhibition of Tomorrowland concept art and took inspiration from the designs therein.

Perhaps the most obvious of these influences is the presence of a PeopleMover transportation system running through the middle of the club and elite decks, in a style very similar to the PeopleMover at Tomorrowland. The evolution of Disney's PeopleMover concept began with the 1964–65 New York World's Fair, for which the Ford Motor Company asked Disney to design an attraction to compete with General Motors' *Futurama II* exhibit. The resulting Magic Skyway gave fairgoers an opportunity to ride in a driverless Ford convertible—including the just-launched Ford Mustang—through a diorama that transported them from prehistoric times to a futuristic space city.

Following its success at the World's Fair, the traction system behind Magic Skyway was adapted into a new feature for Tomorrowland's 1967 relaunch. The new attraction, known as the WEDway PeopleMover, enabled Walter Elias Disney to follow Axel Lennart Wenner-Gren (of ALWEG monorail fame) in naming a futuristic transportation mechanism with his initials. It also provided an ideal inspiration for the *Axiom*'s central transport system.

ABOVE: Visitors in Ford convertible vehicles enter the Magic Skyway ride at the 1964–65 New York World's Fair

BELOW: The club deck's circular PeopleMover loading area

BOTTOM: Raised PeopleMover tracks running along the length of the club deck

LEFT: Disneyland's WEDway PeopleMover in 1968, viewed from a car near the Tomorrowland entrance, looking toward the PeopleMover's circular loading area beneath the Rocket Jets attraction

RIGHT: Disneyland's WEDway PeopleMover in 1968, viewed from a car in the main loading area, looking back toward Tomorrowland's entrance

The *Axiom*'s PeopleMover has much in common with its WEDway counterpart. Both are focused on a main circular loading area in the heart of a central plaza, with a long, straight stretch of track extending away from the loading deck. Both give passengers a tantalizing view of surrounding attractions as they are transported from one area to another. Indeed, I am sure Walt Disney would have been delighted to see his dream of future transportation integrated into the *Axiom*'s space-age environment, especially given that Disneyland's People-Mover was a prototype for Walt's grander vision of futuristic living. Walt planned to build a larger PeopleMover installation as part of his Experimental Prototype Community of Tomorrow, or EPCOT—a new and futuristic city to be created from scratch at his planned Disney World Resort in Florida.

In October 1966, Walt recorded a short film pitching his "Florida Project" to industrialists and legislators, including a detailed description of EPCOT's transportation system. In this new city, cars and trucks were to be pushed underground, with the community's twenty thousand residents instead traveling by WEDway and monorail to work, play, and socialize. The concept images below from Walt's EPCOT film give an idea of just how much imagination the creative brains at WED Enterprises applied, under Walt's careful guidance, to everyday living challenges.

TOP LEFT: EPCOT's transportation was planned on a radial system, as this schematic from Walt's EPCOT film demonstrates. City residents use a series of PeopleMover systems (shown here as light blue spokes) to travel from their homes on the outskirts of the city to the central transport hub. Should they need to travel to other parts of Disney World, they then transfer to a high-speed monorail system (shown here in red).

TOP RIGHT: Concept art showing one half of EPCOT's main transportation lobby. The longer-distance monorail service (right) runs through the center of the lobby, with shorter-distance WEDway PeopleMover services departing from the edges of the lobby (left). Cars and trucks are pushed underground into lower levels of the city's transportation network (bottom).

BOTTOM LEFT: In Walt's EPCOT proposal, the city's WEDway PeopleMovers (shown here as light blue spokes) transport residents through the city's greenbelt, past sports facilities and schools . . .

BOTTOM RIGHT: . . . to residential areas in the city's suburban districts, complete with footpaths and children's play areas.

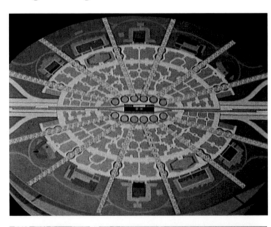 

 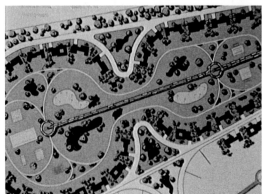

Tragically, Walt Disney died less than two months after his EPCOT introduction was filmed, passing away before the pitch was screened and before New Tomorrowland opened to the public. His ambitious vision of a prototype community did not become a reality, but its name lives on in the Epcot theme park (formerly "EPCOT Center") at Walt Disney World in Florida—although the eventual EPCOT park became more of a permanent World's Fair than a real-life city of the future. The WEDway PeopleMover did not realize its potential, either: The Disneyland attraction closed in 1995, to be replaced by the faster (but short-lived) Rocket Rods ride, which itself closed in 2001.

Disneyland park-goers can still see the PeopleMover's abandoned tracks snaking through Tomorrowland, displaying curved, arched supports that Santiago Calatrava would surely approve of. (Thankfully, a PeopleMover can still be experienced at the Magic Kingdom park at the Walt Disney World Resort in Florida, where the Tomorrowland Transit Authority People-Mover continues to provide a leisurely tour of nearby attractions.)

An overhead section of the now-disused PeopleMover track in Tomorrowland, seen in 2009

BOTTOM LEFT: Illuminated paths provide hover-chair routes throughout the *Axiom* . . .

BOTTOM RIGHT: . . . defining a "final mile" pathway to each passenger's room. Here, the normally blue "human" pathways have turned bright green to indicate that plant life has been found and the *Axiom* is preparing to return to Earth.

Of course, the PeopleMover also lives on via the *Axiom,* whose reimagining of the concept is almost a microcosm of Walt's vision for EPCOT. Aboard the *Axiom,* it's a PeopleMover (not a monorail) that fulfills the role of high-speed arterial transport, with individual BnL hover chairs completing the "final mile" of the journey via preset illuminated paths (blue for humans, white for robots, red for stewardbots). It may not match the scale of Disney's EPCOT dream, but it's nonetheless fitting that Walt's vision of a transportational future made the trip into space.

During WALL·E's tour of the passenger decks, we discover that the *Axiom*'s computer is voiced by none other than *Alien*'s Ellen Ripley. Casting Sigourney Weaver as the disembodied voice of a space-based computer is clearly ironic, especially given her experience with such voices in *Alien* and *Aliens*. *WALL·E* ups the irony by having Weaver narrate not one but two scenes that would feel all too familiar to her xenomorph-hunting counterpart, triggering bonus space-peril associations for *Alien* fans. (Weaver also plays a disembodied voice in Andrew Stanton's *Finding Dory,* aping her narration of nature documentaries.)

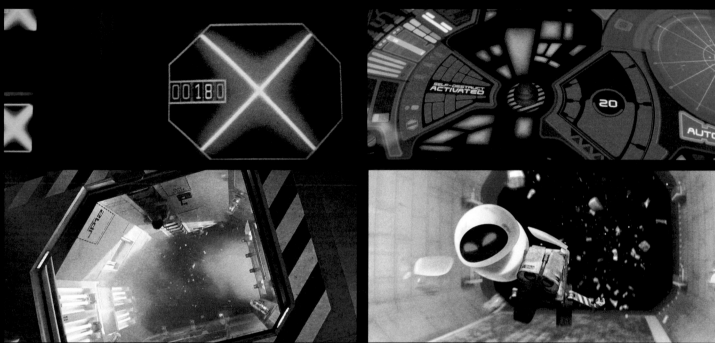

Alien and *Aliens* are not the only sci-fi movies to get a nod from *WALL·E*. On the *Axiom* bridge, we meet AUTO, the ship's autopilot robot. It might be hard to believe just by looking at him, but AUTO is actually an Evil Space-Based Computer. His design is clearly influenced by a certain *other* ESBC—that central red eye is a direct reference to *2001: A Space Odyssey*'s HAL, giving an immediate signal that this robot is not to be trusted.

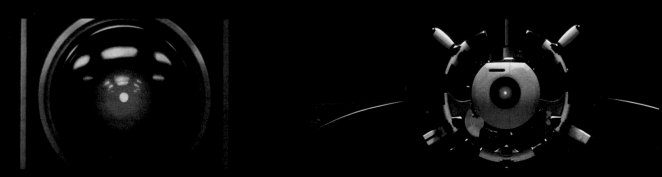

AUTO and HAL belong to a long-standing tradition of sci-fi automata whose glowing red eye(s) give away their evil nature. They really are everywhere in sci-fi movies—from the Model 101 in *The Terminator,* via the replicants in *Blade Runner,* to the evil wriggly thing inserted into Neo's belly button in *The Matrix.*

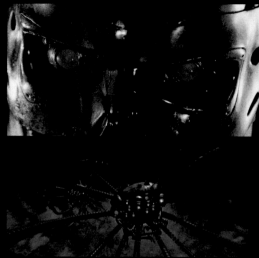

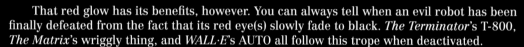

That red glow has its benefits, however. You can always tell when an evil robot has been finally defeated from the fact that its red eye(s) slowly fade to black. *The Terminator*'s T-800, *The Matrix*'s wriggly thing, and *WALL·E*'s AUTO all follow this trope when deactivated.

As *The Terminator*'s T-800 is squished beneath the sheets of an industrial steel press . . .

. . . its evil red eye fades slowly to black.

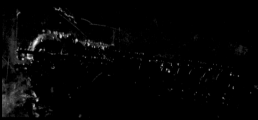

After removing the wriggly thing from Neo's belly, Trinity discards it in the rain . . .

. . . where its evil red eye fades slowly to black.

After the *Axiom* is switched from autopilot to manual control . . .

. . . AUTO's evil red eye fades slowly to black.

AUTO may *look* like the movie's bad guy, but his actions are simply an example of artificial intelligence following its programming too literally. To understand his motives, we must remember that BnL's original plan was for its star liners to return to Earth as soon as an EVE probe found proof that life was once more sustainable. Five years after their departure, however, BnL autopilots were sent a directive by CEO Shelby Forthright telling them to keep their craft in space indefinitely, because the cleanup process on Earth was not going to succeed. Six hundred ninety-five years later, with no subsequent instructions to the contrary, AUTO is simply following this command to the letter, blocking any and all attempts to return to Earth.

In this regard, AUTO is eerily similar to *2001*'s HAL, whose murderous tendencies aboard the *Discovery* were similarly driven by an inability to reconcile a contradiction in his programming. In the movie's sequel, *2010: The Year We Make Contact,* we learn that the basic purpose of HAL's design was "the accurate processing of information without distortion or concealment." We also discover that HAL was instructed (via Directive NSD 342/23) to lie to Dave and Frank about the real reason for the *Discovery*'s mission. After lip-reading that they planned to disconnect him, HAL determined that the only logical way for him to both keep processing and avoid lying was for Dave and Frank to die.

AUTO's own instruction is Directive A113, whose numbering may sound familiar to Pixar fans. "A113" appears in every Pixar film, from a family license plate in *Toy Story* to an underwater camera model in *Finding Nemo.* (Indeed, it's even in *Brave,* where the roman numerals ACXIII appear carved just above the front door of a witch's hut.) The reason for its repeated inclusion is that room A1-13 was the classroom for the Character Animation Program at the California Institute of the Arts, where Pixar alumni John Lasseter, Pete Docter, and Andrew Stanton studied. (This explains why it's also the number on the door of Riley's classroom in *Inside Out* and on the Scaring 101 classroom door in *Monsters University.*) *WALL·E* may be its highest-profile outing, but it's there in every Pixar movie if you keep your eyes peeled.

THE MAJORITY of *WALL·E*'s robots are voiced by Ben Burtt, the Academy Award–winning sound designer and creator of R2D2's bleeps. AUTO's voice, however, is provided by MacInTalk, a speech synthesis technology first used to announce the Apple Macintosh computer in January 1984. (You may also recognize MacInTalk as the lead vocalist on Radiohead's "Fitter Happier," from 1997's *OK Computer* album.)

MacInTalk's inclusion in *WALL·E* makes it one of only two Apple voice synthesis technologies to star in a feature film; the other is Siri, who provides the voice for 'Puter, Batman's high-tech assistant in *The LEGO Batman Movie.* Despite the technology's age, I'm happy to report that MacInTalk voices still ship with macOS today. If you'd like to turn your Mac into an Evil Space-Based Computer, simply open the System Preferences application, select Accessibility and then Speech, and enable the "Ralph" system voice.

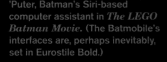

'Puter, Batman's Siri-based computer assistant in *The LEGO Batman Movie.* (The Batmobile's interfaces are, perhaps inevitably, set in Eurostile Bold.)

In addition to AUTO, there are two more nods to *2001: A Space Odyssey* in *WALL·E*, both of which take advantage of preexisting associations for dramatic or comedic effect. The first is WALL·E's brief escapade in a LifePod, the design of which seems clearly inspired by *2001*'s EVA pods. That iconic ball-like shape immediately triggers an association with interstellar peril, which WALL·E soon discovers is entirely justified.

TOP LEFT: One of the *Discovery*'s EVA pods is activated in *2001: A Space Odyssey*.

TOP RIGHT: One of the *Axiom*'s LifePods is activated in *WALL·E*.

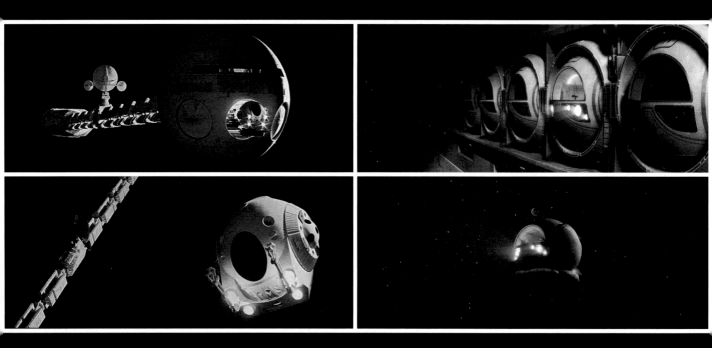

The second *2001* reference is a knowing usage of Richard Strauss's *Also sprach Zarathustra,* when Captain McCrea becomes the first human to stand up and walk in possibly hundreds of years. It's an appropriate enough use of the music—*2001*'s monoliths oversee (and supposedly trigger) several leaps in mankind's evolution, so it's entirely valid to hear those famous chords when the captain makes his first steps (even though this is technically a regression, not an evolution).

Of course, *WALL·E* is not alone in riffing on Strauss's classic melody. It is similarly parodied in *Charlie and the Chocolate Factory* (as a *2001* monolith turns into a bar of chocolate) and *Zoolander* (as Hansel considers smashing Mugatu's iMac with a nearby bone). If that's not enough, it's also in Pixar's *Toy Story 2* and *Cars 3,* plus other animated movies including *Kung Fu Panda 3, The Pirates! Band of Misfits,* and *The Simpsons Movie.* On the live-action front, it's in *Man on the Moon, Catch-22, Night at the Museum: Secret of the Tomb, Clueless, Turner & Hooch,* and *Harold & Kumar Go to White Castle,* to mention just a few. If Craig Huxley's Blaster Beam is the Eurostile Bold Extended of sci-fi audio, *Also sprach Zarathustra* is definitely its Bank Gothic.

ABOVE LEFT: The pod design in *2001* has many similarities with its *WALL·E* counterpart . . .

ABOVE RIGHT: . . . though it does not (as far as we know) include an optional satellite dish, parachute, flare set, or inflatable life raft.

BOTTOM LEFT: Determined to tackle the mutinous AUTO, Captain McCrea steadies himself . . .

BOTTOM RIGHT: . . . and drags himself to his feet, to the tune of *Also sprach Zarathustra.*

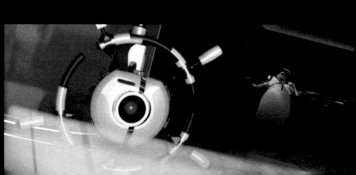

TOP LEFT: In 2005's *Charlie and the Chocolate Factory*, Willy Wonka transports a bar of chocolate via television to the tune of *Also sprach Zarathustra* . . .

TOP RIGHT: . . . transforming 2001's famous monolith into a bar of Wonka Nutty Crunch Surprise.

ABOVE LEFT: In 2001's *Zoolander*, non-evolved male models Derek Zoolander and Hansel smack an iMac chimpanzee-style to the tune of *Also sprach Zarathustra* . . .

ABOVE RIGHT: . . . before Hansel grabs a handy bone to use as a tool.

Despite AUTO's best efforts, McCrea manages to switch him to MANUAL and sets the *Axiom* on a hyperjump trajectory back to Earth. The hyperjump looks exactly like you'd expect, which is exactly like the USS *Enterprise* engaging warp drive in *Star Trek: The Motion Picture.* Once again, *WALL·E* is sneakily using prior sci-fi art as a shortcut, re-creating familiar effects so that the *Axiom*'s quick journey home can be explained without exposition. (It might also account for why everyone aboard the *Axiom* experiences a brief stint of *The Motion Picture*'s wormhole effect during the jump.)

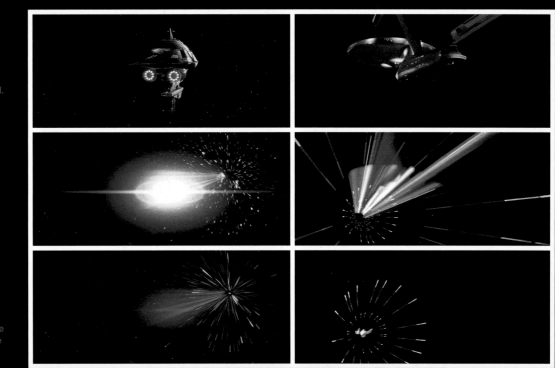

The *Axiom* makes a hyperjump toward Earth in *WALL·E* (left), while the *Enterprise* engages warp drive toward "thataway" in *Star Trek: The Motion Picture* (right).

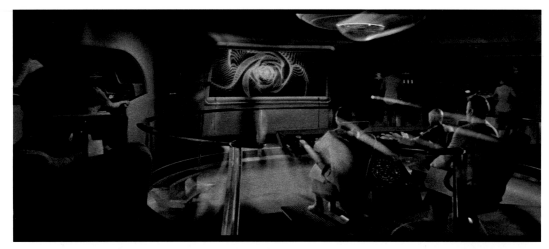

LEFT: The *Enterprise* bridge goes all "wormhole effect" when it engages warp speed while still within the solar system.

BELOW: EVE and WALL·E go all "wormhole effect" when the *Axiom* hyperjumps back to Earth.

AS THESE HOMAGES SHOW, *WALL·E* is not afraid to borrow from its predecessors to gain some free sci-fi association. Indeed, such references are celebrated and elevated, drawing on the production team's clear fondness for vintage sci-fi to create a movie that is both a love letter to the classics and a worthy addition to the list. *WALL·E* capitalizes on our existing associations with the future to communicate complex plot points and motives with minimal dialogue and text. It is, to my mind, Pixar's most realistic vision of an internally consistent world, despite the polar opposites of its Earth- and space-based environments. It's political and satirical, representing utopia and dystopia with enough humor to poke fun at the downsides of both. In short, *WALL·E* envisages a future that could so easily be bleak and pessimistic—but is instead inspired by the naïveté of its inhuman heroes to re-create the optimism that took man into space in the first place.

RALPH EGGLESTON & CRAIG FOSTER

In September 2017, I spoke with Pixar's Ralph Eggleston and Craig Foster about design, typography, and world building in *WALL·E*.

Ralph Eggleston was *WALL·E*'s lead production designer, overseeing the movie's design, look, and styling. His Pixar credits include art direction for *Toy Story* and *The Incredibles*, and production design for *Finding Nemo*, *Inside Out*, and *The Incredibles 2*. He also directed the Oscar-winning Pixar short *For the Birds*.

Craig Foster was a graphic designer for *WALL·E*. His job was to create many of the signs and computer displays that appear throughout the film. His Pixar credits include *Cars*, *Ratatouille*, *Up*, *Toy Story 3*, *Cars 2*, and *Cars 3*.

ADDEY: Starting with the Earth side of the movie—there's a definite world's fair vibe to the city, with a monorail and a Space Needle–style building in the distance. What was your architectural inspiration for its styling?

EGGLESTON: It was really optimism for the future, like [Disney theme park] Tomorrowland. A lot of the films I end up on are, like, "Where's my jetpack?" But in the case of *WALL·E*, it was "Where's my jetpack?" gone horribly wrong. This is like Space Mountain when you were a kid, but completely decrepit, just falling apart. The best of intentions for the future, completely fallen apart because we consumed too much. That was the idea. It almost hurt to have to dream that.

The Earth city subverts the usual "space is lonely" trope. Normally, it's someone on their own on the moon or on Mars or in space. Here, it's the exact opposite: Earth is the place where WALL·E is lonely. How did you use the design and coloring of the city to give it that sense of loneliness?

EGGLESTON: The world of that film, and the loneliness, was a real challenge. Because it's not just the fact that it's a very monochrome world; it's also, he's a bucket of bolts. And how do you make a bucket of bolts interesting for a whole movie? Especially for the first half hour or so, where it's on Earth?

And so the first thing that came to mind was romantic lighting. Not romantic as in "lovey-dovey" but romantic in terms of underlining the character's emotions with lighting. So if you have a monochrome world, which we did—it was basically brown, rust, and orange—how do you do that? Well, oddly enough, with monochrome we can do a lot with lighting and really underline the character's emotions. In this movie, it's very reserved, up until the moment when WALL·E meets EVE. And then you start introducing pink and blue.

The first time you see green in the film is when he finds the plant. And then it's pulled back completely, until you see the plant again. Except for one shot that snuck through a little earlier—but we dulled the green as much as we could. There was also a shot of a Rubik's Cube, which was done for a trailer and then it was approved for use in the film.

Before *WALL·E*, I had just finished *Finding Nemo*, which was a wonderful explosion of color, and we could do lots of things we couldn't do before. On *WALL·E*, I wanted to see how far the other way I could go. The palette of *WALL·E* is extremely controlled—it's pulled way, way back.

One of the fun things we asked

WALL·E discovers a plant growing in a disused refrigerator, introducing us to the color green for the first time on Earth.

WALL·E studies a Rubik's Cube, which has just been solved by EVE. It's the only non-plant-related use of green in *WALL·E*.

The palette for Earth in *WALL·E* is muted, with sun-bleached tones throughout.

BnL branding is on *everything* in *WALL·E*, from signage and billboards . . .

. . . to industrial shipyards . . .

. . . to even WALL·E himself.

ourselves, in looking at [architect] Santiago Calatrava's work for inspiration, is, how many shades of white are there? And so there's a lot of playing with light value in the film. I wanted to see how far we could take that.

Does that lead to that very bleached-out feeling on Earth?

EGGLESTON: Very bleached out, yeah. That was exactly it.

What feeling were you aiming for with the signage and graphic design of the city, through its billboards and advertising?

FOSTER: When it started off, I was using Times Square as a reference. Every color and every advertising motif and every product with a little "BnL" at the bottom—"Brought to you by BnL." But it just got muddy; you couldn't tell that there was any point to it.

Once we saw that treatment, we decided to go to where it's more like Costco. Everything's branded: BnL blotter, BnL shoes, whatever. So when you see it, it's like BnL owns *everything*. To the point where "BnL" is *all* you see; you don't see the products. And then you think, they own those apartment buildings, they own that TV station.

Then we took out all the colors, based on Ralph's direction. And when it

got desaturated with the atmosphere, that blue and red turned this brownish color, and everything fell away—

EGGLESTON: And just melted together, like smog.

FOSTER: We also decided that BnL was very informational in their advertising. So we used Futura. Like, that was it. Everything's just Futura in there. So it wasn't a lot of fun, but that's just what it is, because it's so to the point.

Am I right in thinking that Buy n Large has the same corporate font as Costco?

FOSTER: Yeah. I think IKEA, Costco, Pepsi, and Domino's Pizza all use it, too.

EGGLESTON: We also had a website leading into the distribution and promotion of the film. Disney has go.com, but we didn't want to use go.com to promote the company, because we didn't want anyone to know that Buy n Large was part of it. So we created a Buy n Large site. Adam Gates did it. It's brilliant. It's selling robots. And the small print is better than you can imagine. The small print alone is worth reading.

Many of those Buy n Large ads appear on holographic video screens around the city. Why is it that those screens have scan lines on them? Is that a

trope that's become self-fulfilling?

FOSTER: We had many conversations about that with [previsualization designer] Philip Metschan. I was like, "How's it

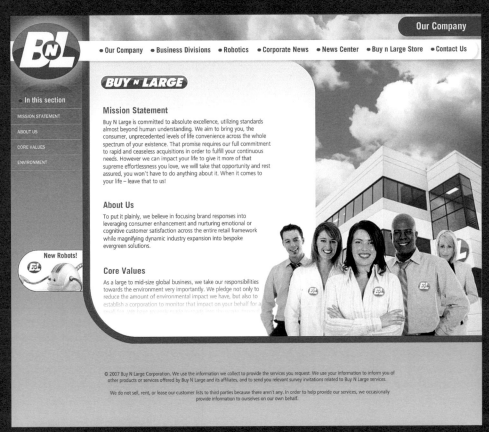

The Buy n Large website, buynlarge.com, created for *WALL·E*'s release. Its small print reads: "We do not sell, rent, or lease our customer lists to third parties because there aren't any. In order to help provide our services, we occasionally provide information to ourselves on our own behalf."

A holographic advertising screen on Earth, with clearly visible CRT-style scan lines

work? Why are there scan lines? Is it scan lines because there's some sort of ionization thing happening?" And he was like, "No—it's because it sells it."

It's what they have because it's what they have?

EGGLESTON: It's an audience identification thing. If you have to spend time explaining what it is, then they're not going to be paying attention to what you need them to pay attention to. That's where it lands, honestly. They understand [from scan lines]: Television.

The Buy n Large corporation is unusual, at least for megacorporations in science fiction, in that it doesn't seem evil—it almost seems slightly naive. Did that change how you approached its branding, the fact that it's more benign?

EGGLESTON: We did talk about that a *lot* for a while.

FOSTER: Yeah. We did a whole bunch of advertising packets for all these different brands, like water and air. And the original stuff I was making was really dystopian; there'd be fashion ads that had jackets with bladders in them, kind of like *Dune,* so you'd get to drink your own sweat. And bottled air, with these glasses that had a little thing on them, and it said, "No one knows you're breathing such-and-such air." But it didn't seem to matter, because it wasn't that they were a *bad* company; it's just that they owned everything.

EGGLESTON: That was the idea, really—that as a corporation they thought they were doing the right thing. They wanted to believe they were doing well. Only when it gets out of control do they realize, "Oops, we made a bad."

I think my favorite BnL ad that I spotted in the background was for a product called Regurgi-shake.

FOSTER: Yeah. I liked that one. And Compost-ies was the cereal.

EGGLESTON: It was also a trick with a lot of these graphics in act one, as well as two and three. It's not that we didn't have funny things, but they couldn't be so attention-stealing that the audience paid attention to them over the characters. And that's one of the really hard things with word graphics: If there's a word on the screen, the audience naturally wants to read it. If there's an important scene going on, and you want them to be looking *here,* you can't put a big word over *here*, because the first thing they're going to look at is that word, and *then* here, and they're going to miss the story point.

At one point, WALL·E rolls over some BnL banknotes. Looking at those very closely, it seems like they say "ten to the power six" on them. And another has what looks like "ninety-nine to the power six," to save you from having to split the change. Did I read that right?

FOSTER: That sounds right. Because inflation was out of control.

EGGLESTON: One of the hardest things and the simplest things was that everything was from Buy n Large's perspective. Their corporate thinking. We actually sat down and thought through the whole company—the board of directors and marketing—just as an idea.

You have BnL selling to people, and then you have to sell the *Axiom* to people, and then you have to sell supplies to get to the *Axiom,* as well as moving materials to get to the trucks that are also owned by Buy n Large. So as we go through all these thoughts, one of the other ideas was, how do you sell the idea that we're moving to a spaceship, and we're going to clean up Earth? That's where that idea was coming from. And a lot of that fell away. We overthink everything in our process here.

They like to say, "Story is king," but that's not true. Story*telling* is king. There's a big difference. It came down to: What is the most important way of telling the story? And it was an angle, from Buy n Large, where they're providing robots to clean up Earth while we're waiting for them in space.

The other thing that was an idea for a long time was that the humans used to speak in IKEA-ese. There was an idea that aliens came to Earth and dropped this robot off. And WALL·E and EVE met, and all this stuff. But only at the end of the film did you realize that the

aliens were human. They would write dialogue like "I'm going to the store," and then they would find words from the IKEA catalog that sounded like it, and they would have the actors record them. The Sklüb-Flark Flyyk-Myliik shelves, you know. But it was another idea that became one other level that we couldn't deal with, so we backed out.

A lot of people say of the humans, "Oh, they turned into big fat lazy people." That wasn't the idea; the idea was that in space, every month you lose three percent of your bone and muscle mass, and over the years everything moves toward your heart. Then you also become gelatinous, and you start becoming translucent. This is the idea, that they're actually going backward and are becoming, retroactively, embryos. They're becoming big babies, basically.

There's quite a disparity between the technology we see on Earth—discarded CRT TVs, WALL·E's iPod—and what we see aboard the *Axiom.* Presumably both of those came from the same era; the craft left at the same time that stuff was discarded. What was the thinking behind that disparity between the two worlds?

EGGLESTON: Well, they were *created* at the same time, because the ship left from there, right? But the difference is the one in space has an ongoing resource, which is birth, to keep it up, and robots and things; whereas on Earth they have robots, but they're falling apart and dying. That was kind of the idea.

And that retro technology that's left behind?

EGGLESTON: It's gone. And he's the last one.

Talking of the *Axiom*: How did its typographic styling evolve?

FOSTER: Basically, we went and looked at all the science-fiction films and tried to use their brand equity to legitimize

our sci-fi, so that it had this emotional authenticity.

EGGLESTON: And immediacy.

FOSTER: Yeah. It's like . . . you just *know* that's the future. Then we'd compile screen captures and send them to Ralph and say, "Look at all these fonts!" And he'd say which fonts he liked.

EGGLESTON: Graphics and fonts are not my forte. I know what's going to work for the story, though.

Visually, as part of the storytelling, it was really important for the audience to know exactly where they were at any given moment. You arrive on the ship and it's very utilitarian, and then you go to economy class and it's almost cement—all the signage is pretty much the same. Then you go to middle class, which was all about Vegas and Disneyland, leading you somewhere to spend more money. And then there's first class, where you already spent so much money that you don't *need* to spend any more money, and it's all very calming—the world comes to you, you don't go to the world. Then we had the captain's area, which was its own thing. But there were basically three regions—for a while, we called them classes—to the ship.

For the Vegas part—the middle part, the largest part—the director wanted signs everywhere. Five thousand of them. My intuition was telling me, don't do that! Because it's just going to become a visual mess. Unfortunately, a lot of time and effort was spent doing that, and the first time he [Andrew Stanton] saw it, he said, "This is a visual mess!" I think we got rid of ninety percent of it and instead had fewer, bigger signs.

FOSTER: We had all these signs that would be for a hamburger, a shake, and fries—

EGGLESTON: Or for clothes—

The *Axiom*'s inhabitants spend their entire lives gazing at their own personal screens, even when sitting around a beautiful lido pool.

FOSTER: And then, when you went around from WALL·E's point of view, they'd line up. It would be like this ad for a complete meal. Or for clothes, it would stack up, like they were lenticular. But when we tried to do it, it was just—

EGGLESTON: A cacophony of nothingness. We were trying to be too clever.

One of the ironies of seeing the humans go through this part of the ship is that, even with all the advertising around them, they are so focused on their individual screens—

EGGLESTON: That they're all together, alone.

Yes. They miss all the visual noise that's happening around them. That styling, giving them a very immediate focus—what was the design thinking behind that?

EGGLESTON: It was more of the storytelling aspect. I mean, the designs on the screens were one thing, but the design for *storytelling* was, literally, "We're together, alone." Buy n Large doesn't want them looking too far. They might see something that they like, that Buy n Large didn't produce. So yeah, that was really it; it's kind of reining them in. Sound familiar? [LAUGHS]

What was the inspiration for the architecture of the *Axiom,* with its arches and curves?

EGGLESTON: We went around the block on that for a long time. The director wanted a cruise ship. We designed—oh God, how many—*lots* of different designs. And he kept coming back to: "I just want a cruise ship." So that was our starting place. The idea is that there's not just one ship; there are many ships out there in space. But the idea for this was it's like a cruise ship, where you have your economy, middle, and first class, and a captain, and a bridge, and it's laid out like a boat. It wasn't a whole lot more than that.

And that Vegas ceiling, where you don't know whether it's day or night.

EGGLESTON: The sky dome, yeah. Myself, Andrew, [producer] Jim Morris, and I think it was [production artist] Dan Holland and [coproducer] Lindsey Collins, we got a location scout and we went to Vegas. We went to every gentleman's club in Vegas. Well, not *every* club. We went to *five* gentleman's clubs in Vegas, for the three hours a day they're all closed and they're being cleaned. And we went to look at the lighting setups above. Because this is like two hundred bucks just to get in the front door, right? They have all this expensive lighting equipment above the stages and all the gears to move things underneath. A lot of that was important to the *Axiom*'s design early on, and then over time a lot of it fell away. Although a lot of that lighting, we ended up using that sort of lighting in the captain's bridge, for the large panels of glass buttons and things.

That captain's bridge computer interface feels like it's almost designed for robots; it has very rotational controls.

EGGLESTON: It was actually designed for production friendliness. Because at the time we needed to hand that over to be produced, it hadn't been written yet. And so we needed to have lots of buttons that we didn't know what they needed to do yet. Originally, it was going to be carved out, with cut buttons, and what we ended up saying was, "Well, the best we can do is give you eight-by-eight, four-by-four, two-by-two, and individual pods of buttons, so you can decide later on what you need them to do." Then these guys came up with a language for that.

What was that language?

FOSTER: That "orbiting" business? That came from the animator, who said, "The captain's going to run the clock backward at the beginning, and the sun's going to go 'Zrrrrup!' and we want to be able to have a control to animate that, but we need the interface." And we're like, "Well, what would that be?" And the animator was like, "Well, [rotating his wrist] we think *that* would be cool," like he's actually turning it. So I made this sundial thing that he could move.

And when the captain does the dirt analysis, we actually built a whole interface—an operating system that would've been for the command staff, the captain. I called it the Fisher Price system. It's these little pieces that come in; it was a dumbed-down high-tech. Everything was in these little blocks, and they floated around.

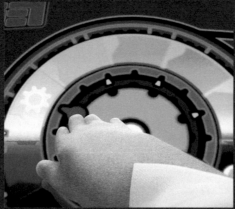

Captain McCrea rotates the *Axiom*'s clock from 12:30 P.M. . . .   . . . to 9:30 A.M.

The "Fisher Price" computer interface used by Captain McCrea to discover more about WALL·E's dirt

EGGLESTON: This is one of the tricks that's very different from a live-action film approach. In live-action, in most cases you have a shooting script, and very often by the time you get to doing these kind of graphics, they already have a cut of the film. Whereas we're doing this as story writing is still happening. There's a lot of back-and-forth among story, editorial, art, and graphics—and animation needs to see it, to know where the character needs to look. So things like that are roughed in, put in on a plate; animation can see it and see where to look. Then editorial makes a change, and it has to go through everyone again; sometimes five, ten times before it gets exactly right. Then you move forward from there.

The other thing was we actually went on a cruise. It was the first time a Disney cruise ship came to the West Coast. It was during the fiftieth anniversary of Disneyland, and they went through the Panama Canal to Los Angeles. Out of the blue, a friend of mine from high school, who's now the head of Disney Cruise Line, emailed me and said, "Hey, I heard you guys were trying to get a cruise."

So we went down and we had a three-hour tour of the entire ship—all the way from the top to ten feet from the propeller on the inside. One of the things we discovered was that because ships, especially cruise ships, have international crews, all the signage below deck is visual. No words. So we got the idea that we should utilize that on the *Axiom* as well, as much as possible.

FOSTER: It helps when AUTO comes down and starts touching things; we didn't have to line up with the animation or anything for, like, "Security."

EGGLESTON: Also, our films go international, and we have to translate words, and it can get very overwhelming. We'll do a lot of variations on that kind of stuff. And we like to minimize that, because it can get out of control. It's a lot of work. Swahili, Korean . . . we got a lot.

When you're working with international alphabets, how do you make sure that it reads as "the Future" to non-American viewers?

EGGLESTON: I know we think about that in relationship to color, especially like on a film like *Inside Out;* what does "red" mean to North America, or Western culture, versus Eastern culture? It's very different.

FOSTER: We do meet with our international team, to show them major story points, so they can start thinking ahead how to translate things.

And get the right font?

EGGLESTON: Or even the right tone, you know. Maybe we can't use the same word.

FOSTER: And they'll suggest, "Well, could that be some sort of universal symbol?" or "That will never fit in there in German."

Because it'll be four times as wide?

EGGLESTON: Yeah. Or Finnish.

FOSTER: If they said, "Wow, that font in Asian cultures is the most offensive thing you could ever have chosen to use," then we'd change it. But generally that stuff doesn't seem to come up.

EGGLESTON: Walt Disney was always interested in keeping dialogue to a minimum, so that he could sell overseas. We've kind of kept that same approach. Not that we worry *so* much about that, but we do a lot of international stuff here. All of our films are translated here in the company. It can eat up a lot of time.

The style of the future that we see in the *Axiom,* and also on Earth, is a very aspirational future, a "what could be possible?" future.

EGGLESTON: That's exactly right. Maybe I'm late to the game, but I discovered in my research that during that period after we went to the moon, in the early seventies, when budgets started getting slashed for all kinds of things, including NASA, it ceased to be about what *could* be, and it became more about what *can* be. And it became a failure of imagination.

If you track the artwork from the late forties through the late sixties, it's "what *might* be." And then, starting around 1972, all the way through the eighties, it starts looking like clip art. "We know we can do *this.* And because we know we can do *this,* we know how to budget and schedule it and fit it to our little box here on this parfait chart." And so that's what it became. Rather than "Here's a great idea, let's figure out how to solve it," it became "Well, we've solved the budget schedule; now fit your idea into it." And so we wanted to go back to that original, aspirational principle.

The Disney Tomorrowland films of the fifties were circulated within the government to feed those ideas — to say, "Hey, look what's possible!" Do you think Disney and Pixar have a role in providing that inspiration today?

FOSTER: I would like to think so.

EGGLESTON: Yeah, I would, too.

FOSTER: I think even with non-sci-fi. In *Cars 3,* McQueen is getting caught up in the modern day of "I just wanna win, I gotta be the best," as opposed to "for

A Disney cruise liner, the *Disney Dream*, at port in Nassau, the Bahamas, in 2011

Title cards from four aspirational "Tomorrowland" films from the 1950s, broadcast as episodes of the *Walt Disney's Disneyland* TV show

the love of the sport." It's not sci-fi, but it's saying, "Hey, *enjoy* life." It's a nice thing to remind people.

EGGLESTON: Yeah. And even the look of *WALL·E*—the anamorphic lenses, the wide-screen aspect. We all grew up in the seventies and eighties, including the director, when all of the stuff that we were talking about earlier started falling away. A lot of the design aspects in the film were an homage to our childhood, to growing up with *Star Wars* and *Close Encounters* and *E.T.* and *Blade Runner* and all of those great films. Even the ship. We gave some of the designs to one of our painters and said, "Look at John Berkey's stuff, and just kind of emulate him," and he did. And that worked beautifully.*

A lot of the fun we had with the graphics and the storytelling and Buy n Large was making fun of the things that we wished we could have had as a kid

---

* Berkey painted sci-fi book covers for Isaac Asimov, Philip K. Dick, and Robert Heinlein; concept art for the original *Star Wars*; movie posters for *King Kong*, *Superman III*, and *Dune*; and artwork for NASA's Apollo space program.

that never came true. And what would that be today, really? It would be Buy n Large. That's somewhat ironic, somewhat cynical—but always done with a sense of humor.

Turning to the robot designs onboard the *Axiom*: How much did they have a consistent visual language across all the robots, versus how much were you looking for an identity for each of them, to make them recognizable as characters?

EGGLESTON: We wanted a design consistency. A lot of that design was instituted by [production artist] Dan Holland and followed through by others. And yet WALL·E looks like he was created many, many moons ago, you know. He's a bucket of bolts. Which reminds me: One of the funny things that floats around here is that the film was originally going to be called *WAL-E*. But Steve Jobs came in and read it, and said, *"WHALE?"* So we changed it.

We needed the robots to be individual enough, but what we *didn't* want was "people in a costume." Each of the

robots, including WALL·E, had a specific role, a function. WALL·E's function was to crush trash. That's it. Fourteen-point-two-inch cubes of trash. Then we had the umbrella, whose function was just to go out and be an umbrella. And then we had the fibrillator guy.

So they were *functionally* differentiated, rather than stylistically?

EGGLESTON: Yeah. Every single one had a function. Personality-wise, the jokes that they made with them had a little more personality than their function. But that was one thing the director really wanted—he didn't want any of the robots to come across as though it could just be a person in an outfit.

Were there particular sci-fi movies, in addition to the ones that inspired the *Axiom*'s fonts, that gave you a visual cue for the movie? AUTO is definitely reminiscent of *2001: A Space Odyssey*, for example.

EGGLESTON: Yeah, *2001.*

Any others?

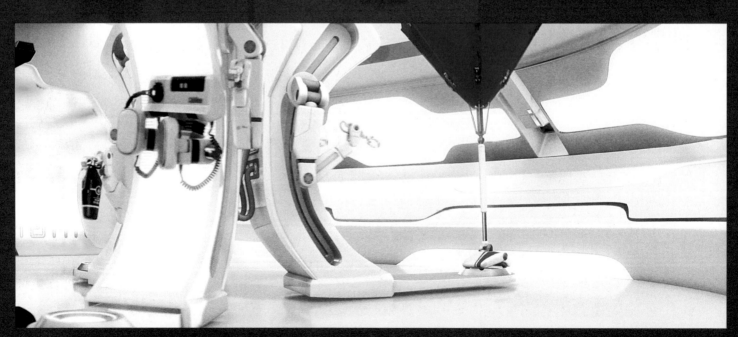

The fibrillator guy (left, floating) and the umbrella guy (right, open)

EGGLESTON: *Things to Come* [1936]. *Blade Runner.* What else?

FOSTER: For me, I was looking at *Space: 1999, UFO,* and, of course, *2001*—but also anything where they had a uniform that was a standard color, with some sort of signifier. When we did the lineup for the robots, Dan had done all their shapes, and we went in and did a color pass and worked out what their graphics would be. We came up with a few stripes, thick and thin—except for command robots like AUTO and GO-4, which were based on ensign stripes. Their stripes were actually command references: four for a captain, one for an ensign.

From my research into *Blade Runner*, it sounds like they designed twenty times as much stuff as finally made it on screen. But by thinking it through, it gave them a much better idea of the world they were creating. It sounds like you went through a very similar process on *WALL·E*.

EGGLESTON: Same thing. Absolutely. And it's not about the end result—it's about world building. And not just graphics. It's characters, sets, textures, everything.

We had a wonderful man who came here a long time ago, Richard Sylbert, who designed *Chinatown* and *Dick Tracy.* He was the only production designer in history to get residuals for a set design, for the TV show *Cheers.* He came to Pixar, and he looked around and saw what we were doing, and said, "You guys get to draw *everything?*" And we're like, "*Get* to? We *have* to!" We have to design *everything.* Because it doesn't exist. And we don't get physics for free, either. Lighting or weight, none of it. It's all made up. And he was flabbergasted.

Fifteen years later, he wrote his autobiography, and in the introduction he wrote, "Me and my boss, William Cameron Menzies"—his mentor, who designed *Gone with the Wind*—"if we were starting out now, we'd be working at Pixar." Which is a huge compliment. And it wasn't about the drawings and the pretty pictures; it was about the thinking and the storytelling. The character *behind* the thinking.

It's very much like a theater, the way we produce our films. Every three months, we have to show everybody what we're working on. And they tear it down and rebuild it. And hopefully it's getting better as you go along. You do a lot of work, and a lot of it falls away, but the stuff that sticks matters most. That's what *everybody's* after, right?

GO-4, whose sides have stripes to indicate his rank as a command robot

The GERTY 3000 "robotic assist" from *Moon* combines a dispassionate voice with simplistic emoji expressions, evoking the emotionless HAL 9000 from *2001* and MU/TH/UR 6000 from Alien, and causing us to assume an evil AI intent.

2009

Duncan Jones's *Moon* is a bleak, lonely, and, above all, beautiful love letter to classic sci-fi typography and design. It therefore seems the perfect movie to round off our study of typography in science fiction.

SAM ROCKWELL

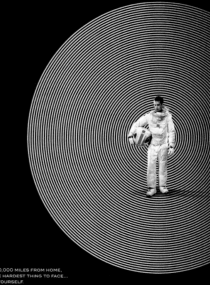

250,000 MILES FROM HOME,
THE HARDEST THING TO FACE...
IS YOURSELF.

MOON

I'll tell you exactly where we are now. We are in the FUTURE; and we are on the *moon*.

The searching question above is the opening shot of an infomercial for Lunar Industries Ltd., whose moon-based mining of Helium-3 is providing a plentiful source of energy on Earth. (On the evidence of this ad, they sound like a great company to work for—certainly at least on a par with the Weylan Yutani corporation.)

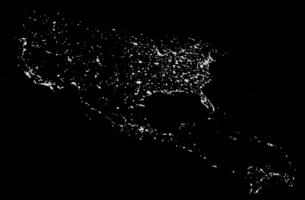

"HE3 = POWER" may sound like science fiction, but *Moon*'s projection of future lunar industry turned out to be remarkably prescient. In January 2014, NASA started accepting applications from companies who want to mine the moon. This film isn't science fiction—it's inevitable science *fact*.

Fittingly, the infomercial finishes with an animation of the words *sun / moon / earth / energy / future* and a transition to the Lunar Industries logo:

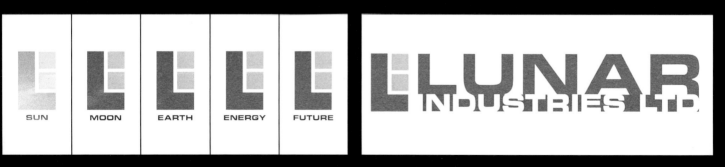

As introductions go, it doesn't get more Eurostile Bold Extended than that.

And that's where I have bad news, I'm afraid. The font seen opposite is not Eurostile. It's not even Eurostile's precursor, Microgramma. According to *Moon* conceptual designer Gavin Rothery, it's actually Microstyle Bold Extended, a just-different-enough take on the original created by the Agfa corporation in 1991.

Microstyle Bold Extended

ABCDEFGHIJKLMNOPQRSTUVWXYZ

You're probably wondering how to tell the three apart, right? Don't worry—it's trivially easy, as the big number *2* to the left (created by superimposing the three typefaces over one another) will illustrate. Eurostile is in blue; Microgramma is in red; Microstyle is in green.

I'm glad we've cleared that up. (For ease of cross-referencing, I'm going to put my fingers in my ears and continue to call it Eurostile anyway.)

Eurostile is joined in *Moon*'s introduction by the *other* classic bold extended sci-fi font, Bank Gothic. A clever 3-D layout of Bank Gothic Medium is used for much of the film's title credits, superimposed in and over each of its positioning scenes.

Bank Gothic Medium

ABCDEFGHIJKLMNOPQRSTUVWXYZ

One of these scenes introduces us to the film's central character. Look! It's Sam Bell, running on a treadmill to keep fit during his three-year stay on the moon. But what's that on his T-shirt?

Haha! It's a meaningless, throwaway gag about running. Because "runners don't quit," do they? Unless this comedy 1980s typography has a deeper, hidden meaning . . .

One of my favorite things about *Moon* is its constant foreshadowing of the movie's central twist. "Wake Me When It's Quitting Time" is a neat forward reference to events later in the movie, slotted neatly into its opening in a way that is easy to miss. (Although for the type purists among you, I'm afraid to say that isn't Helvetica on Sam's T-shirt—it's Arial, Monotype's identically spaced sans-serif imitation. You can tell from the *Q* and the *G*.)

Helvetica

ABCDEFGHIJKLMNOPQRSTUVWXYZ

ABCDEFGHIJKLMNOPQRSTUVWXYZ

Arial

This opening sequence is also the first time we discover that the moon base is called "SARANG - 사랑," which is essentially a duplication. *Sarang* is a transliteration of the Korean word 사랑, which means "love" or "affection." (*Sarang* is also etymologically and graphically close to *saram,* or 사람, which can mean either "person" or "people.") In either case, it's an unfortunate choice of name for Sam's permanent home on the moon, many thousands of miles away from his beloved wife and daughter.

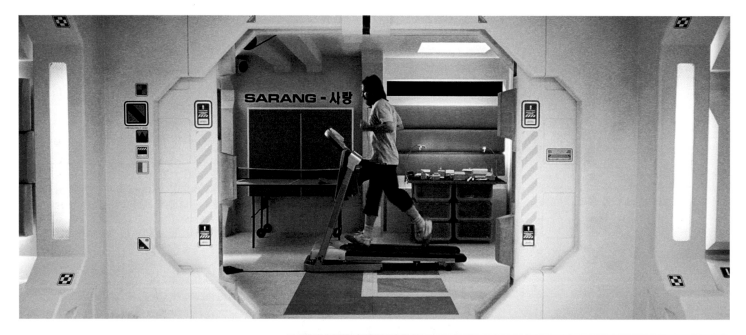

You may remember another *Moon* opening shot from page 59 of the *Alien* chapter, where we saw it as a classic example of the "foreshadowing inventory" trope introduced for the *Nostromo*. In *Moon*'s case, the foreshadowing is extremely accurate—the base does indeed have a crew of one (Mr. Sam Bell), and the moon-based contract of Mr. Sam Bell lasts exactly three years. It's just that "CREW: 1" can be taken rather more literally than an innocent first-time viewer might expect. (More on that front shortly.)

The foreshadowing inventory's typeface is OCR-A, designed in 1968 for use in optical character recognition systems. Not only is it an ISO standard for character recognition, it looks like the FUTURE and therefore makes a perfect choice for on-screen interstitial positioning shots. We saw it earlier for Deckard's video call in *Blade Runner*, but you'll also find it in *The Matrix*, *District 9*, *Pacific Rim*, and *Jurassic World*, to name but a few.

OCR-A

ABCDEFGHIJKLMNOPQRSTUVWXYZ

TOP LEFT: All of Neo's database records in *The Matrix* are set in OCR-A, including some impressively technical-looking numbers and characters down the side.

TOP RIGHT: OCR-A provides some handy timing exposition in *District 9.*

BOTTOM LEFT: *Pacific Rim*'s Shatterdome Jaeger Station is introduced via some OCR-A that also adopts the "CRT scan lines" trope we saw in *Alien*.

BOTTOM RIGHT: Raptor Delta's HUD (heads-up display) in *Jurassic World* uses OCR-A for a shot that clearly foreshadows the fact that this guy is going to get eaten before the movie is over.

BACK INSIDE THE BASE, Sam notices that one of the four HE3 harvesters has a full load ready for collection. The on-screen display is classic Bold Extended sci-fi, with bonus points for yellow-and-white text and barber's-pole patterning. Also notable in this movie still is a juxtaposition of the harvester's precise on-screen display with Sam's handwritten customization of the surrounding fascia. This human customization of a clinical surrounding is something we certainly didn't see in *2001: A Space Odyssey*, but it's a common theme in *Moon*. Sam's boredom keeps finding creative and subversive outlets within the strict design confines of the moon base environment.

As Sam heads out to collect the HE3, we note that his pressurized suit has three fabric mission patches. Sam's patches follow the Apollo mission patch trend toward Bold Extended typography, as seen in the *2001* chapter. However, apart from their typography, Sam's patches are very different from those of the Apollo era. NASA astronauts always had creative input into the patches for their missions. In his book *Carrying the Fire,* command module pilot Michael Collins described the design process for the *Apollo 11* mission patch typography:

"I also penciled APOLLO around the top of my circular design and ELEVEN around the bottom. Neil didn't like the ELEVEN because it wouldn't be understandable to foreigners, so after trying XI and 11, we settled on the latter and put APOLLO 11 around the top."

Sam's patches are the exact opposite of those from the Apollo era—rectangular rather than round; corporate and branded rather than personal and decorative. As in *Alien,* the message is clear: The corporation owns you, and you are entirely expendable.

SAM RECORDS a message for Lunar Industries back on Earth. He's unable to speak to them live, owing to an ongoing problem with the long-range communication system.

This on-screen interface is once again all about the Bold Extended. More importantly, if you look very closely, you'll see that one of the buttons to the right of the screen is labeled "Wake Up." (I wonder what it does.)

SAM ISN'T HAPPY about the fact he's been on the base for nearly three years. "I'm talking to myself on a regular basis," he says. (Be careful what you wish for, Sam.)

Sam's attempts to customize and personalize his environment continue in the living quarters. He's keeping count of his time on the moon with a dry-erase marker on the bathroom wall. By my count, this is 156 smileys for 156 weeks—exactly the three years mentioned in the plot.

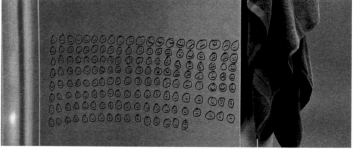

However, according to a commenter named DUNCAN JONES on the Typeset in the Future blog, this count was accidental: "There was one for each week, but I think I lost count, as there should have been two less than the full three years." The facial emotions represent Sam's mental state week by week, as DUNCAN continues: "Each face was meant to represent how the week had gone. Smile/good! Sad face/shit." The smileys are also a neat parallel to the simple expressions seen on the front of GERTY, Sam's AI companion on the base. GERTY communicates his emotions to Sam via the GERTY Unit Primary Emotional Interface, which is a small LCD screen on his frontmost robotic side. GERTY has a stock set of ten emoji faces, which will be familiar to users of instant messenger emoticons. It's notable that GERTY's voice remains entirely emotionless throughout the film, regardless of which icon he is displaying. As with HAL in *2001,* the effect of a neutral AI voice as events descend into chaos is disarming, terrifying, and extremely effective at reinforcing Sam's isolation.

ABOVE: The complete set of emoji seen on the GERTY Unit Primary Emotional Interface

BELOW LEFT: Sam's hand-drawn scene in *Moon*

BELOW RIGHT: Sergeant Pinback's hand-drawn floral scene on the wall of the *Dark Star* dormitory. As his facial expression attests, the scene's jollity is not working.

SAM HAS DRAWN a window and pastoral scene on another metal wall, surrounded by family photos. This customization of a clinical environment by a clearly bored employee evokes the similarly long-term residents of *Dark Star* (1974), in which Sergeant Pinback draws a sunny scene on a metal wall to summon memories of a world he cannot experience. It's a low-tech form of the "TV as outdoors" trope we saw in *Total Recall,* and even less effective at replacing what is being missed.

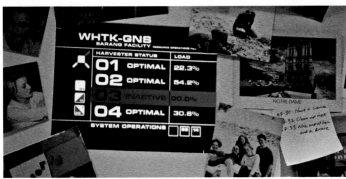

THE FUNCTIONAL Eurostile of a harvester status screen is similarly customized with Sam's family photos and postcards. Just readable among the photos is a Post-it note detailing his plans for starting the day:

07.30: Have a wank
07.32: Clean up mess
07.33: Nice cup of tea and a bickie

Sam might be American, but the film's director and designer are definitely British. (To explain for Americans: *Bickie* is British slang for *biscuit,* the British word for *cookie. Wank* is British slang for an activity I'd best not mention in a family-friendly book of typographic futurism.)

NEXT UP is a gratuitous shot of Sam having a shower. If this isn't a "backside of the moon" gag, I'll be sorely disappointed.

I've had a closer look, but I can't see any typography. And if there's no typography, it's time for us to move on.

AFTER HIS SHOWER, Sam gets his hair cut by GERTY, who uses a futuristic vacuum-based device that sucks up Sam's hair and cuts it to the perfect length.

Hang on a minute. What's that written on the transparent plastic tube? Crop. Zoom in. Move left. Zoom in again. *Enhance.*

That embossed text appears to say:

www.haircut.com
2" EXTENDER

Is this the *Moon* production team saying that at some point in the future, haircut.com will be purchased by a futuristic hair-cutting company that makes robotic trimming devices?

No, dear reader, it is not. Because that future is already here *today.* It turns out that haircut.com is the present-day home of RoboCut Inc., maker of the RoboCut BumbleBee DIY. That's right—the product you see in *Moon* is a product you can buy yourself *today,* via the magic of the Internet. Head over to haircut.com, pick up a BumbleBee DIY, and attach it to your household vacuum cleaner to give a speedy trim to family, boards, and pets.

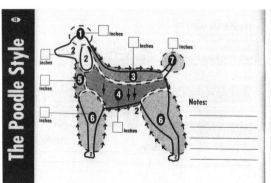

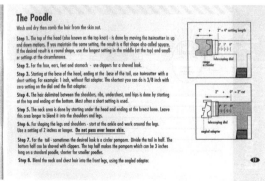

RoboCut BumbleBee DIY instructions for trimming a poodle, from the haircut.com hair-cutting guide

Haircut completed, Sam expresses his annoyance that LunarSat (aka long-range comms) still hasn't been fixed. GERTY notes that it's fairly low on the company's priority list right now. His passive role in this scene is fascinating. If you watch *Moon* after watching 2001, you can't help but be suspicious of GERTY, in the same way that Ripley can't help but be suspicious of Bishop in *Aliens* after her experience with Ash in *Alien*. GERTY is a calm, relaxing AI voice with a glowing camera lens and corporate logo on the front. *Moon* certainly isn't afraid to play with our expectations. After all, what could possibly go wrong?

Sam listens to a message from his wife and daughter. He can't talk to them live owing to the LunarSat mishap, but he's delighted to see them nonetheless. Just look at the joy on his face.

No. *Don't* look at his face; look at his clipboard. That's where the typographic interestingness is most likely to be found.

Crop. Zoom in. Rotate ninety degrees. Zoom in again. *Enhance.*

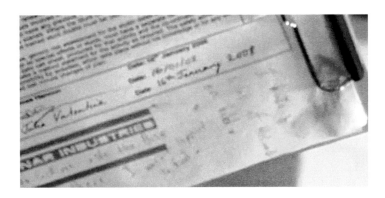

Hold on a minute—it looks like this clipboard was signed on January 16, 2008. But that's not the FUTURE—indeed, it's not even after *Moon* was released! Moreover, the signature looks remarkably like the name of the film's line producer, Julia Valentine. (Damn you, high-definition film releases.)

After his call, Sam tends to his plant collection, which he's growing inside old food containers. The names of these plants—Ridley, Stanley, Stephen, Kathryn, and Doug—might sound familiar to sci-fi fans. Following a Twitter conversation with director Duncan Jones, I can confirm that these plants are indeed tributes to sci-fi moviemakers Ridley Scott (*Alien*), Stanley Kubrick (*2001: A Space Odyssey*), Steven (misspelled Stephen) Spielberg (*Close Encounters of the Third Kind, Minority Report*), Kathryn Bigelow (*Strange Days*), and Douglas Trumbull (*Silent Running*).

LEFT: Sam tends to his plants (from left to right), Doug, Stephen, Stanley, Kathryn, and Ridley.

BELOW: Organic Material / Soylent Storage

AS HE MAKES a cup of tea, he spots a strange girl in his chair. While he's distracted by the plot, let's take a look at a typographically interesting poster in the background, just visible beneath the prepacked food boxes (right). "Soylent." Hmm. That sounds familiar. Surely this isn't the same organic material made by the Soylent Corporation in 1973's *Soylent Green*? Because if it is, that would be remarkably worrying. Spoiler alert: Soylent Green is people!

This signage may be an incredibly subtle nod to Richard Fleischer's seventies dystopia, but it's an appropriate connection nonetheless. In *Soylent Green*'s overpopulated future, elderly detective Sol Roth discovers the reality of the Soylent Corporation's human-sourced foodstuff and commits suicide in despair, unable to deal with the truth. He describes this terminal process as "going home"—an emotion that *Moon*'s Sam Bell could surely sympathize with.

Still, at least we can be confident that *Moon*'s Soylent isn't made from people. After all, where would you get them from? There's only one person on this moon base, and that's Sam Bell.

SAM BURNS HIS HAND while distracted by the mystery girl. GERTY fixes him up in the infirmary. Just visible behind Sam's head is a screen with the comforting advice to "TRUST ROBOTIC ASSIST."

ROBOTIC ASSIST is the official name for GERTY 3000, Sam's AI companion on the base (voiced by Kevin Spacey doing his best HAL impression). And why *not* TRUST ROBOTIC ASSIST? I'm sure the 3000 series has a perfect operational record.

SAM GOES TO BED. Beside his bunk is issue 15 of *Take Off* magazine, a 132-issue aviation partwork published in the 1980s by British magazine company Eaglemoss. This particular issue features V-bombers and biz-jets. It's not quite the wistful outdoors video wall from *Total Recall*, but like Sam's hand-sketched pastoral scene, it illustrates his desire to escape nonetheless.

As he snoozes, Sam has a sexy dream about his wife. It does not contain any typography.

Sam is rudely awakened by his Karlsson Digibell LCD alarm clock. Sam's future version of the clock has a bonus feature compared to the one you can buy in shops today. That's right—Sam's version plays Chesney Hawkes songs. Specifically, it wakes Sam by playing Chesney's 1991 hit single, "The One and Only."

"I am the one and only," croons Mr. Hawkes. You heard me right—unbelievable as it sounds, director Duncan Jones is foreshadowing upcoming events in the movie *via the lyrics of a Chesney Hawkes song.*

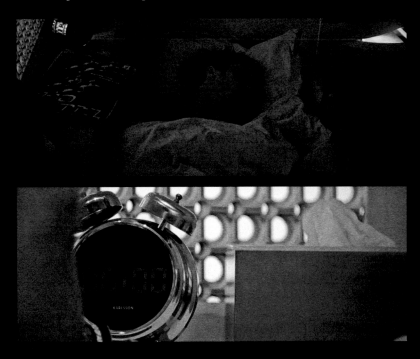

This is not the one and only appearance of "The One and Only" in a Duncan Jones movie. The song also appears in 2011's *Source Code,* as the ringtone for Christina's cell phone. Moreover, Chesney recorded a special lute rendition of his pop hit for 2016's *Warcraft: The Beginning.* Sadly, his medieval version did not make the movie's final cut, but it can be enjoyed as part of the DVD and Blu-ray extras.

SAM SPOTS that Matthew, one of Sarang's harvesters, has a full load of HE3 ready to send back to Earth. He learns this fact via the moon base's laser display board, whose surrounding wall iconography owes a large debt to *Alien*, with rounded, outlined rectangles and abstract shapes aplenty.

This iconography is not *Moon*'s only nod to *Alien*. Sarang's computer is named Old Man, which is slang for "father"—a knowing tribute to *Alien*'s MU/TH/UR by conceptual designer Gavin Rothery. Also visible during Sam's later message from Lunar Industries is a small PURGE panel in the bottom right of his screen, reminiscent of the PURGE screen seen in both *Alien* and *Blade Runner*.

Sam heads out to retrieve some of the HE3 from Matthew in a moon rover. On the way, he sees a second vision of the mysterious girl and crashes into the side of Matthew, damaging both himself and the rover. The rover's emergency sign once again asks him to "TRUST ROBOTIC ASSIST." There's a clear message coming through from these on-screen text displays: If things go wrong, ROBOTIC ASSIST should be TRUSTed to make things right. Let's fade to black with that sensible advice in mind.

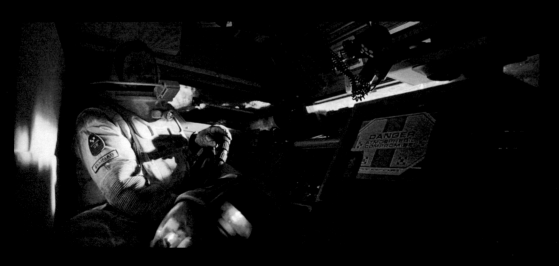

FADE UP FROM BLACK. Why hello, Sam! You're looking remarkably fresh-faced for someone who's just nearly killed himself in an accident. Shortly thereafter, we over-hear GERTY saying something to Lunar Central about "the new Sam." It turns out that Dingbat Sam is an *entirely brand-new Sam*—a clone of the original Sam Bell, who has just been woken up by GERTY.

This might get confusing rather quickly, so let's lean on our good friend "typographic convention" and use subscript to refer to him henceforth as Sam$_2$. (Trust me, it'll make life a lot easier once you know where we're going with this.)

Sam$_2$ spots that Matthew has stalled. He asks GERTY to unlock the doors so that he can go and fix it. GERTY says, "I'll pass on your message." (This is Lunar Industries–speak for "I'm sorry, Sam. I'm afraid I can't do that.")

Sam$_2$ has a dream about his wife. This time, it's not sexy at all—it's psychologically *and* typographically disturbing. There's a scary Sam$_1$ under the bedclothes, and he works for RANUL SEIRTSUDNI, on the 랑사-GNARAS base:

LUNAR CENTRAL tells Sam$_2$ to stay put. GERTY apologizes for being under strict orders not to let him outside. He's acting like some kind of . . . *benevolent* HAL 9000, which actually endears him to me considerably.

GERTICON:
STRICTORDERSFACE

BOTTOM LEFT: "SARANG ROVER –
PLEASE DRIVE CAREFULLY – NAV
– COM"

BOTTOM RIGHT: A selection of three-letter acronyms from HAL interfaces in *2001: A Space Odyssey*

Sam$_2$ tricks GERTY into letting him go outside anyway. He notes a missing space suit and rover, and sets out to investigate. On the way, his rover's computer screen displays some familiar text, with the abbreviations "NAV" and "COM" clearly visible in Eurostile Bold Extended. These three-letter combinations are reminiscent of HAL's *Discovery* screens in *2001*, which display "NAV," "COM," and other NASA-style abbreviations for informational purposes. It's a subtle touch, but like the *Alien*-style iconography aboard the Sarang moon base, this homage to classic sci-fi gives *Moon*'s viewers a subconscious association with space-based danger effectively for free.

Sam₂ finds an unconscious Sam₁ in the crashed rover and brings him back to the base. GERTY tells Sam₂ that the person he's found is also Sam Bell. He is understandably confused.

During a subsequent interstitial shot, a passing satellite shows an aerial view of the effect the Lunar Industries harvesters are having on the moon. The white crosses seen in this shot are examples of fiducials, used to detect and correct film distortion in geographic photography. You might recognize them from Apollo mission photography, such as the iconic portrait of Buzz Aldrin walking on the moon during the *Apollo 11* mission. If you look closely at any of these Apollo photos, you can spot the distinctive crosshair pattern of regularly spaced fiducials overlaid on the image for calibration purposes.

A satellite view shows gouges in the moon's surface created by Lunar Industries' HE3 harvesters, overlaid with white fiducial crosses.

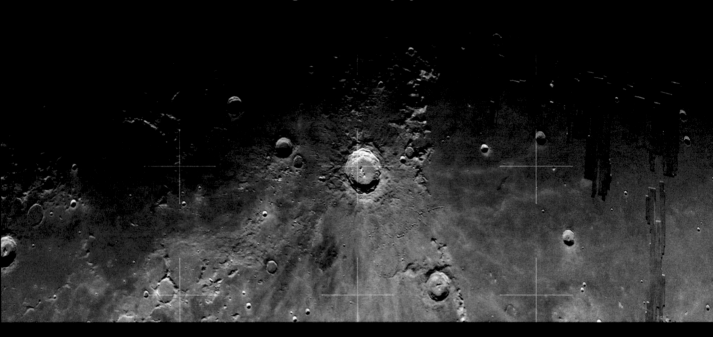

Astronaut Buzz Aldrin walks on

Apollo 11's fiducials came from a thin glass plate known as a Réseau plate, which was attached to the body of the Hasselblad film camera used to take lunar surface photographs. When each photo was taken, the plate's accurately printed crosshairs would block a small amount of light from reaching the film, superimposing black lines on the resulting photo. If the film were to slip or warp within the camera, these distortions could then be detected from variations in each crosshair's location.

Moon's fiducials are white, not black, which means they come from an alternative process whereby fiducials are preexposed onto the film, bleaching out the calibrated area. Their inclusion in this positioning shot adds nothing to our view of the harvesters' effect on the moon—indeed, it could be argued that they distract from the primary detail in this image. Nonetheless, the use of fiducials plays on our subconscious recognition of NASA photography, giving this satellite shot an authenticity and scientific validity without the need for special effects.

Before long, a message comes through from Lunar Industries to say that the crew of the *Eliza* is on its way to "rescue" Sam$_2$:

They look like a friendly bunch, don't they? The instructions next to their mugshots say:

> *Lunar Industries rescue crews have your best intentions at heart. Please try not to panic until they arrive. Remain on-station and make sure you obey their instructions no matter how strange they may seem. After all they're here to help!*

I'm sure it's entirely coincidental that the *Eliza* crew of Rothery, Ward, and Shaw looks a lot like *Moon* conceptual designer Gavin Rothery, first assistant director Mick Ward, and director of photography Gary Shaw.

GERTICON: FALLINGAPARTFACE

GERTY AND SAM$_1$ have a chat, during which GERTY works his way through an entire Unicode block's worth of emotions. He starts out sad at Sam$_1$'s deteriorating physical state . . .

GERTICON: YAYPROGRESSFACE

. . . but briefly turns cheery in response to Sam$_1$'s recollection of a brief stint separated from his wife, during which he changed for the better.

GERTICON: THATDOESSEEMPUZZLINGFACE

As Sam$_1$ presses him for the truth about the hundreds of messages he's sent home to his wife, GERTY replies, "I can only account for what occurs on the base." (His emoticon doesn't look convinced by this distinctly corporate line.)

GERTICON: NOTMYPROBLEMFACE

Sam₁ quizzes GERTY further about the reality of recent events. GERTY reiterates his base-only responsibilities with a cheery ear-to-ear smile.

GERTICON: NOTHINGTOSEEHEREFACE

Unperturbed, Sam₁ presses GERTY to tell him if he really is a clone. GERTY trots out his stock line about a small crash followed by Sam₁ waking up in the infirmary with minor brain damage and memory loss.

GERTICON: OHNOFACE

Unexpectedly, GERTY then changes tack and tells Sam₁ the truth. There was no accident. Rather, Sam₁ was being woken up, and the tests were for genetic abnormalities in a new clone. This truth makes GERTY sad.

GERTICON: SADTRUTHFACE

Sam₁ asks GERTY about his wife, Tess, and his daughter, Eve. An even more sad GERTY discloses that they are nothing more than memory implants from the original Sam Bell.

The simplicity and directness of GERTY's emoticons make this scene surprisingly effective. In the absence of emotion from Kevin Spacey's voice, GERTY's icons become Sam₁'s emotion distilled. Combined with Clint Mansell's haunting soundtrack, this makes the movie's crucial plot reveal (and Sam₁'s subsequent devastation) all the more powerful, with only a robotic emoji to represent the viewer's empathy.

The Sams head out to find out why long-range comms aren't working. They discover some suspicious signal-blocking antennas. Sam$_1$, who is increasingly falling apart, returns to the Sarang base. He tries to access his three-year mission log, but his ACCESS is DENIED. Out of nowhere, GERTY's robot arm arrives and enters a special password on a Windows keyboard, unlocking the entire history of Sarang's video diaries.

GERTY enters an override password on the moon base's Windows keyboard. The password begins with the text "KLGAN," but unfortunately the security-conscious Duncan Jones cuts away from the keyboard just before we can hack into his email.

Sam$_1$ learns that Lunar Industries understands "termination" and "contract" in much the same way as the Mafia. Meanwhile, Sam$_2$ finds more long-range-comms-blocking aerials and prints out their coordinates on a handy receipt printer.

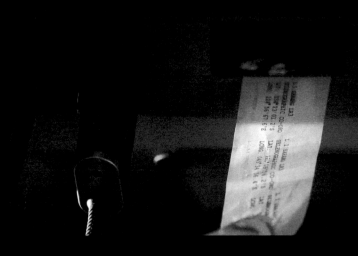

These are selenographic coordinates, used to refer to locations on Earth's moon. Specifically, the coordinates are:

LAT 034°23'01.2"S, LONG 124°56'67.6"E
LAT 121°09'56.2"S, LONG 045°34'56.4"E

We'll gloss over the fact that one of these numbers has sixty-seven seconds in a minute. However, it's a little hard to ignore the latitude value of 121 degrees south, given that the maximum value that latitude can take is 90 degrees south, which occurs at the south pole of a sphere. Maybe Sam mistyped it because of his stubby space-glove fingers.

Back at base, the Sams discover a hidden room. Look at that: It's Sams all the way down!

LEFT: Sam$_1$ enters Sarang's Sam storage facility.

RIGHT: The simple but effective use of a four-digit-padded number for each tray in the storage area makes the scale of Lunar Industries' Sam duplication terrifyingly clear.

Trays 0001 through 0006 have already been opened, as can be seen from their red side indicators. Sam$_{0005}$ and Sam$_{0006}$ *(for it is they)* decide to open tray 0007:

It's the small details of this scene that I find most disturbing. Every prepacked Sam$_n$ has a prepacked "Wake Me When It's Quitting Time" T-shirt. The person at Lunar Industries responsible for this whole macabre setup not only had the temerity to subject Sam Bell to his own personal *Groundhog Day;* they also had the gall to leave cynical in-jokes for every iteration to endure.

After leaving this sinister tunnel of clones, Sam$_1$ asks GERTY why he helped him with the password earlier on. "Helping you is what I do," says GERTY. (See, Sam$_1$? I told you you should TRUST ROBOTIC ASSIST.)

SAM$_1$ DRIVES THE ROVER a very long way from the base, reestablishes video contact with Earth beyond the range of the signal jammers, and calls his family back home. It turns out his wife is dead, but his now-fifteen-year-old daughter has a chat with him anyway. She ends by shouting off-screen to her dad to say that someone is asking about Mom. We hear the distinct voice of a certain Sam Bell in reply. Sam$_0$ is still alive!

Sam$_1$ calls home and speaks to his daughter, Eve.

The known-to-be-alive-ness of Sam$_0$ provides an alternative, cheerier way of looking at the prepacked T-shirt dilemma for the less depressingly morbid of you. Presumably, Sam$_0$ is complicit in the fact that thousands of Sams are in cold storage on the moon. If he's complicit in the scheme, could it be that these small personal details—even that seemingly sinister T-shirt— have been chosen with Sam$_0$'s involvement, as homely comforts to soften the terror of Sam$_n$'s cloned reality?

I don't think that's the truth of it at all. But if it helps you sleep at night, you're more than welcome to run with it.

Back at the base, Sam$_1$ continues to fall apart. Sam$_2$ tucks him into bed, then spots and watches his video call with Eve. Sam$_2$ realizes that he and Sam$_1$ will be killed when the *Eliza* crew arrives, and convinces GERTY to wake up a new clone, whom we'll refer to henceforth as Sam$_3$.

This section of the film gives us a rare close-up of the base's operational notifications board:

Among other things, this board tells us that Lunar Industries Ltd. is a registered company of the United Kingdom, number 06346944. Delightfully, this is indeed the case—Lunar Industries Ltd. is the name of the production company that made *Moon,* and its directors are none other than Duncan Jones and Stuart Fenegan (the movie's director and producer, respectively).

In addition to its scrolling Eurostile, the operational notifications board has a big countdown clock (in a pseudo-LED font), reinforcing the time pressure of *Eliza*'s imminent arrival. (It was conveniently fixed at 88:88 before the *Eliza* plot point came into effect.) Notable on all of its displays is an illustrative dot-matrix resolution substantially lower than the actual resolution of the fonts displayed thereon.

Moon's one-sheet US theatrical poster, showing Sam Rockwell's name repeated in triplicate

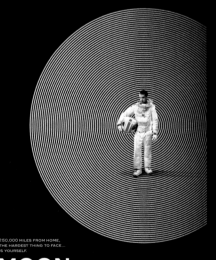

SAM$_1$ WAKES UP to a second rendition of "The One and Only." Once again, Chesney's foreshadowing alarm clock preempts our introduction to a new Sam clone. This time, it's Sam$_2$ discovering Sam$_3$ in Sarang's infirmary.

Talking of foreshadowing: On the movie's theatrical poster, Sam Rockwell's name is backed by three shadow renderings of "Sam Rockwell" (right).

Strictly speaking, this is an accurate cast list. The film now stars Sam Rockwell$_0$, Sam Rockwell$_1$, Sam Rockwell$_2$, and Sam Rockwell$_3$. To put it another way: The movie's poster is four-shadowing the foreshadowing. (This is surely deliberate.)

After much debate, it is decided that Sam$_1$ will go back into the crashed rover; Sam$_2$ will take the HE3 launcher back to Earth; and Sam$_3$ will stay in the infirmary to be discovered by the crew of *Eliza*. He's still unconscious, so he doesn't know this yet, but it's a decision made by a quorum of hims, so he can't really complain.

Once he's dropped Sam$_1$ off, Sam$_2$ loads up the HE3 launcher. GERTY suggests turning him on and off again so that he can't provide any incriminating evidence to the *Eliza* crew. "I'm here to keep you safe, Sam. I want to help you."

Sam₂ asks GERTY if he'll be okay. "Of course. The new Sam and I will be back to our programming as soon as I've finished rebooting."

GERTICON: YAYPROGRAMMINGFACE

Sam₂ replies: "GERTY, we're not programmed. We're people. You understand?"

As GERTY turns around, we see that Sam₁ has stuck a "KICK ME" Post-it on GERTY's backside:

Sam₂ turns GERTY off. After a short, poignant pause, he removes the Post-it from GERTY's back.

GERTICON: REBOOTINGFACE

Sam₂ gets ready to launch back to Earth. Just as in *Alien,* an emotionless female computer voice counts down as Sam₂ awaits the *Eliza*'s arrival.

At the very last minute before launch, Sam₂ realizes he can use the HE3 harvesters to disrupt the base's signal-blocking aerials and prevent Sam₃ from suffering a fate similar to his own. He grabs the piece of paper from earlier with lunar coordinates on it and types a long series of numbers into a keyboard with great precision despite wearing space-suit gloves. The harvester coordinates update. Go Sam₃!

Eliza crew members find Sam₁ in his rover. Sam₂ has a psychedelic trip through space, continuing the fine tradition of psychedelic trips through space begun by Dave Bowman in *2001: A Space Odyssey* and continued by Spock in *Star Trek: The Motion Picture*. As Sam₂'s flight takes him homeward, an HE-3 harvester crashes into an aerial, long-range comms come back online, and we hear audio news reports of Lunar Industries stock crashing as "clone six" (now returned to Earth) gives evidence against his former employer.

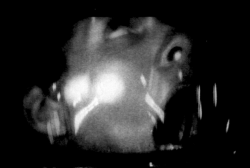

ABOVE LEFT: Dave Bowman takes a psychedelic trip through space in "Part 4: Jupiter and Beyond the Infinite" in *2001: A Space Odyssey.*

ABOVE RIGHT: Spock takes a psychedelic trip through space while trying to mind-meld with V'Ger in *Star Trek: The Motion Picture.*

RIGHT: Sam Bell takes a psychedelic trip through space when returning to Earth in *Moon.*

AS WE'VE SEEN throughout this chapter, *Moon* borrows cleverly from sci-fi history and plays with our expectations while doing so. It gains free association from *2001*'s Eurostile-led typography and dispassionate computer, combining them with *Alien*'s foreshadowing inventory and uncaring corporation to keep its viewers on edge. Despite these appropriations, however, *Moon* never feels like parody or homage. Rather, these borrowed tropes are its secret weapon, preparing us for one set of expectations before subverting them with another. Based on his name and voice, we assume GERTY 3000 is an Evil Space-Based Computer; it turns out he is Sam's only companion and ally, and is genuinely "here to keep you safe." Similarly, we assume *Moon* is about the loneliness of a three-year industrial contract a long way from home; the reality is far more sinister, with the added twist that Sam himself is in on the corporate act. The design of *Moon*'s lunar environment, also grounded in sci-fi tradition, is sufficiently humanized by Sam's personalization, layered over a worn, clinical foundation, that it creates its own rebellious identity. (Indeed, *Moon*'s environments are so effective at evoking Sam's enclosed world, it's easy to forget this modern sci-fi classic was created by a small production team on a miniscule budget when compared to the budgets of its forebears.)

Without our existing expectations to draw on, *Moon*'s story line would require far more exposition, at the expense of character development and atmosphere. Instead, the movie shows that modern sci-fi can be smart about its history—and use that history to build a believable future of its own that tells every bit as compelling a story.

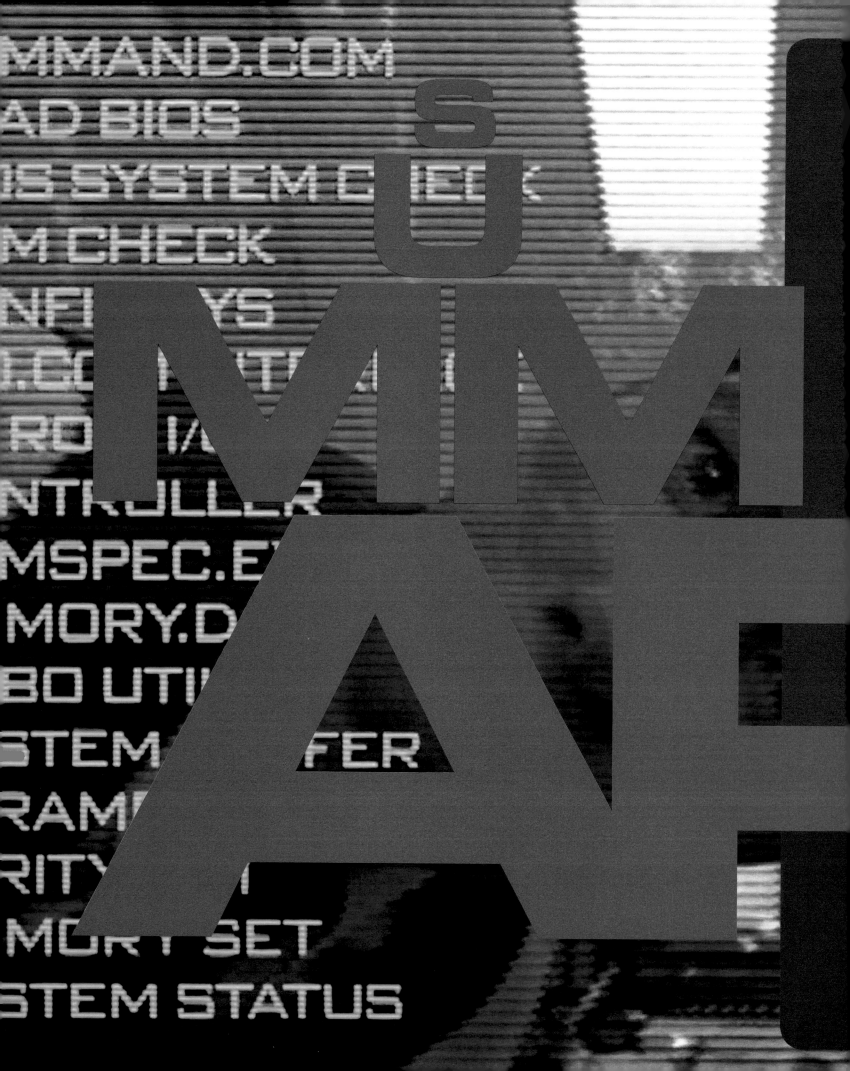

MMAND.COM
AD BIOS
IS SYSTEM CHECK
M CHECK
NFI YS
.CO T
RO I/O
NTROLLER
MSPEC.E
MORY.D
BO UTIL
STEM FER
RAM
RITY M
MORY SET
STEM STATUS

SÜMMAF

There's one overriding fact
that the movies in this book
have demonstrated:
Visualizing the future is *hard*.

OPPOSITE: Murphy's post-resurrection POV from *Robo-Cop* combines technical-sounding DOS commands (set in classic sci-fi Bank Gothic) with CRT scan lines to make it clear we are viewing the world from the viewpoint of a machine. This heavily stylized HUD reinforces the injustice of Murphy's transformation, and sets up his attempt to regain his humanity.

In our interview, Paul Verhoeven described the process thus: "I don't think that these movies have anything to do with the real future. I don't think the brain can invent something completely out of nowhere—it's always based on details of the now." It should be no surprise, then, that extrapolating from the present is a long-standing technique for imagining the future. The movie *2001: A Space Odyssey* used real prototypes from major corporations of the time, borrowing those companies' projections to show a future that viewers in the present would find believable and relatable. *Blade Runner*'s serial-numbered snake scale came from a contemporary book of electron microscope photography, and the sequel, *Blade Runner 2049*, imagined its own cutting-edge technology—surveillance drones—as used by law enforcement thirty years hence.

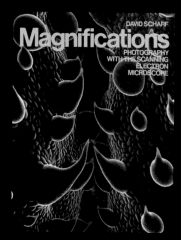

The front cover of *Magnifications: Photography with the Scanning Electron Microscope*, by David Scharf (Schocken, 1977). The image seen in *Blade Runner* is a photo taken from the book of a female marijuana flower, with the serial number added to the photo by hand.

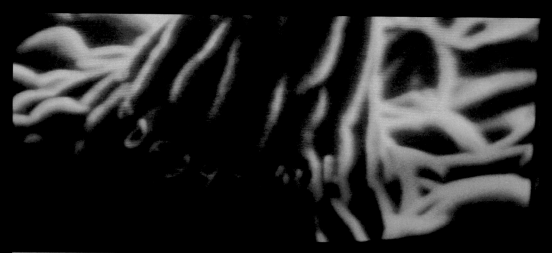

Extrapolating from the technologies and paranoias of the day is the essence of many twentieth-century and contemporary sci-fi stories, from militarized police in *RoboCop* to genetic modification in *Jurassic Park* to sentient AI in *Her*. Rod Serling's *The Twilight Zone* (1959–64) included many such conceits, sidestepping censorship by addressing contemporary issues in alternate-future settings. Since 2011, Charlie Brooker's *Black Mirror* has picked up where Serling left off, with nearly every episode taking a modern-day subject or technological paranoia to its logical extreme.

Projecting the future is not restricted to the creative worlds of movies and TV, either. In 2012, author Ari Popper founded SciFutures, a company whose business is writing science fiction tales for real-world corporations. Popper's network of more than one hundred sci-fi authors has created narratives for the products and services of present-day companies including Visa, Ford, and PepsiCo. They've even worked with the US Navy and NATO, for whom they envisaged worst-case scenarios such as a smart gun that gets hacked, nearly causing a massacre.

TOP LEFT: Electron microscopes were an exciting new technology in 1982. Using an image from such a microscope as a visualization of a replicant's serial number would have been futuristic yet relevant to *Blade Runner*'s audience.

ABOVE LEFT: In *Blade Runner 2049*, K's flying car has a drone in place of a sunroof. He uses the drone as a security monitor during his initial encounter with replicant Sapper Morton.

ABOVE RIGHT: K also uses his drone to survey the Las Vegas terrain from the safety of his car before setting out to find Deckard.

episode "Number Twelve Looks
Just Like You" (1964). This episode
is set in a dystopian version of the
year 2000, in which young adults
have their bodies modified via
"the Transformation," changing
their looks to match one of several
idealized models. When eighteen-
year-old Marilyn (right) rebels
against the Transformation, she
is taken to a hospital from which
she fails to escape, ultimately
succumbing to the process.

TOP RIGHT: In the episode's finale,
Marilyn is shown transformed into
number 8 (left), an identical match
to her previously transformed
friend Jan (far right). In his closing
monologue, series creator Rod
Serling notes: "Portrait of a
young lady in love—with herself.
Improbable? Perhaps. But in an age
of plastic surgery, bodybuilding,
and an infinity of cosmetics, let us
hesitate to say 'impossible.' These
and other strange blessings may be
waiting in the future—which, after all,
is The Twilight Zone."

BOTTOM LEFT: *Black Mirror*'s
season-four episode "Metalhead"
(2017) features a mechanical
dog that is essentially a Boston
Dynamics robot envisaged as a
Terminator-like ruthless hunter,
filmed in chilling black and white.

BOTTOM RIGHT: A Boston Dynamics
SpotMini robot, shown in "cute and
yellow" mode

A sample set of cards from *The
Thing from the Future*

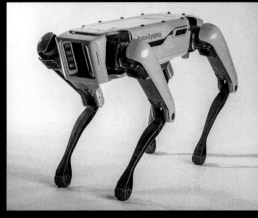

As designers, then, we can help ourselves imagine the future by extrapolating from the present rather than from a blank piece of paper. If you're keen to get started on your own future products, Stuart Candy and Jeff Watson of Situation Lab have created a useful card deck, *The Thing from the Future* (available from situationlab.org), which provides triggers for creative inspiration. The deck contains three types of cards that together form a prompt for a future product to be envisaged.

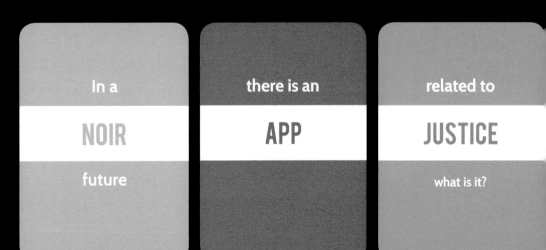

In a | NOIR | future

there is an | APP

related to | JUSTICE | what is it?

Despite all this extrapolation, there is a flip side: We can't assume that the things we see in sci-fi movies are examples of *good* futuristic design. While movie designers can experiment and push the boundaries, free from the constraints of having to make their designs work in reality, they are nonetheless driven by one overriding principle: It's all about the story. This means that on-screen sci-fi design is not always great design in real life.

This is particularly true for the text we see on screen. In essence, this text is either *(A)* something you need to read in order to understand the plot or *(B)* something you should *not* read, because it will distract you from the plot. *B* is typically visual noise that exists to make the things on screen realistic. You won't see a computer screen in the real world with just the words "BEGIN SELF-DESTRUCT SEQUENCE," at least not without an "OK/Cancel" dialogue hovering somewhere nearby. It's important to add visual decoration, typographic or otherwise, to make a sci-fi design believable. The job of a movie designer, then, is to ensure that *A* cannot be missed and that *B* is as non-distracting as possible, while still creating a visually interesting world on screen.

There's a second complication, too: Human beings can process only one linguistic input at a time. Presenting two conflicting inputs—such as an actor speaking dialogue and some text on a computer screen—causes the viewer to struggle to comprehend *either* source, because speech and reading are processed by the same part of the brain, and it can't do both at once. (This is why PowerPoint slides full of text are ineffective: Audience members reading the text cannot listen to the presenter's voice, causing the message to be lost.) It is therefore even more important that ancillary text is visually diminished when a character is speaking, no matter how scientifically interesting or well thought-through that on-screen text might be.

Thankfully, there are some tried-and-tested ways to downplay secondary text that can easily be adopted into your own futuristic designs. Here are ten tricks movie designers use to make sure words don't distract from the story.

TRICK NO. 1: WRITE IT IN TECHNICAL

Humans are natural pattern recognizers. We are innately wired to spot words we know, including when they appear on a movie screen. If you change those words into abbreviations or combine letters and numbers to make technical lorem ipsum, it's much easier for a viewer to tune out the text. Sci-fi movies, which by their very nature require the invention of specialist terminology, often take advantage of this fact to fill screens with technical-looking text that the brain is not tempted to read.

HAL's interfaces in *2001: A Space Odyssey* are perhaps the original example of "writing it in technical" to avoid distracting from spoken dialogue. HAL's displays do not show distinct words but still look technically meaningful.

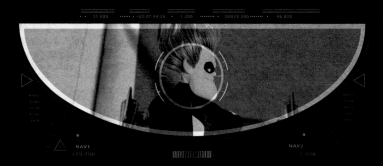

The surrounding text of the Omnidroid HUD (heads-up display) in *The Incredibles* is decorated with number-letter combinations, with a HAL-like "NAV1" and "NAV2" added to the mix for good measure.

Alien's MU/TH/UR interface makes great use of abbreviations and number-letter combinations to create a display that looks meaningful and complex, without ever becoming readable.

Background scenery can also benefit from number-letter combinations to look technical without becoming distracting, such as in this example from the airlock finale in *Aliens*.

This computer display in 2009's *Star Trek* makes it clear that there is "EXTREME DANGER" due to an "EMERGENCY WARP CORE EJECT." Other details, such as "D2V1Y" and "ASYS 7018," do not catch our attention.

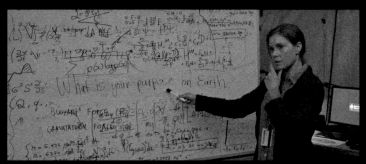

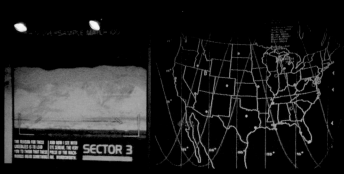

Writing things in technical doesn't have to involve a computer screen. As this example from 2016's *Arrival* demonstrates, a whiteboard can work just as well to give the illusion of technical complexity without distracting anyone but the most attentive mathematician.

In 1996's *Independence Day,* the narrow white text reads: "THE REASON FOR THESE GREEBLES IS TO LEAD YOU TO THINK THAT THESE WORDS MEAN SOMETHING." "Greeble" is sci-fi model-making terminology for fine detail added to an object's surface to make it seem more complex than is strictly necessary.

TRICK NO. 2: WRITE IT IN NUMBERS

Human beings do not parse numbers as multicharacter words, with the possible exception of exciting things like phone numbers and the dates of birthdays. If aspects of the text on screen are written entirely in numbers, therefore, it is unlikely viewers will read meaning into them.

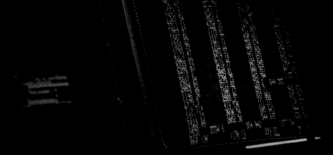

The *Nostromo*'s computer displays information about LV-426's atmosphere in *Alien*. These numbers are nonsensical to the viewer, but android Ash is able to translate their meaning, saying, "Inert nitrogen, a high concentration of carbon dioxide crystals, methane . . . I'm working on the trace elements."

A series of random numeric coordinates is shown in Starfleet Command when power is restored at the end of *Star Trek IV: The Voyage Home*. They are clearly important, and easily ignorable.

Sergeant Vrataski's Mimic-slicing sword in *Edge of Tomorrow* is decorated with a random numeric string in a stencil font that makes the sword look like a futuristic military-issue weapon, all without catching our attention.

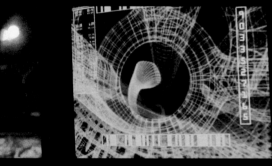

Many of the interfaces in *The Matrix* are constructed from arbitrary numbers in an OCR font . . .

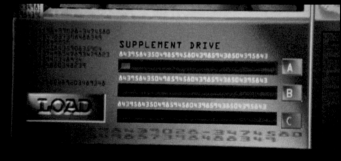

. . . with words included only when it's important we know something is about to LOAD from a SUPPLEMENT DRIVE.

The visual detail on the left and right of this wide-screen interface from *The Incredibles* is made entirely out of numbers. This ensures that only the plot-significant "PHASE 3" text at the top of the screen catches the viewer's attention.

Hackers takes numeric backgrounds to their logical extreme, combining a hexadecimal data dump with the numbers one through nine superimposed in sequential order. This avoids distracting us from the Cookie Monster virus in the foreground.

TRICK NO. 3: WRITE IT IN FOREIGN

If you want an interface or environment to look visually rich, but you don't want its text to be read by the audience, write it in a foreign language. This works perfectly until the inevitable moment when someone in your audience can *read* that foreign language, in which case your text might distract them even more. (Trick number 4, below, provides a handy alternative.)

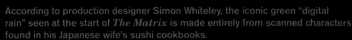

According to production designer Simon Whiteley, the iconic green "digital rain" seen at the start of *The Matrix* is made entirely from scanned characters found in his Japanese wife's sushi cookbooks.

Egyptian hieroglyphics, from 1994's *Stargate*. It is unlikely many viewers will be distracted by reading a dead language that has gone unused since the fifth century CE.

The Eye World store from *Blade Runner*. The store's name is in English, but the graffiti on its wall and nearby trash can is in traditional Chinese characters, to avoid distracting English-speaking viewers.

The 2012 *Total Recall* remake envisages a multilingual world where street signs are in Russian, Chinese, and a host of other languages. The primary purpose is to present the movie's future as a cultural melting pot; it also conveniently avoids linguistic distraction for English-speaking viewers.

K fills in some paperwork in *Blade Runner 2049*. The forms are in Japanese, apart from "LAPD," which tells English-speaking viewers K is with the Los Angeles Police Department. (The red kanji across the top translates as "Farmland Assessment Sheet 358.")

Later in *Blade Runner 2049*, K meets three prostitutes in a crowded downtown area. Signs are visible in a wide range of languages, including a Hebrew ad for Coca-Cola whose letters flash on and off from left to right, even though Hebrew is written from right to left. Despite the myriad languages present in this scene, they are primarily languages with non-Latin alphabets, making them less likely to distract English-speaking viewers.

Firefly envisages a future in which English and Chinese are the dominant intergalactic languages. In the opening episode, "Serenity: Part 1," Dobson's communication device is unable to connect because of interference. The Chinese characters on screen are a literal translation of the English "UNABLE TO CONNECT," adding visual noise without distracting either English- or Chinese speakers.

TRICK NO. 4: WRITE IT IN ALIEN

If you make up an entire alien language—or at least something that *looks* like an entire alien language—you can be reasonably confident that no one will read it by mistake. Setting your text in an alien script is a guaranteed way to fill space on screen without distracting a multilingual audience, as long as that audience does not include one of the estimated several hundred people in the world who are fluent in Klingon.

Additionally, if you make up a language that viewers do not understand, you can show a textual translation on screen *without* overloading the brain's linguistic processing capabilities. This provides a great opportunity to use an appropriate choice of typeface to communicate the speaker's personality.

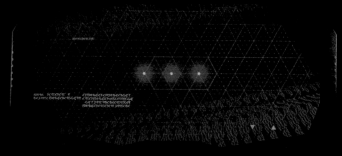

The Klingon tactical display in *Star Trek: The Motion Picture* features several lines of nonsense Klingon characters. Despite their lack of meaning, the characters make it look as though important tactical information is being communicated.

Android and linguist David studies symbols from Mala'kak, the language of the Engineers, in *Prometheus*. He later manages to hold a brief conversation with an Engineer in his native tongue.

When Rocket scans Quill in *Guardians of the Galaxy*, all the text and data on his screen is in a non-distracting alien language, except for the plot-significant information about a bounty on Quill's head, which is in English, in Eurostile.

At the start of 1983's *Star Wars Episode VI: Return of the Jedi*, Lord Vader's shuttle crew sends a transmission that allows his shuttle to pass through the Death Star's deflector shield. This transmission is written in Aurebesh, a writing system for Galactic Basic. The use of an alien typeface here avoids the transmission's text distracting from the plot.

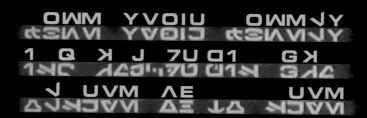

Vader's transmission does look curiously familiar, however. Having studied it in detail, I suspect that someone in the *Return of the Jedi* design department constructed it by futzing around with a sheet of Letraset Eurostile Bold Extended, rotating or flipping characters and removing random segments to make the script seem more alien.

The Na'vi language in *Avatar* is translated into English via subtitles set in Papyrus. This typeface has shipped as a system default on every Windows PC since 2000, and on every Mac since 2003, leading it to become the overused default for bistros and boutiques around the world.

Arrival (2016) is a movie *whose entire story line* is about alien typography that is hard to read. Its circular alien "coffee-cup stain" language, inspired by sketches created by artist Martine Bertrand, is translated into English via some suitably futuristic Futura.

TRICK NO. 5: WRITE IT IN CODE

If you write text on screen in computer code, you can make your sci-fi environment look highly technical without people parsing the text. This trick does, however, suffer from the same problem as "write it in foreign"—if your audience can read computer code, there's a danger you'll pique their interest and distract them from the plot.

(I should note that I am indebted to John Graham-Cumming for much of the detail in the examples below. John's *Source Code in TV and Films* blog, moviecode.tumblr. com, provides many great images of computer code on the big and the small screen and is well worth a spare afternoon of your time.)

In *Jurassic Park,* Dennis Nedry's Mac is shown with some impressive-looking code on screen. The important plot detail here is the big red EXECUTE button, which (when pressed) will run his code and shut down crucial safety systems across the park. The code *surrounding* this button exists to make Nedry look like he knows what he's doing, thereby justifying the fact that no one in the park can undo his technical hack. In reality, he has simply opened some example code from the Macintosh Programmer's Workshop, as shown by the "NEDRYLAND:MPW:Examples:" text in the top left of his screen.

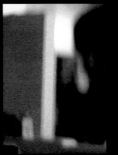 

At the beginning of *Ex Machina,* programmer Caleb Smith writes a linked-list implementation in C, which is nowhere near as interesting or eye-catching as the plot-significant "VIP EMAIL RECEIVED" he sees a few seconds later.

One of the very few snippets of code seen in *Hackers* is a configuration file from Lantastic, a peer-to-peer local area network operating system. It looks impressively technical but is insignificant to the plot.

In the season-one *Westworld* episode "Contrapasso," Elsie Hughes learns that a transmitter inside an android's body contains corrupt GPS data. The code seen beneath the plot-significant "GPS DATA CORRUPT" is real GPS satellite data from the US National Oceanic and Atmospheric Administration. Despite being an appropriate chunk of data for the scene, it is sufficiently technical, and written in a small enough font, to avoid distracting from the tablet's headline.

Arnold Schwarzenegger's HUD in *The Terminator* features 6502 assembly code from an Apple II computer, overlaid on the Terminator's red view. The snippet at the bottom of this shot is from the September 1984 edition of *Nibble*, an Apple II programming magazine, and serves no plot purpose other than to make it clear we are viewing the world from the vantage point of a machine.

TRICK NO. 6: WRITE IT ON SOMETHING TRANSPARENT

It's harder for humans to parse words when they are written backward. *Minority Report* (2001) takes advantage of this fact to place its text on transparent computer screens and to then film *through* those screens, making the text easier to ignore, especially when the camera's focal point is not on the text itself.

The shot-framing opportunities provided by transparent screens have led many sci-fi movies and TV shows to follow *Minority Report*'s lead, to the point where a see-through or holographic display is now pretty much expected for a modern sci-fi interface. This trick also often exploits the fact that humans are innately programmed to look at faces, and so placing an actor behind the screen further distracts from the text.

More generally, the very act of placing text on a transparent surface reduces its visual prominence, making it harder to distinguish from the background of the scene. Indeed, placing text on a transparent screen is almost always a terrible interface design decision, but it's great for framing a shot without needing to cut to an opaque display in order to impart information.

Minority Report's transparent displays often sit in front of an actor's face in close-up. The presence of a face catches the brain's attention and discourages the viewer from reading any backward text.

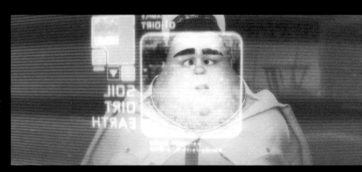

WALL·E's pop-up holographic screens are semiopaque, enabling compositions such as this neat shot in which Captain McCrea's face is framed by a video on-screen.

Another advantage of making a computer screen transparent is that you can make it *entirely* transparent when you want to see through a space that previously contained text.

In this pair of images from *Minority Report*, a series of computer screens becomes a series of empty frames as the camera's vantage point rotates to stand behind the movie's central character.

Firefly episode "Ariel" (2002) shows Simon manipulating a medical interface that is conveniently transparent, with backward-written text, enabling us to view the emotion on his face as he assesses his sister's health.

The 2012 *Total Recall* reboot takes the "transparent" trick to the extreme, turning nearly every see-through surface into a display for a video call or computer.

Minority Report may have been the first sci-fi movie to make computer displays transparent, but the principle of see-through scenery goes back further. *Independence Day* was doing it in 1996 for its illuminated world map . . .

. . . but the originator of the trend is surely 1977's *Star Wars Episode IV: A New Hope,* whose rebel base on Yavin IV includes beautiful illuminated see-through tactical displays.

There's a subgenre of design that also takes advantage of this trick, providing first-person HUDs layered over a human head. *Iron Man* (2008) and *District 9* (2009) both provide great examples of how a close-up on a human face, coupled with naturally reversed information for that human's use, can keep us in touch with that human's emotions even though they are wearing an enclosed exoskeleton suit. (All of which is another way of saying that you don't pay Robert Downey Jr. millions of dollars to be in your movie and then film two hours of a metallic face mask.)

Iron Man's Jarvis UI is perhaps the definitive example of an exoskeleton HUD. It's unclear whether Tony Stark would be able to read this much information so close to his face, but for storytelling purposes the trick enables us to keep in touch with Tony during his extended scenes as Iron Man, without being distracted by the text in his reversed UI.

Toward the end of *District 9,* Sharlto Copley's character—fast turning into a prawn—dons an alien exoskeleton whose HUD is not only reversed but reversed in *alien,* making it even less distracting for the viewer. (For bonus points, the fast-moving alien text in front of his face does a great job of reinforcing his descent into prawn biology.)

During a police investigation in *Minority Report,* we see one of the officers wearing a head-mounted see-through screen. Easier to follow than an exoskeleton close-up, the screen gives her a full-vision overlay of textual data while still keeping the shot focused on the actor's face.

Avatar (2009) features a curved personal screen that rotates with its operator, ensuring that the operator's primary and peripheral vision are always full of information. This also enables us to see the operators as they go about their work.

Another emerging take on the "make it transparent" trope is a trend toward 3-D maps and visualizations around which characters can have a conversation, with overlaid text conveniently positioned or rotated to minimize distraction. This enables characters to study terrain and details with their faces clearly visible and without having to cut away to a paper or computer map. In addition, where the map's labels are symbolic rather than word-based—such as individual letters or numbers indicating the current location of characters— they can be oriented toward the camera, without causing distraction. (These recent 3-D maps are a great example of how advances in present-day visual-effects technology have improved our visualizations of future technology.)

Sully and Quaritch study a map of Pandora in *Avatar*. The map's wordy labels are oriented away from the viewer to avoid distraction, while still keeping the actors' faces visible.

Prometheus crew members track the locations of their expedition party within an alien structure. Party members are reduced to single initials, and reconnaissance drones to numbers.

These letters and numbers are oriented *toward* the camera in every shot, as this second angle of the same map demonstrates. This means that they are displayed back to front for the characters in this scene.

Gamemakers in *The Hunger Games* sit around a dynamic 3-D map that shows the current location of each tribute. The map's numbers are conveniently oriented toward the camera in every shot.

Rebels study a 3-D map of the Nut in *The Hunger Games: Mockingjay— Part 2*. An ensemble shot showing this many characters would not be possible without the transparent 3-D visualization.

Once again, however, *Star Wars* got there first. *Return of the Jedi*'s Death Star II briefing scene uses neat 3-D visualizations of Endor and the Death Star to keep everyone in shot during Admiral Akbar's update.

Indeed, the 3-D visualization worked so well in *Return of the Jedi* that its sequel, *The Force Awakens,* used essentially the same shot during a rebel briefing about Starkiller Base. Here, the opacity of the projection is dropped back slightly to allow characters to be seen behind it.

TRICK NO. 7: WRITE IT NEAR THE EDGES

The human eye's peripheral vision is poor at detecting color, shape, and detail. This means that if the eye is focused on the center of a screen, it's less likely to be distracted by text around its edges. (There's a reason Mac users do not immediately read "Finder File Edit View Go Window Help" whenever they turn on their computers.)

This trick is used when laying out textual elements for suit cams, environment cams, and CCTV-like video logs, to avoid drawing the eye unnecessarily. These layouts also take advantage of a second human trait, which is that once we become used to an on-screen layout, we're less likely to be distracted by it. A recurring on-screen design located around the periphery becomes easy for viewers to tune out, with only the data they see changing (such as a character name or location) catching the eye. Our familiarity with the layout gives filmmakers a shortcut to explaining character or scene transitions, because we're already trained as to what that data represents.

The Martian (2015) makes extensive use of suit cams and environment cams to keep track of geography and time during Mark Watney's extended stay on Mars. In addition to showing the passing of time and clarifying the current location, these cameras provide a great in-world excuse for Mark to narrate his survival strategy to the audience. As we grow accustomed to the camera's peripheral layout, the on-screen text informs without distracting, becoming a helpful and voyeuristic storytelling tool for both the movie's central character and the director.

The individual suit cams in *Aliens* have identical layouts, with only the name (and some irrelevant technical nonsense) changing from character to character. This is used to good effect during the Marines' initial exploration of the terraforming base, to introduce us to their personalities and to associate their voices with their military-use surnames. The same layout helps build tension and clarify who is killed when the Marines are ambushed by aliens.

Europa Report (2013) goes even further than *The Martian*, constructing an entire movie from found footage captured by the crew and cameras of *Europa One*. The use of peripheral location and timing text within this video is subtle but vitally important—the movie's nonlinear timeline would be confusing without it, and the ever-present detail around the edges reinforces the claustrophobia and uncertainty of the movie's found-footage conceit.

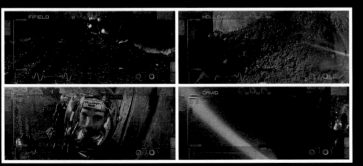

Overlaying data on suit-based cameras offers a great opportunity to represent a character's quickening heartbeat as the audience experiences drama through their eyes. This trick is subverted in *Prometheus*, where android David shows zeroes for his vital statistics, and a flat line for his pulse, as he races through an alien structure alongside panicking human colleagues. He is also the only character referred to without a surname, reinforcing his artificiality.

RoboCop (2014) shows a battle-training exercise through the HUD of its eponymous cyborg, with a simple yet effective overlay in the top right corner of the screen tracking the number of remaining threats. The display does not distract, but ticks ever downward as he progresses through the exercise. Its payoff is a significant tick to zero as the Big Bad is disabled in the scene's final shot.

Jurassic World plays with our expectations of first-person cameras and their surrounding text in two clever scenes late in the movie. After learning that four velociraptors have green-tinted cameras attached to the sides of their heads, we are shown a montage of all four raptors turning to view their trainer, which tells us that they have chosen to side with the dinosaurs.

During the subsequent raptor battle, we cut quickly between dino cams and human cams to see the fight from both sides of the food chain. The two kinds of cameras have the same information arranged in different layouts, with color further differentiating the factions and with names overlaid in OCR-A. (Sadly for the humans, the raptors take the "LIVE FEED" text a little bit too literally.)

TRICK NO. 8: OVERSATURATE THE INFORMATION

With enough information on screen, text can become an oversaturation of detail, with no one item naturally drawing the eye. Used carefully, especially with repeated regular elements, this trick can offer a way to fill a screen with textual detail without causing distraction.

In the opening scenes of *WALL·E*, we encounter an oversaturated vista of Buy n Large ads, with billboards filling every space. There's nothing for us to be distracted from—the omnipresence of BnL is the point of this scene—but the level of detail means we see the whole, not the elements, especially given the multiple uses of the company's logo.

A similar advertising density in *Blade Runner 2049*, coupled with movement and language variance, reduces the likelihood we will focus on a single ad's text. (It's also a tribute to the recognizability of TV that these flat-screen ads, set thirty years into the future, still have curved-rectangle silhouettes to evoke CRT displays.)

The ads in *Idiocracy*'s court scene are so regularly organized and densely packed that they become visual noise.

It's not immediately obvious what's going on in this dense control screen from *Jurassic World*, but it is clearly Very Bad, and that's really all that matters.

TRICK NO. 9: USE ICONOGRAPHY

There is, of course, an easy way to avoid distracting a viewer with text—just don't use any text. Switching to iconography for some or all of your on-screen detail has the added benefit of encouraging viewers to apply their own meaning to the iconography, triggering a different part of the brain from the one used for word recognition.

Alien uses subtle wall iconography to create a functional, believable navigation system that can appear in the background of any shot without distracting the viewer.

In this scene from *WALL·E*'s finale, the plot-significant detail is that AUTO is about to be switched to "MANUAL." Despite the clear labeling of this crucial switch's states, the accompanying blue buttons are marked with meaningless iconography to suggest function the viewer does not need to parse.

The *Axiom*'s instructions for its plant-transferal process are similarly schematic. The movie's designers were inspired to reduce the amount of on-screen text after they took a tour of a Disney cruise liner, whose behind-the-scenes signage was predominantly illustrative to support its international crew.

A hospital control panel in *Firefly* episode "Ariel" shows an almost entirely iconographic interface, presumably to assist a multilingual interplanetary staff in a similar way to the *Axiom*'s controls in *WALL·E*.

The use of iconography is subverted for a medical scene in *Idiocracy*, where the gag is that people have become too stupid to read actual words, and thus pictographs have to be used instead.

In 2013's *Her*, virtually all communication with the movie's AI character takes place via the spoken word. The configuration screen used when setting up her AI is therefore entirely iconographic, with interactions triggered solely by voice.

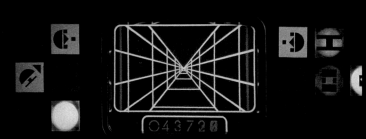

The tie-fighter display in *Star Wars Episode IV: A New Hope* is, like much of the movie, almost entirely without on-screen typography. It instead uses iconography to suggest controls and meaning, with numbers (for distance) as the only visible text.

TRICK NO. 10: DON'T WRITE ANYTHING

If switching to iconography *still* isn't enough, you can take things to their logical extreme, eschew text and iconography altogether, and simply use color or sound to communicate meaning.

The most iconic example of not using icons is 1977's *Close Encounters of the Third Kind*. In its climactic finale, humanity speaks to alien life for the first time, via a colored light display and synthesizer keyboard.

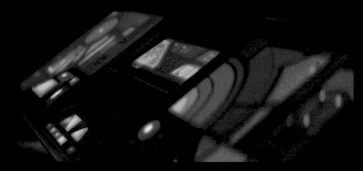

We saw earlier how *WALL·E*'s finale uses iconography to keep distraction to a minimum. Some of the movie's earlier interfaces go even further. The LifePod launch control in this shot is essentially just a series of colored blocks.

Once again, 1977's *Star Wars* led the way in minimizing distraction on-screen. Its visualization of the Death Star's approach to Yavin is an incredible piece of design minimalism that nonetheless clearly conveys the Empire's evil intent.

BONUS TRICK NO. 11: BREAK THE RULES

Having defined these ten techniques, I should note that moviemakers sometimes go against them for in-world product placement. It's a difficult balance to strike—you don't want product placement to interrupt narrative flow—but if a company is paying to have its name or logo on screen, you probably shouldn't write it backward.

Nokia's presence in *Minority Report* includes this subtle use of its logo, which is oriented toward the viewer despite being a detail on a screen that otherwise faces the character in the background.

The primary purpose of this display from 2014's *RoboCop* is to explain that crime boss Antoine Vallon is no longer a suspect in the murder of Alex Murphy. Its peripheral detail, however, includes not one but three unnecessary search engine features—Recent Searches, People Also Searched For, and Similar Results—whose distracting nature is surely connected to the presence of real-world Internet search engine Bing in the screen's title.

Jurassic World's opening scenes include the ironically named Samsung Innovation Center at the head of the park's downtown area. Real-world sponsorship of theme park attractions is entirely realistic—Disneyland has been doing it since the fifties—but the inclusion of three Samsung-branded displays in a subsequent interior shot suggests that product placement may be more of a driver in this case.

Of course, designers aren't limited to using just one of these tricks at a time. Here are some examples of how these ten tricks can be combined to create visually rich designs that still keep the plot on track.

Technical + Numbers + Oversaturated =
Star Trek: Generations

Alien + Code = *Arrival*

Technical + Numbers + Transparent =
Hackers

Code + Numbers + Iconography =
not distracting from an important countdown clock
in *Independence Day*

Technical + Foreign + Iconography + Oversaturated =
Alien's psychedelic keyboard

Foreign + Numbers + Transparent =
Blade Runner 2049

During Tony Stark's first flight in *Iron Man,* we see a shot through his transparent HUD of the Santa Monica ferris wheel, showing not one but two faces; scan lines, so we know it's video; dense text for the ferris wheel description; technical details in the top right; significant-looking numbers on the left; and iconography along the bottom. (I think we may have a winner.)

A space-suited hand reaches out to make contact with the TMA-1 monolith in *2001: A Space Odyssey*. Like all of *2001*'s predictions, these suits were inspired by cutting-edge technology of the time—in this case from illustrations by Harry Lange, who joined the production from NASA's Future Projects Division to bring realism to *2001*'s suits, sets, and spaceships.

Like all good sci-fi movies, our brief trip to the future must come to an end.

Over the course of this book, we've seen how design tropes can provide a visual shorthand for viewers and storytellers alike, offering shortcuts to exposition that are strengthened through repetition. We've discovered how the right choice of typeface can locate a movie in both place and time, and how a font's divergence from handwriting can give it a technical, even alien feel. And we've learned that movies set in the future have a bonus design challenge to solve: Their on-screen worlds must be as convincing as any other cinematic creation, even though they do not yet exist. Extrapolating from the present day can help, but it still takes imagination, discipline, and consistency to make an imagined world feel real.

In particular, we've focused on how design inspiration can bring these future worlds to life. This is not a one-way street, however. As Mike Okuda put it in our interview: "Science fiction has a duty to *entertain*. And part of the process of entertaining is telling stories that happen to inspire. In the process of telling a story, you sometimes predict the future, or you warn of dystopia, or you present alternatives. But having that brilliant idea means nothing if you don't tell an entertaining story."

The sci-fi classics herein tell great stories first and foremost, whether it be *Alien*'s claustrophobic horror or *Total Recall*'s philosophical ambiguity or *Blade Runner*'s tech noir thriller. When we look to science fiction for design inspiration, we must remember that its primary driver is narrative, not design, and this does not always lead to practical creations, however fantastic they seem.

If you take the design tricks from these movies into real-world creative work, then, I encourage you to take Mike's words to heart. Keep these tricks close at hand, but remember that they are only tricks. Great design cannot bring the future to life without a compelling story to tell.

ACKNOWLEDGMENTS

The author wishes to thank the following people who helped bring this book to life.

Thanks to everyone who posted suggestions and corrections on my original blog posts, especially Simon Flummox and David Large (for identifying the Matrix Color Graphic Camera System), and Duncan Jones and Gavin Rothery (for *Moon* design and production trivia). Thanks also to font-spotters Indra Kupferschmid, Marc Rouault, Tim Mountford, Heather (surname unknown), Rumsey Taylor, Mark Simonson, James Heartney, and Susan Bradley. Equal gratitude is due to the people whose own painstaking research has helped me along the way, with notable mentions to Yves Peters, Drew Stewart, Martin Belam, John Sisson, Greg Tyler, Rick Sternbach, and Dominic Kulcsar.

Thanks to the many friends who have offered their support and opinions, including Ben Pickering, Tim Sismey, Rob Hale, Dan Rendall, Tim Isted, Rian van der Merwe, 'Deep Jawa, Sydney Padua, and Bill Thompson. Particular thanks go to John Gruber of Daring Fireball for spreading the word with each new blog post, and to Michael B. Johnson for introducing me to the fantastic folks behind *WALL·E*. I am also grateful to the many experts and historians who have helped me along the way, including A. Michael Noll, Stephen Coles, Mike Okuda, Antonio Cavedoni, Paul Verhoeven, Ralph Eggleston, Craig Foster, James Hutchinson, Robin Love, Irelys Martinez, Christo Datini, Andy Davies, Cathy Wilbanks, Beverly Bradway, Robert Chisholm, John Knight, Bill Caughlin, Ed Eckert, Jim Orr, Caroline Quinn, John Overholt, Leslie Morris, Ian Wheeler, and Geoffrey A. Landis.

I am indebted to three people in particular for bringing this book to life:

My editor, Eric Klopfer, for his skill, patience, and intimate knowledge of sci-fi minutiae. This book is infinitely better for his influence, and could not have found a better home than with Eric at Abrams.

The book's designer, Martin Venezky, for making imagined futures from the screen look equally amazing in print.

Movie-critic extraordinaire Matt Zoller Seitz, for introducing me to Abrams, and for saying so many nice things about me in the book's foreword.

Finally, I am eternally grateful to my lovely wife, Keri Maijala, for her suggestions, patience, and resilience in the face of sci-fi inanity. It means everything to me that while watching an episode of *Buffy the Vampire Slayer*, Keri sent me a photo of on-screen coffee shop Espresso Pump, noting its use of Pump Demi. For you, dear reader, we have sacrificed our ability to watch movies and TV like normal people. I am sure you'll agree it was worth it.

Editor: Eric Klopfer
Designer: Martin Venezky
Production Manager: Denise LaCongo

Library of Congress Control Number: 2017956872

ISBN: 978-1-4197-2714-6
eISBN: 978-1-68335-334-8

Text copyright Dave Addey © 2018

pp. 2–3, 15: Nebula photograph courtesy of NASA / STScI. • p. 8: Starfield photograph by Steve Parker (flic.kr/p/cRJTTf), CC BY 2.0. • pp. 11, 46, 72 (bottom right), 127 (bottom right), 132 (top right, middle right), 136 (bottom right): Photographs © 2018 Dave Addey. • p. 18: Earthrise photograph courtesy of NASA. • pp. 23, 24, 33, 36, 39, 44: "2001: A Space Odyssey" Exhibitor's Campaign Book © 1969 Metro-Goldwyn-Mayer. • p. 26: "Runabout" photograph courtesy of General Motors. • pp. 30, 31: Picturephone sketch and photograph courtesy of AT&T Archives and History Center. • pp. 42, 228: Apollo mission patches courtesy of NASA. • pp. 49, 144 (top), 145 (top right), 147: Type specimens reproduced with kind permission of Letterform Archive. • pp. 60–61: Set photograph and Semiotic Standard production sketches from *Alien* © 1979 Twentieth Century Fox. All rights reserved. • p. 72: Giger Bar photographs © 2018 Andy Davies | HR Giger Museum. • p. 77: Fly agaric photograph © 2018 Christian Payne. • p. 92: "Charter of the United Nations and Statute of the International Court of Justice," United Nations, New York, as available on treaties.un.org/Pages/CTCs.aspx, October 18, 2016. • pp. 92–93: "Charter of the United Federation of Planets" and "Official Type Style" from *Star Fleet Technical Manual* by Franz Joseph, copyright © 1975 by Franz Joseph Designs. Used by permission of Ballantine Books, an imprint of Random House, a division of Penguin Random House LLC. All rights reserved. Any third party use of this material, outside of this publication, is prohibited. Interested parties must apply directly to Penguin Random House LLC for permission. • p. 96: MULTI illustrations courtesy of thyssenkrupp. • p. 99: Details from "The Inboard Profile" and "Deck 6 Plan—Crew's Quarters" from *Star Trek Blueprints* by Franz Joseph, copyright © 1973 by Franz Joseph Designs. • p. 101: Da Vinci Surgical System photographs © 2018 Intuitive Surgical, Inc. • p. 103: *Pioneer 10* plaque illustration and photograph courtesy of NASA. • p. 104: USS *Enterprise* (1799–1823) illustration NH 63534 and USS *Enterprise* (CV-6) photograph NH 77349 courtesy of the Naval History & Heritage Command. • p. 105: Space Shuttle *Enterprise* photograph courtesy of NASA. • p. 106: White House memos courtesy of U.S. State Department. • p. 108: VSS *Enterprise* photograph © 2013 by MarsScientific.com/Virgin Galactic. • p. 109: Voyager Golden Record photographs courtesy of NASA. • p. 110: *Pasadena Star-News* cover image courtesy of the Pasadena Star-News/Southern California News Group. • p. 117: STS-125 mission patch courtesy of NASA. • p. 130: Ennis House photograph by Edward Stojakovic (flic.kr/p/7hzXrQ), CC BY 2.0. • p. 132: Ennis House schematic courtesy of Library of Congress, Prints & Photographs Division, HABS CAL,19-LOSAN,58-. • p. 135: Bradbury Building entrance photograph by Jack E. Boucher. Courtesy of Library of Congress, Prints & Photographs Division, HABS CAL,19-LOSAN,11–2. • p. 135: Bradbury Building photograph by Carol M. Highsmith. Courtesy of Library of Congress, Prints & Photographs Division, LC-HS503-506. • p. 137: Million Dollar Theatre photograph by Carol M. Highsmith. Courtesy of Library of Congress, Prints & Photographs Division, LC-HS503-473. • p. 146: Ave Maria photograph by Ottavio Atti. Courtesy of Tallone Editore. • p. 149: "Acerbis," "Baral-

dini," "Baroni Legno," and "Dominator" photographs courtesy of Antonio Cavedoni. • p. 149: "Barbiere" photograph courtesy of Claudio Piccinini. • p. 149: "Palazzo di Guistizia" photograph courtesy of James Clough. • p. 149: "Sacchi" photograph courtesy of Antonella Carnicelli. • p. 161: Tarzan®, Edgar Rice Burroughs®, John Carter of Mars™, Tars Tarkas™, Gods of Mars™ trademarks owned by Edgar Rice Burroughs, Inc. Cover art for *Gods of Mars* © 1979 Edgar Rice Burroughs, Inc. Used by permission. • p. 166: Form (left) and photograph (bottom right) courtesy of NASA. • p. 189 (top left): Photograph courtesy of Library of Congress, Prints & Photographs Division, LC-DIG-ggbain-03961. • p. 189: Seattle Center monorail and Space Needle photograph by Smart Destinations (flic.kr/p/6Ns9ie), CC BY-SA 2.0. • p. 189: Disneyland Monorail photograph by Robert J. Boser (en.wikipedia.org/wiki/File:6308-DisneyLandMonoRail-ParkStation.jpg), CC BY 3.0. • p. 195: Apple Macintosh 128k photograph by Ian Muttoo (flic.kr/p/5UTQB5), CC BY-SA 2.0. • p. 196: Magic Mouse photograph by Yutaka Tsutano (flic.kr/p/7F83fo), CC BY 2.0. • p. 197: Sputnik and Space Shuttle helmet photographs courtesy of NASA. • p. 197: Apollo 14 command module photograph by gordonplant (flic.kr/p/nFr8MZ), CC BY 2.0. • p. 200: Contemporary Tower photograph by Sam Howzit (flic.kr/p/aCmeqK), CC BY 2.0. • p. 201: Las Vegas Strip photograph by iStock.com/rabbit75_ist. • p. 201: Forum Shops Arcade photograph by anokarina (flic.kr/p/XMaHuq), CC BY-SA 2.0. • p. 201: Fremont Street photograph by dconvertini (flic.kr/p/BUXLBo), CC BY-SA 2.0. • p. 203: Museum Café, Milwaukee Art Museum photograph by Peter Alfred Hess (flic.kr/p/eae7XA), CC BY 2.0. • p. 203: Lyon-Saint-Exupéry Airport Railway Station photograph by Ingolf (flic.kr/p/cosGR9), CC BY-SA 2.0. • p. 203: Palau de les Arts Reina Sofia photograph by Kent Wang (flic.kr/p/nu8K6B), CC BY-SA 2.0. • p. 203: Exterior detail, Milwaukee Art Museum photograph by joevare (flic.kr/p/82YLtB), CC BY-ND 2.0. • p. 203: Adan Martin Auditorio de Tenerife photograph by Rick Ligthelm (flic.kr/p/dmTZZa), CC BY 2.0. • p. 204: Magic Skyway photograph from the collections of The Henry Ford. • p. 205: WEDway PeopleMover photographs from the collection of davelandweb.com. • p. 206: PeopleMover track photograph by dconvertini (flic.kr/p/7992RM), CC BY-ND 2.0. • p. 215: Buy n Large site © Disney/Pixar. Site created by WDDG Inc. Image provided by James Hutchinson. • p. 219: Disney Dream photograph by Christian Lambert (flic.kr/p/bEAw6z), CC BY-ND 2.0. • p. 236: Buzz Aldrin photograph courtesy of NASA. • p. 247: *The Thing from the Future* (2nd Edition) image courtesy of Stuart Candy and Jeff Watson, Situation Lab.

Cover © 2018 Abrams

Printed and bound in the United States
10 9 8 7 6 5 4 3 2 1

Abrams books are available at special discounts when purchased in quantity for premiums and promotions as well as fundraising or educational use. Special editions can also be created to specification. For details, contact specialsales@abramsbooks.com or the address below.

Abrams® is a registered trademark of Harry N. Abrams, Inc.

ABRAMS The Art of Books
195 Broadway, New York, NY 10007
abramsbooks.com